Portrait of a Hunt

FRONTISPIECE: Captain Charles Barclay with hounds at Brent Pelham (detail)

Portrait of a Hunt

The History of the Puckeridge

and

Newmarket and Thurlow Combined Hunts

MICHAEL BRANDER

Hutchinson Benham,
London

Hutchinson Benham Limited
3 Fitzroy Square, London W1

An imprint of the Hutchinson Group

London Melbourne Sydney Auckland
Wellington Johannesburg and agencies
throughout the world

First published 1976
© Michael Brander 1976

Set in Monotype Spectrum

Printed in Great Britain by
The Anchor Press Ltd, and bound by
Wm Brendon & Son Ltd, both of
Tiptree, Essex

ISBN 0 09 127800 7

Contents

Author's Preface and Acknowledgements   xi

Introduction   xiii

1 The Early Beginnings   1
2 Notable Events of the Eighteenth Century   7
3 The First Quarter of the Nineteenth Century   17
4 The Period up to 1845   27
5 The Years from 1845 to 1875   41
6 The Years from 1875 to 1900   55
7 The Years from 1900 to 1920   71
8 The Years from 1920 to 1945   89
9 The Years from 1945 to 1975   105

Appendix Extracts from the Hunt Diaries of the
Newmarket and Thurlow, Puckeridge, and Puckeridge
and Thurlow Hunts.   121

Rules of the Thurlow Hunt Club   183

List of Masters   184

Bibliography   186

Index   189

List of Illustrations

Colour plates

Frontispiece: Captain Charles Barclay with hounds at Brent Pelham. Photograph by John Freeman, reproduced by kind permission of Captain Charles Barclay

Between pages 56 and 57

The Layston meet of the Puckeridge hounds, 12 February 1859. Photograph by John Freeman, reproduced by kind permission of Captain Charles Barclay

The Newmarket and Thurlow at Six Mile Bottom, by J. F. Herring Senior. Photograph by John Freeman, reproduced by kind permission of Captain Charles Barclay

Captain Charles Barclay. Photograph by John Freeman, reproduced by kind permission of Captain Charles Barclay

The joint Masters of the Puckeridge hunt for the season 1947–8. Photograph by John Freeman, reproduced by kind permission of Captain Charles Barclay

Mr J. D. Webb. Photograph by John Freeman, reproduced by kind permission of Mr J. D. Webb

Mr and Mrs E. H. Vestey, and Tony Champion. Photograph by John Freeman, reproduced by kind permission of Mr and Mrs E. H. Vestey

Black-and-white plates

Between pages 24 and 25

George Mure of Herringswell, Suffolk, Master of the East Suffolk. Photograph reproduced by kind permission of Arthur Ackermann & Son Ltd

A meet at Chippenham Park with George Mure, Master of the East Suffolk, and his huntsman William Rose. Photograph reproduced by kind permission of Arthur Ackermann & Son Ltd

Chaunter. Photograph reproduced by kind permission of *Country Life*

Mr Sampson Hanbury of Poles. Photograph reproduced by kind permission of *Country Life*
Mr John Chapman. Photograph reproduced by kind permission of *Country Life*
Mr John Dalyell. Photograph reproduced by kind permission of *Country Life*
Mr Nicholas Parry. Photograph reproduced by kind permission of *Country Life*
Mr Richard Simpson. Photograph reproduced by kind permission of *Country Life*
Mr John Josselyn
The Noble Science. Photograph reproduced by kind permission of *Country Life*
Brewer. Photograph reproduced by kind permission of *Country Life*
A letter from John Leech. Photograph reproduced by kind permission of *Country Life*
Abraham Firr. Photograph reproduced by kind permission of *Country Life*
Mr John Sworder. Photograph reproduced by kind permission of *Country Life*

Between pages 72 and 73

Mr Thomas Purkis. Photograph reproduced by kind permission of *Country Life*
Mr George Bowen.
Mr Robert Gosling. Photograph reproduced by kind permission of *Country Life*
Mr Frederick C. Swindell
The Hon. Lancelot J. Bathurst
Mr Edward Barclay. Photograph reproduced by kind permission of *Country Life*
The Revd Sir William Hyde-Parker, Bt.,
Mr Richard Bower
Mr Herbert Jones
Mr Walter K. Cannon
Mr Robert W. King
Major Maurice E. Barclay. Photograph reproduced by kind permission of *Country Life*
Robert Gardiner. Photograph reproduced by kind permission of *Country Life*
Miss G. Cotton-Browne, with her harriers and hunt servants
Mr Robert C. Gosling

Between pages 88 and 89

Mr Frank Debenham and Mr Edward Barclay. Photograph reproduced by kind permission of *Country Life*
Mr Edward Barclay on Epsom
Mr Frank Stacey. Photograph reproduced by kind permission of *Country Life*
Major Henry A. Anderson
Mr Hugh Smyth
Mr George Smyth

Mr Thomas Stubbing

Mr Colledge Leader

A group of the Newmarket and Thurlow hunt staff and supporters *circa* 1927

A day out with the Newmarket and Thurlow, 1925

Between pages 104 and 105

Woodcock, 1942

President, 1948

Gravity, 1950

Poetry, 1951

Charles Field with hounds in Linton, 1955. Photograph by Jim Meads

Acting joint Master Mr J. D. Webb, heading the Newmarket and Thurlow across country, 1956. Photograph by Jim Meads

Colonel D. R. B. Kaye, D.S.O., Master of the Newmarket and Thurlow 1958-9

The Newmarket and Thurlow, 1963. Photograph by Jim Meads

The Newmarket and Thurlow, 1966

Mr and Mrs E. H. Vestey and members of the Puckeridge and Thurlow hunt. Photograph by Jim Meads

Captain and the late Mrs Charles Barclay and Mr E. H. Vestey

Ned Paxton

Captain Charles Barclay

Vestey Fox, by William Garfit. Published in the *Shooting Times & Country Magazine*, 19 February 1976. Reproduced by kind permission of the artist.

Author's Preface and Acknowledgements

THERE may be those who wonder why a Scot living in a non-hunting part of Scotland should write a history of two hunts covering parts of Hertfordshire, Essex, Suffolk and Cambridgeshire within commuting distance of London. The short answer is that I was asked and chose to do so because both my school and university days were spent on the edge of this country when I came to know and like it well. Apart from writing on hounds, horses, hunting and the country-side I have also written a number of books on changing social customs over the centuries and this seemed a challenging opportunity to combine these varied interests to produce a social portrait of a hunt.

Almost inevitably, I found a number of Scots involved over the years. The Newmarket and Thurlow was founded by James I and VI, followed as Master in due course by others such as George Mure and Captain Gordon-Miller, while the Puckeridge had such notable Scottish Masters as Mr John Dalyell and, of course, pre-eminently, the Barclay family. Yet it was not so much the characters involved – although, English or Scots, they proved immensely interesting – as the countryside itself, the changing social habits, the slowly altering methods of farming, of building, of transport, of communication and even of dress and speech, set against the background of history, of war and peace, revolution, boom and recession, which proved most fascinating of all.

The numerous hunt diaries, particularly those in the crabbed hand of Mr Thomas Purkis of Barham Hall, Linton, stretching from 1880 to 1932, were re-warding if difficult reading. The famous hunts collected from these and other sources are included in an appendix and it is not only the keen foxhunter who will find them of absorbing interest. To follow these accounts of various hunts, year by year, over the centuries, is to come to know the countryside as well as if one had hunted it oneself, and no one is likely to have a more intimate knowledge of an area of country than a foxhunter.

This is therefore a book about some six hundred square miles of countryside close to London, showing the changes that have taken place there over the centuries, not only in the countryside itself, but in the people, their customs, habits, way of life and sport. It is possibly also an explanation, for those confirmed town dwellers who care to read it, of why and how country ways of life survive today. There is a continuity in the countryside which too often has been lost elsewhere. It is my hope that those who read this account of the development of the hunts concerned will find it as interesting as I found it to write.

My very grateful thanks for their help and co-operation are due to many people, but first and foremost to the Masters of the Puckeridge and Thurlow Hunt, Captain C. G. E. Barclay and Mr and Mrs E. H. Vestey, also to many past Masters of the Newmarket and Thurlow and to officials of the Puckeridge and Thurlow, particularly, in alphabetical order, since to place them otherwise would be invidious, Mr E. Cooper-Bland, Colonel and Mrs E. H. Deacon, Colonel D. R. B. Kaye, D.S.O., Mr H. N. Sporborg, C.M.G., and Mr J. D. Webb, also to all those whose memories of the hunts stretch back many years who have helped with the facts, anecdotes or documents, amongst whom I would like to include the Reverend E. S. Barrington Barnes, Mrs Vera Berry, Mr. R. E. Way, Mr Albert Williams, and many more. My thanks for the loan of their diaries, or hunting notes, must also go to many others, particularly Mr Jack Webb for his fine collection of old Newmarket and Thurlow records, including the Purkis and Hicks diaries. Finally I must make grateful acknowledgement to Mr Michael F. Berry for permission to plunder his very well written *History of the Puckeridge Hunt*, of which I availed myself freely. I must merely add that for any errors or omissions I am solely responsible.

Introduction

HUNTING is more than a sport of the countryside. It is unique in forming a bond between all classes of countrymen, uniting them in a common interest and enthusiasm for the chase. There can be few combined hunts which portray so well the development of foxhunting over a period of some two hundred and fifty years as the Newmarket and Thurlow and the Puckeridge hunts, now merged as the Puckeridge and Thurlow. Throughout this time each of the hunts has relied almost entirely on the support of the farmers, countrymen and landowners living within their boundaries – despite their closeness to London, less than thirty miles to the south. It is this remarkable survival of close-knit country enthusiasm for their sport so near to the concrete jungle now annually encroaching on their boundaries which makes them such an interesting study.

Although the Puckeridge is the best documented of the combined hunts, having been the subject of a well researched and very readable history by Michael Berry, published by *Country Life* in 1950, it is undoubtedly the case that the Newmarket and Thurlow has older origins, even if less well attested. Both, however, at one time probably formed part of the King's Forests and were subject to the Forest Laws first introduced by Canute and greatly extended by the Norman Kings from William I onwards. One of the earliest references to foxes in the area may have been that contained in a grant of land to Thomas Engaine during the reign of Edward III (1327–1377) 'by service of finding at his own proper costs certain dogs for the destruction of wolves, foxes . . . and other vermin . . .'

At that period, of course, the fox was not highly regarded as a beast of the chase. In his famous *Master of Game*, written between 1406 and 1413, the Duke of York listed the fox seventh, beneath the hare, the hart, the buck, the roe, the wild boar and the wolf in that order. Hunting then was conducted in the woods with the aid of snares, nets, long bows or cross-bows and spears as well as very varied trencher-fed hounds. It was not until 1591 that Sir Thomas Cockaine wrote for the first time of hunting foxes in the open. In a delightful account of how to find sport, entitled *A Short Treatise on Hunting*, he listed foxhunting as his first pleasure, placing hare hunting second, and recorded that he had 'killed a fox distant from the covert where he was found fourteen miles aloft the ground with hounds'.

Sir Thomas Cockaine was undoubtedly ahead of his time, but the increasing speed of the enclosures during the seventeenth century was beginning to change the face of the English countryside thus favouring conditions for foxhunting of this kind. The old open field system of farming of the mediaeval days was slowly giving way to the hedged fields we know today and the old overgrown forests were being relentlessly felled and cleared. The change was a very gradual one and with it came a gradual realization that the type of hound used made considerable difference to the sport.

Throughout the seventeenth and greater part of the eighteenth centuries hare hunting remained generally more popular than foxhunting, with small privately owned packs of hounds hunted by individual squires replacing the old trencher-fed packs of hounds of the mediaeval days.

By 1781, in his brilliant *Thoughts on Hunting*, Peter Beckford had crystallized the more advanced feeling of his time that there should be different types of hound for hunting hare or for hunting fox, each bred especially for their purpose. He wrote feelingly:

It is the dash of the foxhound which distinguishes *him*, as truly as the motto of William of Wickham distinguishes *us*. A pack of harriers, if they have time, may kill a fox; but I defy them to kill him in the style in which a fox ought to be killed; they must hunt him down. If you intend to tire him out, you must expect to be tired also yourself. I never wish a chase to be less than one hour, or to exceed two; it will seldom be longer, unless there be a fault somewhere; either in the day, the huntsman, or the hounds. What Lord Chatham once said of a battle is particularly applicable to a foxchase; it should be *short, sharp and decisive*!

Yet the difference between different parts of the country was as marked then as today for in 1783 the *Sporting Magazine* printed an account of hunting in Yorkshire with the hounds of the famous all-round sportsman Colonel Thomas Thornton of Thornville Royal near Boroughbridge as follows:

Upon the 19th of February 1783 a Fox was unkennelled near Boroughbridge, Yorkshire, at twenty-seven minutes past *nine* and except half an hour taken up bolting him from a rabbit burrow the hounds had a continued run until fourteen minutes past five in the evening, when they killed. During the space of nearly *eight* hours hard running several horses died in the field and many others were hurt as never to be perfectly recovered.

By the beginning of the nineteenth century the advance in agriculture had revolutionized the farming scene and completed the changes begun by the enclosures. The introduction of new machinery and new farming methods, of new root crops and crop rotations, improved stock breeding and land drainage, as well as the increased use of marl and manure, had vastly altered the country-side. Inevitably these changes led to larger farms, to a drift away from the countryside to the new industrial towns or to London, and to altered methods of hunting. Hare hunting at last began to take second place to foxhunting and the speed of hounds specially bred for their country began to increase as Peter Beckford had foreseen. In the area, within thirty miles of London, covered by the combined hunts of the Puckeridge and the Newmarket and Thurlow today, all these factors had their effect.

During the nineteenth century all these changes intensified. The speed of communications increased immensely, first with the introduction of the steadily improving stage-coach services on the turnpike roads, then with the spread of the railways. Although the latter were at first seen as the death knell of fox-hunting they proved eventually a fillip to the sport by allowing foxhunters to hunt with more than one pack much more easily than was previously possible. With the introduction of the *Foxhound Kennel Stud Book* in 1866, its records in some cases going back almost to the turn of the century, the science of foxhound breeding entered a new phase producing even faster hounds. The end of the farming boom in the 1870s also tended to enhance the popularity of hunting since many farmers relied on the rabbits on their farms or the subsidies from the hunt for damage to crops or livestock as part payment for their rents. By the end of the century foxhunting had far exceeded hare hunting in popularity and even the introduction of barbed wire in the 1880s and the motor-car in the 1890s had little impact at the time.

The First World War brought hunting almost to a standstill in 1918, but the 1920s and '30s saw a surprising revival of hunting as a country sport, with more packs than ever run by subscription rather than as private packs. The Second World War saw hunting again almost completely halted, with packs and horses put down wholesale, although even so a nucleus remained. Above all the countryside retained its enthusiasm where the farmers themselves were directly concerned with their sport. It was thus in an area close to London, in conditions of war-time rationing and restrictions, that somehow the combined hunts retaining only a handful of hounds and served by elderly hunt servants and Masters, or by part-time enthusiasts, still managed to show a few days sport on a greatly restricted scale.

Despite post-war austerity, despite the growth of motorways and of new towns in the 50s and 60s, despite the threat of airports and other aspects of the concrete jungle encroaching on the countryside, and quite apart from the increasing mechanization of farming, including the use of dangerous new sprays and artificial fertilizers, hunting revived again after the war. In the six hundred or so square miles covered by the combined hunts within commuting distance of London, intersected by roads and railways, bounded by motorways, with the new towns of Stevenage and Haverhill growing rapidly on each boundary, it remains a remarkable phenomenon that this should be so. Yet it was only in the late sixties that the hunts felt the need to combine and consolidate their country under joint mastership, as a single unit.

It must be remembered, of course, that this was never a 'fashionable' hunting country. To the north above Newmarket the Fen country was the boundary and from there to the south as far as Stevenage, Saffron Walden and Ashdon extended the chalky subsoil to be found in the Chilterns, providing well drained light land without ditches and with few fences – ideal for galloping, but with not many coverts for foxes. For the rest, the land was plough country, varying from heavy to very heavy indeed, with good coverts, but with deep ditches forming formidable obstacles. To stay with hounds in this country and to kill foxes requires skill and understanding of a high order. Yet, far from being a dying sport, it remains essentially the sport of the farmers and of the countryside. Here indeed the combined hunts of the Puckeridge and the Newmarket and Thurlow, as the Puckeridge and Thurlow continues to thrive.

Chapter 1

The Early Beginnings

ALTHOUGH Sir Thomas Cockaine acknowledged his favourite sport to be foxhunting, and claimed, as 'a professed hunter and not a scholler', to have 'killed a fox distant from the covert where he was found, fourteen miles aloft the ground with hounds', the Elizabethans were primarily hare and deer hunters. Elizabeth I herself enjoyed hunting with harriers, but she also thoroughly enjoyed buck hunting within the enclosed confines of a park. The essence of this form of hunting lay in matching the hounds for sound rather than for size. A variegated pack would be loosed on a buck (sometimes lamed with a cross-bow bolt beforehand) and the hunters then rode to a knoll in the centre of the park where they listened to the hounds giving tongue on the scent, naming each in turn, and so followed the progress of the hunt.*

On the death of Queen Elizabeth I in 1603 James VI of Scotland and I of England succeeded to the throne. A poor rider and a far from lovable character, he was nevertheless fond of hunting and hawking. In 1605 he first visited Newmarket and found he could hawk or hunt hares and buck to his heart's desire on the chalk land of the Heath and the surrounding countryside. There are no records of his having actually hunted or killed a fox and – indeed it is unlikely that with the slow Talbot hounds of the day he would have succeeded in doing so unless an elderly fox with a full stomach was caught in the early morning on a keen scenting day. Yet there can be little argument that the Newmarket hunt owes its origins to the first of the Stuart monarchs, even if the records since then are far from continuous.

On the death of James VI and I in 1625 he was succeeded by his son Charles I, a far better horseman and a lover of both racing and hunting, who frequented Newmarket for both these sports. After his execution in 1649, during the dark

*Until quite recently a similar form of hunting survived in the Kentucky mountains with the 'coon hunters listening from a verandah to the progress of the hunt in the valley beneath while they drank mountain dew'.

days of the Commonwealth, racing was forbidden and hunting was frowned on to a large extent. On the Restoration of Charles II in 1660, however, it was not long before Newmarket came into its own again, for the King spent a great part of his time in the town with his favourites the Earl of Rochester and the Duke of Buckingham, as well as his numerous mistresses, notably the notorious Nell Gwyn. During this period James, Duke of York, kept his pack at Newmarket and was reputed to hunt the fox, but with the passing of the Stuarts in 1689 the town, the Heath and the hunt lapsed into obscurity for a period.

Without historical records it is difficult even for the fortunate minority who live in the English countryside today to visualize it as it was in the seventeenth and eighteenth centuries. Evocative names such as Six Mile Bottom, Stocking Pelham, Lords Fields and Horseheath may now have a very different significance from their original meanings. Bogend may now be a well-drained Council housing estate and Ditchfield a well-wooded copse with only their names as a reminder of a very different – if quite recent – past, for such are the inevitable changes wrought by time. Each generation of countrymen tends to alter the appearance of the countryside, obliterating old landmarks and erecting new ones, so that each decade there is a gradual, scarcely noticeable, change, although there is usually a spirit of continuity apparent and traces of the past are generally still visible to the keen observer.

It is, of course, easy to think of the seventeenth and eighteenth centuries as halcyon days of peace and plenty, although the reverse was generally the case. It must be remembered that from 1642 until 1660 there had been civil war and revolutionary government with neighbours, friends and families often deeply divided and fighting on opposing sides. The bloodshed and bitterness caused by the political and religious dissensions of the time resulted in deep-rooted animosities which were slow to heal, for countrymen have long memories in such matters. There was a strong Puritan and Quaker element in East Anglia as well as numerous royalist supporters and in the isolation of the village communities old grudges tended to fester and grow rather than die an early death. It was well into the eighteenth century before many of these old feuds were forgotten or overlaid by time.

Just how extremely localized country life was in early eighteenth-century England it is hard to appreciate fully today. That people could be born, live their lives and die without stirring further than ten or fifteen miles from their homes throughout their life was rather the rule than the exception as far as the country yokels and yeoman farmers were concerned. The small squire, distinguished only from his yeoman neighbour by possession of a coat of arms and a small stable with his pack of four or five couple of hounds, would probably only visit London once or twice in a decade on business, but otherwise scarcely stirred from his own few acres. The wealthier squire might find it incumbent on him to visit London for the season, but by June he would be home again, preparing happily no doubt for the sport of the autumn and winter months.

Yet already there were the beginnings of social change, heralding the greater changes which were to come in the nineteenth century. Although the eldest son might enter the army prior to inheriting his father's estate, the numerous younger sons – if they survived the rigours of the age and attained their majority – were sent abroad to seek their fortune, or else apprenticed to a City merchant, where their future depended on their own exertions. In the nature of things those who were successful, attaining positions of power and influence in the East India Company or the City, generally wished to return to the land, they bought an estate, sometimes of considerable size, as much for the social prestige connected with landowning as any other reason. There was thus a constant, if gradual, change in the countryside, especially within comparatively easy reach of London.

In an age when there were so many local squires and larger landowners with their own private packs of hounds content to hunt whatever quarry, whether hare, deer or fox, they encountered, it is understandable that precise early records of hunts devoted solely to foxhunting are hard to find or substantiate. Furthermore, even as late as the early nineteenth century, in many parts of the country it was not uncommon for several packs to be found hunting in the same area since there were still no clearly defined boundaries between hunts and it was generally thought that a pack of hounds was entitled to hunt wherever they cared as of ancient right. It was thus often the case of the first pack to find their quarry being the only one to enjoy sport, on the only hare or fox on that ground. For the greater part of the eighteenth century hunting in England remained extremely haphazard with little overall attempt at organization.

It is an interesting feature common to almost all aspects of social history that there is generally a gap of around a hundred years between the introduction of new ideas and their adoption on any scale. It was thus with Sir Thomas Cockaine's early advocacy of foxhunting in 1581, for it was over a hundred years before foxhunting began to be accepted as a sport in its own right preferable to hunting either hare or deer. The old country tenet handed down from the days of the Forest Laws that the hare and the deer were warrantable beasts of the chase whereas foxes were merely classified as vermin may have had its share in this lack of ready acceptance for the sport. Lack of foxes in many areas, as well as the practical countryman's view that 'Us only hunts what us can eat', may

3

also have had their due effect. It was certainly only during the early part of the eighteenth century that this change really began to take effect, althought by the end of the century there was no doubt that foxhunting was the pre-eminent sport of the three.

It is not difficult to trace the stages by which this change came about, for the process once started inevitably snowballed. Even then the business of breeding hounds for a country, although by no means the science it was to become, was in the hands of experienced men who knew what they wanted. Some favoured the slow old Elizabethan Talbot type of hounds with deep belling cry something akin to the bassett hound of today. For puzzling out the scent of a hare and for a slow interesting hunt these probably provided sport enough for many. There were other hounds with longer legs, badger-pyed and faster, moving with more drive, which made for faster hunting, more suited to deer or foxes.

Many of the variegated packs of the day probably contained a mixture of these strains. Even when caught at dawn with a full belly, as most foxes were in those days, a lengthy three-or four-hour hunt was likely to ensue, with hounds probably two fields ahead of the hunt for much of that time and few opportunities to watch them hunting. By the end of the day both hounds and the rather heavy cobs ridden by all but the wealthier squires would no doubt have been exhausted. Especially when the fox was not killed, many must have queried the pleasures of foxhunting – although others, the younger and more thrusting, must have had other opinions.

Here and there, slowly at first, various squires and landowners yielded to the fascination of foxhunting, determining not to be beaten, and started to rear their hounds with a view to killing foxes. The natural result of this was to breed for more speed from the faster hounds and to draft the slower members of the pack. Another was that where coverts suitable for foxes to lie up or breed in were lacking they started to lay them down. Living close to nature, the countrymen of the day knew well that foxes liked to make their lairs in badger earths and thus badgers were encouraged as much for this reason as for the more dubious one of badger baiting. Once foxes were to be found in plenty naturally those who had hesitated about the sport of foxhunting began to appreciate what they had been missing. By the end of the eighteenth century foxhunting was the principal sport of the countryside.

For a large part of the century it still seems to have remained the general practice to start hunting at dawn. Apart from having been the widespread custom and apart from the cogent argument that it left 'a good long afternoon for drinking', for many of the hunt followers their second favourite pastime next to hunting, there were a number of good reasons for this. Since there was a scarcity of foxes it was generally necessary to spend some time finding the stale line of the fox's wanderings during the previous night before working up to the point where he was lying up for the day. Since hounds were generally still slow for their task and the foxes in short supply, much hunted, fit and fast, hunts were liable to take several hours to kill their fox. Since the hunt might cover a distance of as much as fifteen or twenty miles this could mean a long hack home, and possibly being overtaken by darkness on a short dark winter's day – no pleasant prospect in the sparsely populated countryside of the times, even though it was accepted practice for any country household to provide hospitality for both huntsman and horse in such circumstances.

In those days of much undrained boggy ground and of poor, grass-grown roads, mostly heavily rutted and winding, communications were still a major problem with whole areas cut off totally by flooding or snow in wintertime. The average hunt of the period seldom covered more than eight or nine parishes at the most. To hunt an area regularly, such as the three hundred square miles of the present Puckeridge country, was a physical impossibility. From Ware and Hertford in the south to Stevenage in the west, as far north as Royston and Duxford and Hatfield Broad Oak in the east, was an area no single hunt was likely to cover regularly at that period.

When there were so many local squires with their own private packs of hounds hunting various quarries in areas now covered by one hunt it is understandable that exact records of the start of many modern packs of foxhounds are hard to find and even harder to substantiate. The origins of the Newmarket hunt, amongst the oldest, are easy enough to place accurately enough, even if subsequent records are patchy, but those of the Puckeridge, also a hunt of considerable antiquity, are not quite so easy to establish. From various sources, however, it is clear that in the early 1720s a member of the Calvert family started hunting regularly with some friends in the area between Hertford and Cheshunt, which is now some five miles south of the Puckeridge hunt boundaries.

Both Felix Calvert of Furneux Pelham (1693–1755), of the senior branch of the family, and Felix Calvert of Albury Hall (1700–1755), his second cousin, were the descendants of Felix Calvert, a tallow chandler of Little Hadham (1596–1674). His sons had made enormous fortunes in brewing and finance, acting as money-lenders to the Stuart kings in return for the right to collect certain taxes. By the mid-eighteenth century the Calverts were established as the wealthiest and most influential family in East Hertfordshire. For almost two hundred years they were to be closely connected with the Puckeridge hunt.

5

Whether it was Felix of Albury Hall – as seems probable – who founded the hunt, or his cousin, scarcely matters. The important fact is that around 1727 earth-stopping apparently warranted the employment of a man by the hunt solely for that purpose, thus establishing the fact that they were hunting the fox. Colonel John Cook, himself a Master of the Newmarket and Thurlow, in his well-known book *Observations on Foxhunting* (1826), noted that 'The Hertford-shire [Mr Hanbury's] can lay claim to considerable antiquity with justice – as an earth-stopper has lately proved his grandfather's employment with the pack, then Mr Calvert's, so far back as 1727'. Mr Hanbury himself, on his retirement in 1833, mentioned seeing an earth-stopping card sent out by the Calvert family over a hundred years previously. A third, if more dubious, authority writing in 1828 in the *Sporting Magazine* under the pen-name of Ansty claimed that his neighbour at a dinner had stated, 'Here's our Hertfordshire Hounds, just one hundred years' old.' Since this was pure hearsay evidence, and he admitted that his informant was drunk at the time, this would scarcely stand up by itself were it not for the backing of the other two. On the whole, however, it may be safely taken that the Puckeridge hunt was already hunting foxes regularly in 1727.

Chapter 2

Notable Events of the
Eighteenth Century

THE end of the seventeenth century and the start of the eighteenth saw the importation of some notable Arab stallions, which were to have an immense effect on the breeding of British bloodstock, becoming literally the foundation sires of the British thoroughbred. The Byerly Turk, the Darley Arabian and, lastly, the famed Godolphin Arabian, imported in 1729, were to leave their imprint on subsequent generations down to the present day. Although more closely associated in the public mind with racing, there can be no question of the effect they also had on hunting. The speed and stamina which they brought to the hunting field, combined with the increasingly specialized breeding of faster hounds, were to revolutionize the sport of foxhunting even if, like most changes in social history, there was to be a time-lag of something close to a hundred years before the full effects were noticeable.

In the same way, although foxhunting was gaining in popularity throughout the eighteenth century, it must not be imagined that the process was anything but gradual. There were still those who preferred hunting either hare or deer and some who were not particular which they hunted so long as they enjoyed a day's sport following hounds. There were still small private packs to be found well into the nineteenth century, often overlapping the same ground as other packs – indeed sometimes drawing the same coverts. This must on occasion have led to confusion and a degree of ill-feeling, but in general there appears to have been remarkably little friction and a philosophic acceptance that there was room for all.

For a large part of the eighteenth century few packs of hounds or horses were fit enough to hunt more than two or three days a week and hunting was still a slow business by later standards. While such circumstances existed it is easy to understand that each local hunt, the squire and his friends were part of the country scene. When they went hunting, whether after hare, deer or fox, the countrymen would be interested in all that happened and would remember and recount details of each hunt for years afterwards. It was, after all, an interruption in the very even tenor – not to say boredom – of their daily lives, spent for the most part in the grinding irksome toil of the fields. It was something of an adventure, something out of the ordinary, to watch the hunt pass and records of notable hunts over the years became part of the local legend and folklore, growing larger than life in the process.

It was partly the fact that when a huntsman was out with hounds he both enquired from the people he passed as to the whereabouts of the hunted quarry and acknowledged their response with genuine thanks that endeared hunting to the countryside. It was also a sense of their own participation in the hunt, even if only by proxy. The shepherd, or labourer in the fields, who saw the hunted fox or hare headed by a flock of sheep, or herd of cattle, slinking into a copse, was generally ready to share his knowledge with the huntsman. To this extent he shared in the day and gained a vicarious satisfaction in the kill. Thus hunting remained essentially a sport of the countryside, bringing a temporary equality to all concerned and enjoyed by both rich and poor alike.

Although this aspect of hunting scarcely altered – and indeed remains much the same today – there were two significant developments during the latter half of the eighteenth century. Those wealthy landowners or squires who felt disinclined to attend to the management of hounds themselves, or lacked the necessary knowledge to do so, sometimes employed a full-time huntsman to take charge of the hounds and, in the way of things, occasionally to hunt them. In some of the smaller hunts, such as those run by yeoman farmers, it was the custom to share the expenses of any hunt servants employed as earth-stoppers or the like. When it was necessary to economize, similar methods were sometimes employed by larger hunts. When friends and guests turned out to the meets of private packs, especially close to London, it gradually became accepted custom for the hunt servants to be allowed to take a cap round for emoluments from these hunt followers, thus to some extent sharing the costs of the hunt. It was a short step from this to subscription hunts whereby the hunt followers themselves subscribed to the cost of the hunt and appointed their own Master, but this was a change which only appeared towards the very end of the century.

During the early part of the eighteenth century, when few of these changes had begun to take effect, the centre of the Newmarket hunt gravitated northwards to Euston, whence in truly ducal style the 2nd Duke of Grafton hunted a vast area covering most of the present Suffolk hunt country as well as much of the Newmarket and Thurlow. On 2 December 1745, when Prince Charles Edward Stuart, the Young Pretender, was at the gates of Derby, little more than a hundred miles away, the Duke of Grafton, showing a fine contempt for the panic which had infected the whole of southern England including the City of London, or else determined to set an imperturbable example, chose to go hunting, apparently oblivious of the general commotion. In the event he proved to have his priorities right, for a fox was unkennelled in Euston Park which was hunted through no less than twenty-eight parishes before being killed south of Stowmarket and although Prince Charles took Derby on the 3rd his army was back in Edinburgh by Christmas with the rebellion all but over as far as England was concerned.

While this particular hunt was well outside the bounds of the present Newmarket and Thurlow country, it still gives an indication of the remarkable distances sometimes covered by hunts at that time. No doubt the Duke was capable of as deep incursions into the Thurlow country when hounds ran in that direction. His successors, the 3rd and 4th Dukes, also enjoyed their hunting and continued to hold sway over much of the country for a large part of the century.

Although it has been attributed to various packs, it was almost certainly these hounds hunting close to Newmarket in the Newmarket and Thurlow end of the country which were responsible for the strange incident in the latter half of the century involving Sir Robert Walpole's grandson George, the eccentric 3rd Earl of Orford (1730–1791). Amongst the 3rd Earl's eccentricities was the habit of driving from his home at Houghton Hall to Newmarket in a four-in-hand drawn by a team of tame stags harnessed instead of horses. Close to Newmarket the pack picked up the scent of the stags and started after them in full cry. Lord Orford was unable to control his panic-stricken team and the alarm of the passers-by in Newmarket may well be imagined as he rocked into the High Street at full speed with the hounds close behind him. The situation was saved by the prompt action of the ostler of the Ram Inn, which then stood on the site now occupied by the Rutland Arms (built in 1815). As the coach wheeled sharply in at the gates of the courtyard, he slammed them safely shut in front of the noses of the leading hounds.

Although the Dukes of Grafton continued to hunt the northern end of the Newmarket and Thurlow country into the late eighteenth century, the Suffolk country was really more convenient for them and their hunting appears to have been concentrated largely in that area. They were not in any event the only hunts in the Newmarket and Thurlow country, for there were others at the Thurlow end in the south. Notable amongst these was the hunt based on

Stoke College, the home of the Elwes family, notorious throughout much of the eighteenth century for their parsimony and eccentricity.

This hunt probably originated in the late seventeenth century in the time of Sir Gervase Elwes, who died in 1705 leaving his estate so encumbered with debt that his grandson Sir Harvey Elwes only inherited an income of a hundred pounds a year. Determined to relieve the estate of debt, he became famed for his miserliness, accumulating over a hundred thousand pounds before his death in 1763. The trait of avariciousness seems to have run in the family, as his sister, left a widow with a similar sum at her command, starved herself to death. Her son John Meggot, Sir Harvey's nephew, changing his name to Elwes, inherited the fortunes left by his mother and his uncles as well as the estate.

From 1763 to 1777 John Elwes hunted the country from Stoke College, spending about £300 a year on hounds and horses, enough in those days to provide modest sport. He then entered Parliament as member for Berkshire and gradually the family failing appears to have overcome him. He took to avoiding the turnpikes rather than pay the trifling sum involved and to living on hard-boiled eggs and scraps of stale bread which he carried about with him. Faced with the prospect of an election, he resigned rather than face the expenses involved in contesting the seat.

He withdrew to Stoke College and dismissed most of his servants, living in conditions close to penury in many respects. Yet he continued to hunt after a fashion and also plunged heavily on the turf at times, paying his debts of honour promptly. He only employed one servant-cum-huntsman and man-of-all-work whose daily itinerary was formidable. He rose at 4 a.m. each day, milked the cows, prepared breakfast for his master and friends, then donned a green coat and saddled the horses and brought out the hounds. After the meet and the day's sport he would rub down the horses before returning to the house to lay and serve dinner. When that was over he still had to feed the horses and hounds and litter them down before finally milking the cows again. No doubt Elwes's standards of hunting – like his establishment – left a good deal to be desired, but in one respect he triumphed, for he left his two natural sons half a million pounds on his death.

Probably much better from the point of view of sport was the yeoman farmers' hunt known by the lively name of the Hempstead Invincibles. The Master was Mr Thomas Andrews (1765–1847) of Wincelow Hall, Hempstead. He does not seem to have been particular where he hunted, frequently invading the territory of either the Puckeridge or the Newmarket and Thurlow.

It is said that on one occasion George Willis, Mr Andrews' kennel huntsman, reported to his Master that the hounds had escaped from their kennel in the middle of the night and he could hear them running in Hempstead Wood. He was promptly ordered to saddle up his horse and collect them. Fortunately for him the conditions were in his favour, for it was a bright moonlit night and there was also snow on the ground, so that he was able to follow their tracks, but even so it was not until he was at Hare Street, close to Buntingford, in the middle of the Puckeridge country, after close on a sixteen-mile point, that he was able at last to pick them up.

A similar yeoman farmers' pack, known as the Talents, also hunted the southern end of the country towards the turn of the century and likewise did not hesitate to trespass over the neighbouring hunt boundaries on occasions. Nor were these the only packs in the area known to hunt the Thurlow end of the country at times. Yet another pack was to be found in the direction of Bury St Edmunds. It was around 1792 that Sir Charles Davers of Rushbrook Hall first started hunting quite a wide stretch of country from this centre.

Few details of either of these hunts have survived, although it is reported that Sir Charles Davers' hounds were regarded as of high repute, even if his country was notably short of foxes. In such circumstances it is easy to understand that he might more often than not have found the need to make sorties into the Thurlow country. There must certainly have been occasions when this multiplicity of overlapping hunts caused some degree of confusion.

Yet, despite the Dukes of Grafton to the north and the other hunts in the south, it was not until 1770 that the Newmarket and Thurlow could really claim once more to have their own hunt centred on Newmarket. It was then that Mr Thomas Panton, who had for some years previously been acting as joint Master of the Puckeridge, moved up to Fen Ditton near Newmarket and started to hunt the country there with his own pack of hounds. The close connection between the Newmarket and Thurlow and the Puckeridge hunts may be said to date from this period. It would be interesting to know whether either or both were affected by the outbreak of distemper which swept the country for the first time in the 1780s, causing the death of many hounds.

Thomas Panton's father had much to do with the development of early racing and was 'Master of the King's Running Horses'. Born around 1731, Thomas Panton spent his early days with his friend Mr John Calvert in the Puckeridge country before taking over his father's property near Newmarket. Although chiefly known as a respected member of the Jockey Club and a racehorse-owner who won the Derby with Noble in 1796, he was also a keen hunting man. His hounds certainly seem to have been able to show good sport and there was no shortage of foxes then in the Newmarket and Thurlow country if the record of one hunt is any criterion. On 15 October 1793:

They found at Abbassy Wood, near Thurlow, when the fox broke covert and ran in two rings to Blunt's Park and back to Abbassy. He then flew his country, and went in a line to Lawn Wood, Temple Wood, to Hart Wood, where there were a brace of fresh foxes. The pack then divided, fifteen and a half couples went away close to the hunted fox, to West Wickham Common, Weston Colville and over Willingham Green, thence through open country to Six-Mile Bottom and Newmarket; headed by a chaise, he took a line for the Gogmagog Hill, and was run from scent to view, and, laying down, was killed in the open heath at the bottom of the hill; he stood up 1 hour and 45 minutes without a check. The six and a half couples of hounds killed a second fox at Withersfield and one couple of hounds killed the third at Thurlow Park gates.

Mr Panton's hounds were also said to have killed a fox close to the Rubbing House, Newmarket, after a twenty-five-mile run without a check, although no time was given for this feat. It is noteworthy that Mr Panton was accustomed to hunt with twenty-five couple of hounds. How many times a week he hunted, or how far his country extended, is unfortunately not on record. Let it suffice that he seems to have provided good sport and reunited the country after a considerable gap.

Soon after his Derby win with Noble in 1796 Mr Panton seems to have further cemented the connection between the Newmarket and Thurlow and the Puckeridge by taking a house in Ware and hunting with the Puckeridge once more. He died eventually, approaching eighty years of age, in 1808 in Newmarket. It would be interesting to know just how much change he noted in the Puckeridge country on his return after such a long gap and how he found the hunting in the two countries compared. At that time, especially, the difference of twenty-five miles in proximity to London made a very great difference.

Being farther south and closer to London, Hertfordshire was developing faster than traditionally 'sleepy' Suffolk. Vast quantities of barley, wheat and straw, as well as fresh vegetables, cattle, sheep and game, were required to satisfy London's requirements and Hertfordshire was one of the favourite sources. As a result, the roads were mostly turned into turnpikes before the middle of the eighteenth century, although this in itself was at that time no real guarantee as to their passability. It was not finally until the coming of Macadam in the early nineteenth century that they were really improved in anything approaching modern terms and even then the Hertfordshire lanes were noted for their narrow, winding, twisty ways.

The development of Hertfordshire resulted in many lawyers, doctors and other wealthy professional men of the expanding middle classes moving into the country from London. Successful brewers, merchants, industrialists, business men or tradesmen of various kinds also moved out of the city when they retired. All these, however, tended to regard London as the centre where they made their living and still maintained close ties with it.

During the late eighteenth century the village of Broxbourne on the edge of the Puckeridge country was typical of this sort of change, which naturally extended downwards to all classes. The Reverend William Jones, curate and vicar of Broxbourne for forty-four years from 1777 to 1821, noted that he was unable to 'remark any one house tenanted by the same mortals with whom I conversed thirty six years ago. Most of the houses have frequently changed their tenants.'

Although this dramatic rate of change had not really begun in the early half of the century there is no doubt that, being so close to London, the Puckeridge hunt developed at a different rate initially from the Newmarket and Thurlow. The original pack which hunted between Cheshunt and Hertford from around 1727 appears to have lasted until the 1740s when it was embodied in another hunt based on Redbourn and hunting towards St Albans in the present Vale of Aylesbury country. The uniform of this pack seems to have been a blue coat with a red collar. On the death of Felix Calvert at Albury Hall in 1756 his son Mr John Calvert the Elder moved this pack temporarily to Albury Hall before finally moving it in 1760 to Furneux Pelham. From this date onwards the Puckeridge hunt was in being, hunting much the same country as it does today.

The joint Masters of this early Puckeridge hunt, the first to hunt the Puckeridge country, were Mr John Calvert the Elder, Mr Thomas Panton, who went in 1770 to become Master of the Newmarket and Thurlow, and also Mr William Plumer, M.P. for Hertfordshire (1736–1822), who was a Member of Parliament from 1768 to 1822. Son of a previous M.P. for Hertfordshire, William Plumer (1687–1767), he does not appear to have left much of a mark behind him – at least as regards the hunt. His wife, however, of New Place, now Gilston Park, lived in great state, driving round the countryside in a large family chariot flanked by two outriders to the consternation of anyone she met in the narrow country lanes. On her husband's death she married twice more before her death in 1831 at the age of sixty-three and, according to report, behaved 'very much like a young lady in love'. Just how many times she headed the fox with her family chariot is not recorded.

Despite the fact that Mr John Calvert the Elder and Mr Thomas Panton obviously had the lion's share of the work, the joint mastership of the three, assisted by a huntsman named King, appears to have been successful enough. Whether the latter was the same King who was subsequently huntsman to Lady Salisbury when she started her pack of small harrier-type hounds nearby at Hatfield in 1775, amongst the first of many distinguished and long-lived female M.F.H.s, is not clear. One of the few references to him is a not very complimentary mention contained in an early letter about the hunt written some time around 1760 by Jacob Houblin of Hallingbury (1736–1783) to his cousin John Cotton. He wrote:

> Hounds met at Hormead Park, and Conyers and I lost a good day's sport through the obstinacy of King, who would not go off with two couple of hounds when the Pack followed a fox almost in view. We found at Shales [sic] Park – I think the place is called – and ran almost to Newport, where the hounds, for want of a huntsman, would not go on after the first check. A charming country, which made it all the more provoking.

At some time in the 1760s King was succeeded as huntsman by Will Crane, who it seems likely had been an innkeeper at Rivenhall in Essex with a considerable local reputation as a huntsman and a good man with hounds. When Mr Thomas Panton went off to the Newmarket and Thurlow in 1770 John Calvert the Elder remained in effect the dominant figure in the hunt. The principal hunt servants were Will Crane as huntsman and a whipper-in named Tom Hubbard, the son of a farmer, described as a hard rider and a great enthusiast.

On Will Crane's death in 1779 he was succeeded by Tom Hubbard. Shortly afterwards Mr William Plumer seems to have retired and for a brief year or two John Calvert the Elder remained as sole Master. It was not long, however, before he took his son John Calvert the Younger (1758–1844) into partnership and in 1785 at around the age of twenty-seven the latter took over the sole mastership.

It is perhaps typical of human nature that hitherto it had always been the Albury branch of the Calvert family – by far the least wealthy compared with those at Furneux Pelham and Hunsdon – who had dissipated their money on hunting although the latter had always been prepared to hunt when they felt like it. At this stage the financial burden appears to have begun to tell, for it was not long before John Calvert the Younger, keen sportsman and considerable authority on hunting as he was according to that rather dubious source Ansty, felt impelled to let Hubbard 'farm' the hounds. In other words John Calvert paid him a lump sum in return for maintaining horses and hounds to provide sport when required. Inevitably such a system was open to abuse since the Master did not have the same control over feeding and unscrupulous huntsmen were known to economize on feed to increase their income. It seems, however, to have worked well in this instance and the establishment continued as a private pack with no subscribers, for the benefit of John Calvert and his friends.

The first published account of a day's hunting with the Puckeridge appeared in *Bell's Life* in 1789, as follows:

> December 5th 1789. Old Hall Green: – Found at Woodcroft's and lost fox very soon. In going for Woodhall Springs the hounds struck a scent, which they hunted well to West Mill,

through Stonebury to Hormead Park, where the fox waited. Here their scent mended and they had an extraordinary fine run by Beeches and the sides of all the great woods, without touching one (none of which the fox appeared to know), to the edge of Rockalls; then over the champaign to Littlebury Green, and turning up to Green Wood they killed. It seems to be agreed by everybody out, that this was one of the best chases ever seen in the country. A favourite hound, called Liberty, had run so severely, that soon after the death of the fox she dropped dead! The horses were all tired; and it appears that not any one went completely the chase but Mr. Isaac's grey horse, bought of King!'

Allowing for the period flavour of the journalism there seems to be one or two possible inferences or innuendoes in this report which should be noted. Could the writer possibly be implying that, since it did not appear to know the great woods, they had been hunting a bag-fox? Are we to infer that since only one horse went the complete chase that some of the others were following the example introduced by Lord Sefton in the latter half of the eighteenth century and hunting with a second horse? Or could the King mentioned be the erstwhile huntsman and is this a sally at someone, possibly the current huntsman Hubbard? Regardless of these queries this was a point of twelve miles and clearly a good day's sport, although by no means the best they had during Hubbard's period as huntsman. Another good hunt two seasons later was described much more briefly thus:

November 7th, 1791. Bygrave: Found immediately and the fox killed before he could get away; again at Clothall Bury, from which we had as fine a run as ever was seen. The fox went straight away to King's Wood Springs, through Munches Dell and Westy to Sandon Row, where he took the champaign, and was killed at Morden in Cambridgeshire. It is supposed that we ran him at least fourteen miles over the open.

To be strictly accurate, Munches to Steeple Morden is only a seven-mile point, but this estimate need not necessarily be much of an exaggeration as hounds ran. By any standards it sounds like a very fine hunt, but despite the good hunting they were having with Tom Hubbard as huntsman it all seems to have been proving too much for John Calvert the Younger's finances. Up to the year 1794 the title of the hunt was without question 'Mr. Calvert's'. In that year he finally decided to turn it into a full subscription hunt with a committee of fourteen members running its affairs.

So great was John Calvert's popularity, however, or the Calvert influence in the country, that no one wished to change the name of the hunt. It was Mr Calvert himself who insisted on calling it 'The Hertfordshire Hunt', but such is the countryman's resistance to change that it remained in most people's minds 'Mr Calvert's'. Whether he liked it or not, he remained as the figurehead in charge, deputizing as Master, or Field Master, in such duties as had not already been handed over to Tom Hubbard, who still continued to farm the pack.

It was only in the year 1799 that John Calvert the Younger finally managed to hand over the management of the hunt to his friend and neighbour Mr Sampson Hanbury of Poles. A Calvert cousin, Mr Nicolson Calvert of Furneux Pelham and Hunsdon (1764–1841) came in as joint Master with Mr Hanbury and Mr John Calvert the Younger remained in the background as a shadowy joint Master with them. It was thus that the Puckeridge hunt moved into the nineteenth century.

Chapter 3

The First Quarter of the
Nineteenth Century

THE last two decades of the eighteenth century saw Britain's fortunes abroad apparently declining steadily. The American War of Independence ended in 1783 with the ignominious recognition of the United States of America as an independent nation, a republic owing no allegiance to the Crown. The outbreak of the French Revolution in 1789 brought fears of a similar upheaval at home, soon followed by declaration of war with France in 1793. The rise of Napoleon and the long-drawn-out struggle for very existence which followed, with defeat succeeding defeat on land and the only victories at sea, continued over the turn of the century. For the first time since the Armada militia forces were raised with a view to defending the coast against invasion. Yet, despite the calamities abroad and the threat to her own shores, life in England continued almost without change. Agriculture, aided by new inventions and improved methods of crop management, was flourishing and the countryside remained seemingly unaltered with the same country pursuits and interests as of old. Despite the war abroad, the essential countryside of England remained to outward appearances almost untouched.

It may be that there were more military uniforms to be seen about, sometimes even in the hunting field. Certainly it presented a colourful enough appearance at times, with a medley of red, green, brown and blue coats to be seen on occasions, although in general a red coat was the commonest wear. As far as headgear was concerned, the cap with a peak, similar to the present hunt cap, had replaced the tricornes of the early and mid-eighteenth century, even if there may have been some diehards who still clung to the old fashions for hats or wigs, which had also begun to disappear around the 1780s. The flattish beaver hat, or more pronounced top-hat, were the other modes in general use by the end of the eighteenth century. Of course, women in the hunting field riding side-saddle were still very much a law unto themselves as regards dress.

In the first decade of the nineteenth century there were two major developments which were to affect hunting radically throughout the country for the rest of the century, and even to the present day. The first of these was due to the inventive mind of an obscure Aberdeenshire minister of religion. The second was the culmination of bad blood between two titled half-brothers in Hertford-shire. That the Puckeridge and the Newmarket and Thurlow hunts were close to the source of the latter of these developments may have helped to ensure that they were the less affected by it.

It was in 1807 that the Reverened Alexander Forsyth, the minister or Belhelvie in Aberdeenshire, a keen wildfowler, who had for a long time been experimenting with a method of preventing misfires in wet conditions, finally patented a means of percussion ignition. This was the long-awaited breakthrough which led eventually to the flintlock becoming obsolete. Since it enabled faster loading and shooting, it also led inevitably to more battue shooting, hence to more intensive game preservation. This in turn led to a conflict of interests between hunting and shooting, which in some areas was to cause ill-feeling and unnecessary strife between rival sportsmen for many years to come.

In 1808 the Earl of Essex was the plaintiff in the court in Hertford in a civil action for trespass against his half-brother whom he detested, the Honourable and Reverend William Capel, M.F.H. of the Old Berkeley hunt. A fanatically keen game preserver and shooting man, the Earl sued his half-brother for damages for trespass with his pack of hounds and hunt followers in his coverts. It was in this particular instance really a personal matter, but there were much larger issues at stake. It had always been understood that foxhounds had an ancient common law right to ride on anyone's land in pursuit of vermin without requiring permission. Lord Ellenborough's judgement in this case came out clearly against this supposition. The Earl of Essex won his case and despite the fact that he only received a shilling's damages he had made his point at his half-brother's expense and was personally satisfied.

The immediate reaction was that this was the death-knell of hunting but, surprisingly, it had directly the opposite effect. It forced foxhunters throughout the country to reconsider their position and ensure that anyone whose ground they might wish to ride over was approached beforehand and also recompensed for any damage incurred. It ensured that the hunts, in order to survive, remained on friendly terms with everyone living in the countryside. In this respect hunting was always to have the edge on shooting, for while hunting remained basically the sport of the countryside in which all took part, or to

18

some degree were involved, shooting too often became the sport of outsiders who took ground solely for the shooting and gave little or nothing back to the countryside.

Where it was not already common practice it became essential for each hunt to have a regular dinner and ball each year and to present such attractions as a cup or prize for a farmers' race in the hunt races. These sort of attentions to public relations were henceforward necessary to survival, especially where subscription packs were involved. In the case of private packs, steadily growing less common as the century advanced, it was up to the landowner or squire to make his own arrangements of a similar nature and to ensure that there were no neighbours who objected to his hunting over their ground. Without these or similar precautions, and without ensuring that the entire countryside was involved in the hunt to a greater or lesser degree, it was clear from the decision in the Capel case that hunting could not continue.

Colonel John Cook made this point very clear in his book *Observations on Fox Hunting*, which was published in 1826. Son of a wealthy miller in Hampshire, John Cook obtained his promotion in the army by purchase as was the custom in those days – but showed very little real interest in soldiering. He spent his life and most of his money in following his favourite sport, namely foxhunting. From 1800 to 1804 he was the Master of the Newmarket and Thurlow in succession to Mr Thomas Panton. Although no records remain it seems likely that on Mr Panton's retirement the hunt followers turned the hunt into a subscription pack and invited John Cook to be their Master. Since he went on to become successively master of the Essex and of the Hambledon before writing his book in 1826 his experience by that time was considerable and some of his comments were very relevant.

On the subject of game preservation and foxhunting he wrote revealingly:

For some time . . . there has been a war between the Pheasant and the Fox; during which period (what may seem not a little extraordinary and I state it with regret) the former has generally been victorious . . . I hope my brother Sportsmen of the trigger will not be offended; I am as anxious for the preservation of game as any man; my only fear is that it will be carried to too great an extent, and in the end defeat its object. If I were to say a vixen Fox that had cubs would *not* lay hold of the first eatable thing she met with, whether game, fowl or rabbit, I should be making a false statement; but if there are *plenty of the latter*, Foxes will destroy but little game . . .

He referred to an experience when hunting over the Newmarket and Thurlow country:

I was requested . . . to meet at Chippenham, near Newmarket, the owner of which and his keeper said we might *by chance* find a fox, but they were certain no Foxes had been *bred* there, as they had not lost a single head of game. I never in my life saw so many pheasants of every sort, and hares innumerable; and, to the astonishment of all present, in the very middle of the preserve, and lying with the pheasants, so near that they must almost have touched each other, we found a litter of Foxes, six or seven in number. We killed the old dog and one of the cubs. I must observe, however, there were plenty of rabbits – but they were not the keeper's perquisite . . .

On the subject of earth-stopping John Cook also had his own definite and slightly biased views, which were no doubt the product of sound experience at the time. They certainly show a shrewd insight into the minds of the countrymen of the day and also cast an interesting sidelight on the methods employed in overcoming the scarcity of foxes. After expounding on the subject of establishing earths with the aid of badgers where necessary, he continued:

. . . your next consideration must be the appointment of careful earth stoppers, as their duty extends to the taking care of the litters of foxes, as well as to the stopping of the earths; and in order to be certain of having them *well stopped*, you will find it safest to pay for each time of stopping and agree with the people who perform this necessary service, that if the earths are not stopped at the proper time and as they ought to be, *they will not be paid for that day's stopping.*

If, after this notice, you run to ground in any particular man's stop, you had better discharge him immediately. It is nothing more than fair that the keepers should stop the earths in their own manors, it may be the means of saving a litter of foxes. Keepers in general will not refuse a sovereign, so that if you make it answer *their* purpose they will not destroy your foxes unless they have secret orders from their masters to do it. Earth stoppers that are paid *annually*, if it happens to be an open winter, and they have to stop often, think it a hardship; whereas, the man who is paid *every time he stops*, takes pleasure in doing it, knowing he will be recompensed for his trouble. It is in his *interest* also to look after the foxes, for the more he has in his district, the oftener the hounds will be there.

It is plain from Cook's *Observations* that although there was still considerable confusion regarding the boundaries of hunts and quite a few other aspects of hunting certain customs were becoming generally accepted (at least by 1826). Even so, it is apparent that relations between neighbouring Masters were often extremely strained for he warned that:

If you should, after a good day's sport, run a fox to ground in a neighbouring hunt, according to the laws of fox-hunting it is not correct to dig him. If you run him into a main earth, the best way will be to leave the place with as little delay as possible, to prevent any misrepresentation that might lead to a misunderstanding; for no people (I will not even except the riders of the present day) are so jealous of each other as masters of foxhounds. But if you should run your fox into a drain, or any hole that is not a regular fox-earth, it is then thought fair to bolt him in any way you can, except by digging; but on no account must you allow a spade to enter the ground. It may be your hunted fox, or it may not . . .

There was obviously deep feeling behind these comments, which indicates that Cook had suffered numerous acrimonious arguments on such scores. He also seems to have suffered somewhat from the invasions of the Newmarket and Thurlow country by the famed Hempstead Invincibles under their Master, yeoman farmer Mr Thomas Andrews, and his hunstman George Willis, for while writing on the subject of the number of hounds required for hunting he mentioned them with a note of admiration as well as exasperation. He wrote:

The number of days you intend to hunt must be regulated according to your establishment, the extent of your country, and the stock of foxes you have in it. I should say four days a week, *for a pack of fifty couples*, will keep your hounds and horses in regular work. You had better divide them into two separate packs . . . twenty or one-and-twenty couples . . . is as many as you ever ought to take into the field . . . even sixteen couples, that know each other will do the thing . . . How disgusting it is to see a large pack out, and only a few couples at the head! . . . I have known a few hounds, kept by some farmers (not exceeding sixteen couples) that *seldom missed a fox*, – they were named 'The invincibles':

> 'There was
> Invincible Tom and invincible Towler,
> Invincible Jack and invincible Jowler.'

Although they were occasionally a great annoyance to me, and disturbed the cream of the country formerly hunted by the late Mr. Panton, I could not be displeased with them; the farmers who managed them were respectable people, fond of the sport and had as much right to hunt as I had.

There seems to have been no doubt that Mr Thomas Andrews and his hunts-man George Willis were individualists and it is perhaps not surprising that their hounds had something of the same flavour. There is a rare print by J. Walls of Saffron Walden, entitled 'Chaunter, A Favourite Hound, the Property of Mr Thomas Andrews, of Hempstead, Essex. Published July 16th 1810'. It appears that Chaunter had the distinction of having his portrait painted due to the fact that he had hunted and killed a fox single-handed, although whether this feat was performed on his own ground, or on that of the Puckeridge, or of the New-market and Thurlow, is not stated.

When it came to describing remarkable hunts John Cook was again forced to praise Mr Andrews' pack. Considering the hunt seems to have been almost entirely within the boundaries of the Newmarket and Thurlow this was mag-nanimous indeed. He recorded:

. . . the most extraordinary run for distance was one the Hempstead hounds (termed the Invincibles) had from Great Hayles, a covert near Saffron Walden, belonging to Lord Bray-brook, to within four or five miles of Bury St. Edmund's in Suffolk, near Glemsford earth. where they killed him; I should think the distance 25 miles at least as the crow flies . . .

Whether Colonel Cook fell out with his subscribers or not is difficult to say, but the impression gained from the *Observations* is that he probably did. He spent his four years as Master living alone in a cottage opposite the Cock Inn at Thurlow. Obviously by inference he considered that some of his supporters were two-faced on the subject of preserving foxes. The comment attributed to him summing up his feelings on the period of his mastership was: 'Foxes and subscriptions damnably short'.

When he left the Newmarket and Thurlow in 1805 for the neighbouring Essex hunt the Colonel was succeeded by the Reverend Davers, who had taken over the pack of hounds belonging to his brother Sir Charles Davers of Rushbrooke. Although East Anglia has been famed for her sporting parsons from the eighteenth century onwards, the spectacle of a clergyman who was also an M.F.H. was unusual. The attitude of the Church towards hunting has always been ambivalent and a great deal depended on the views held by the bishop. Towards the middle of the nineteenth century the practice of a parson hunting a pack of hounds was generally frowned on rather more than either at the start or the end of the period, but riding to hounds was, of course, unexceptionable.

The classic Suffolk story, relating perhaps to the Newmarket and Thurlow, is of the sporting parson who was up with hounds as they marked a fox to ground and, seeing the preparations being made to dig him out, looked at his watch and remarked: 'That reminds me, I had better go now, I have a burial at four.'

The Reverened William Jones, vicar of Broxbourne at the southern end of the Puckeridge country over this period, had some harsh – but perhaps sometimes not unjustified – comments to make on 'mighty hunting Nimrods of the cloth' and noted that:

> For the accommodation of the latter class of these Reverends daily advertisments appear for the sale of the next presentations of valuable livings, rendered much more valuable as being 'situated in fine sporting countries' – 'plenty of game' – 'a pack of staunch fox-hounds kept in the neighbourhood' &c &c. These men are, of course, rare, charming preachers!

There is little doubt that Jones, poor henpecked man that he was, and with a considerable chip on his shoulder at times, was giving vent to his spleen on this occasion. There is no evidence regarding how well or how badly the Reverend Davers preached. There is even a considerable question as to how long he continued to hunt the country, for some records suggest it was merely for eight years up to 1813, whereas others suggest it was longer. In fact it seems probable there was a hiatus around the time of Waterloo in 1815. The slump in the price of corn due to the sudden ending of wartime scarcities and the influx of men back from the army and navy resulted in a period of unrest in the countryside.

22

It does not seem to have been long, however, before Mr Charles Newman of the East Essex began hunting the Thurlow country as well.

During the season of 1822 he was temporarily ousted by George Osbaldeston, famed as the Squire of All England and perhaps the greatest all-round sportsman of his day. In October, Osbaldeston took over the mastership of the Newmarket and Thurlow, making Thurlow Cottage his headquarters. A writer in *The Sporting Magazine*, in November 1822, noted that Mr Newman's

subscription pack has been obliged to give way to Mr. Osbaldeston, whose quick, animated style of hunting, extraordinary knowledge of breeding, selecting and breaking hounds; the cheerful, good-natured way he meets his friends in the field; with a due sense of the kindness shown him by the nobility and gentry preserving foxes – added to its being no longer a subscription pack – promise a permanence this country desires and deserves . . . Some of their runs have already been very good.

Another writer in *The Sporting Magazine* after praising the beauty of the pack went on:

It is something new to see them stick to their fox and eat him at the end of an hour in an immense wood so thick that it was next to impracticable for a team of spaniels. Mr. Osbaldeston, with his injured leg in a laced boot, rode a neat chestnut and went very steadily and hunted his hounds with great patience and judgement . . . [hence foxes] were very scarce at the end of the season.

As it happens, these eulogistic passages from *The Sporting Magazine* were far from accurate and demonstrate the advisability of not necessarily believing everything written in popular journals. Osbaldeston's mastership was to be anything but permanent. He was merely filling in time while recovering from a severely broken leg, the result of a bad fall while M.F.H. of the Quorn the previous year, before returning to Leicestershire once again in 1823, after serving as Master for only a year. Furthermore 'the Squire' had noted that foxes were scarce when he took over the country and on 19 November he commissioned a reserve of 'bag-men' from Mr Hopkins, of Tottenham Court Road, the well-known supplier of bag-foxes, specifying 'old English foxes, no —— French dunghills'.

Although this was common practice of the day, extending even into the early twentieth century in some cases, his predecessor John Cook would not have approved. He wrote firmly:

. . . whatever you do never turn out a *bag-man*; it is injurious to your hounds, makes them wild and unsteady; besides nothing is more despicable, or held in greater contempt by real sportsmen than the practice of hunting bag-foxes. It encourages a set of rascals to steal from other hunts; therefore keep in mind, 'if there were no receivers, there would be no thieves.' What chiefly contributes to make fox-hunting so far superior to other sports *is the wildness of the animal you hunt, and the difficulty in catching him.* It is rather extraordinary, but nevertheless a well known fact, that a pack of hounds which are kept in sport and blood, will not eat a bag-man.

On George Osbaldeston's abrupt return to the Quorn in 1823 there appears to have been a hiatus for a period during which the familiar anarchy reigned, 'The Invincibles' no doubt vieing with Mr Charles Newman's subscription pack in the southern part of the country and the Suffolk hunting the northern end. Suffice it that in 1827 Mr George Mure, of Herringswell Hall, near Barton Mills, took over most of the Newmarket and Thurlow country as well as most of that previously hunted by the Dukes of Grafton in Suffolk.

Meanwhile the Puckeridge had developed on much steadier lines. This almost certainly had a good deal to do with the fact that it was a lot closer to London. John Cook had noted this as a considerable advantage and gave his reasons plainly as usual:

Should you happen to keep hounds at no great distance from London, you will find many of the inhabitants of that capital (cockneys, if you please) good *sportsmen*, well mounted and riding well to hounds; they never interfere with the management of them when in the field, contribute liberally to the expense, and pay their subscriptions regularly. The sum of fifty or a hundred pounds is nothing out of an individual's pocket; but to a manager of a subscription pack, the fact of *twenty subscribers*, each paying his fifty to a day, is a thing of no small consequence, as he is required to pay for almost every article in advance, old oats, hay, meal &c and the *interest on the money* amonts to one subscription at the least. Whenever I went to town I received the greatest kindness and hospitality from these Gentlemen; capital dinners and the choicest wines. We occasionally went 'the best pace over the mahogany' and often ran the *Portuguese* a sharp burst and whoo-whooped many a long corked *Frenchman*!

Another factor in the steady development of the Puckeridge over this period was the undoubted wealth and popularity of Mr Sampson Hanbury of Poles, who had become joint Master with Mr John Calvert and Mr Nicolson Calvert in 1799. A partner in the firm of Truman, Hanbury and Buxton – later to be better known simply as Truman's – Mr Hanbury combined brewing with foxhunting and was well described by the novelist R. S. Surtees in *The New Sporting Magazine* as follows:

The Squire himself would make an admirable subject for the pen of an Addison or Washington Irving. His low-crowned hat, square-cut coat, flapped waistcoat, big boots and breeches, good natured smile, a word for everybody, added to his slow and cautious style of riding, and the rat-tailed brown horse that walked in and out of his fences, present the beau ideal of an old English country gentleman . . . I have often heard Mr. Hanbury spoken of as the best judge of hounds and one who knows more about pedigrees than any M.F.H. in the country.

24

George Mure of Herringswell, Suffolk, Master of the East Suffolk 1827–45, by J. F. Herring, Senior, 1831

ABOVE: Mr Sampson Hanbury of Poles, Master of the Puckeridge 1799–1832

OPPOSITE TOP: *A meet at Chippenham Park with George Mure, Master of the East Suffolk, and his huntsman William Rose,* by J. F. Herring, Senior, 1832

OPPOSITE BOTTOM: Chaunter. One of the Hempstead Invincibles, Chaunter killed a fox single-handed. From the print published in 1810 by J. Wallis, Saffron Walden

Mr John Chapman, 'from a picture presented to the yeomanry of the Puckeridge Hunt by Francis Grant, Esq., 1840'

OPPOSITE TOP: Mr John Dalyell, Master of the Puckeridge 1835–8. From an illustration in the *New Sporting Magazine* after Francis Grant

OPPOSITE BOTTOM: Mr Nicholas Parry, Master of the Puckeridge 1838–75. From the print after Francis Grant, 1863

Mr Richard Simpson, huntsman of the Puckeridge 1838–51, on Struggles. From a print after R. B. Davis, in *The Hunters' Annual*, 1841

Mr John Josselyn, and hounds, 1865

THE NOBLE SCIENCE.   Tomkins and his friend
(who have been thrown out) congratulate themselves
on falling in with the Squire's second horseman, who
is sure to bring them by a line of gates to the hounds
again – and so he does, only the last of the gates is
locked and over which he 'hops like a bird'.
From the drawing by John Leech, 1858. An incident
said to have been inspired by Brewer

Brewer, second horseman to Mr Nicholas Parry

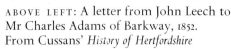

73

ABOVE LEFT: A letter from John Leech to
Mr Charles Adams of Barkway, 1852.
From Cussans' *History of Hertfordshire*

ABOVE RIGHT: Abraham Firr, kennelman
to the Puckeridge Hunt 1814–38 and 1855–76

LEFT: Mr John Sworder of Barkway, 1847–1933

Unfortunately in many ways Mr Hanbury was perhaps too easy-going, for his early choices as huntsman were extremely indifferent. On Hubbard's death in 1802 he moved the hounds to Standon Lordship, still then the property of the Plumer family, and appointed George Sharp as his huntsman. He had been in royal service as huntsman to the Duke of Cumberland's staghounds and did not remain more than a season with the Puckeridge having quarrelled with an influential supporter, finally ending as huntsman with the Royal Buckhounds. He was followed by a man named Holmes, whom 'Ansty' referred to as a poor performer. In 1807 he was succeeded by a yeoman farmer named Canning, who 'farmed' the hounds but gave up after two seasons.

Finally, the whipper-in, John Monk, was promoted to huntsman and stayed in the post from 1809 to 1823. He also 'farmed' the hounds, but appears to have relied too much on his whippers-in, George Barwick, who succeeded him, and Will Church, who became Mr Hanbury's stud-groom. From 1809 to 1814 the hounds were still kennelled at Standon Lordship but, possibly due to interference by the Plumer family, Mr Hanbury moved them to new kennels in Puckeridge in that year. Cook described these kennels briefly but approvingly:

The kennel at Puckeridge in Hertfordshire, which cost about £500 building, is very convenient, dry and healthy, and the hounds have no lameness.

At this period the pack was known officially as 'The Hertfordshire' and unofficially as 'Mr Calvert's'. As late as 1816 this was how Mr Hanbury himself was referring to them in a letter to Lord Hardwicke of Wimpole Hall. In 1819, however, Lady Salisbury, finally grown too old for hunting in her sky-blue habit, handed over her Hatfield Hounds to the Hertfordshire Hunt Club. It is possible that the confusion thus caused resulted in the name 'The Puckeridge' being adopted by the Hertfordshire hunt, for it seems to be about this time that the change occurred, although the earliest mention of the title 'The Puckeridge' in print is in the *Sporting Magazine* of 1828.

Although a good horseman and excellent judge of a horse, John Monk was too keen on horse dealing to wish to damage any of the horses he rode, which he hoped to sell for a good round sum. His slackness finally led to a demand for his removal by the hunt supporters. Although he showed some quite good sport, the best hunts were undoubtedly in his last season when George Barwick was hunting hounds. A good example was on Monday, 6 February 1823. After meeting at Dassels, finding a fox and killing in covert:

They then drew Hormead Park, where they found a second fox, which went away in gallant style through Hormead and thence to Hormead Hall. From Hormead Hall he took straight across country to Scales Park, skirting that on the right without going into it and made away for Clavering Park, leaving Lady Groves Park on the left. He then went straight up the country, crossed Chishall Common, leaving Rofway and High Wood on the right. Here the hounds came to a check, when George Barwick, who was mounted on his favourite brown mare, by young Sir Peter, made a most brilliant cast and set them again to work. They then went away to Pond Street Wood, from thence to Rochelles, and leaving that again faced the open to Green Wood, from thence to Littlebury Hoo, through Shuttle Wood, where he was completely beaten and killed, having run for two hours and a half in the most gallant style.

The clamour for John Monk's removal mounted and finally Mr Hanbury was forced to give way. Monk went off to run a livery stable at Puckeridge and George Barwick succeeded him in 1824. Having been brought up in the famous Colonel Thomas Thornton's hunting stables at Thornville Royal in Yorkshire, Barwick proved to be an excellent huntsman, level-tempered and quick-witted as well as wise with hounds and in the way of a fox. For the next nine seasons he was to provide excellent sport for the Puckeridge hunt.

Chapter 4

The Period up to 1845

THE years up to 1825 saw the turnpike roads, greatly improved by the road surfaces introduced first by Telford then by Macadam, the scene of ever faster travel with the mail- and stage-coaches steadily perfecting their services upon them. Whether in post-chaises or coaches, in carriages or gigs, the horse was the primary motive force and the roads, with their coaching inns at frequent intervals, the dominant feature of travel until 1825. That year, however, saw the opening of the Stockton to Darlington railway and from then on the days of the coach or carriage on the roads as the principal method of travel were numbered. Steam power replaced the horse and the railways replaced the roads with astonishing speed. Railway mania soon had the country firmly in its grip. Despite the efforts of the coach operators to compete, the opening of each new railway saw the closure of yet another coach service. By 1845 almost the last of the stage-coaches still in operation was the Norwich to London via Newmarket and that was to close on 6 January of the following year.

From 1825 to as late as 1835 the coach services continued to fight a losing battle. Combining for once with the railway lobby, they managed in 1831 to check the innovation of steam coach services on the roads, maintaining that their noisy, snorting engines would frighten horses and cause accidents. The requirement of a man walking in front with a red flag was to hold back the introduction of the motor-car for some fifty years, but it did not check the progress of the railways. Although landowners and farmers at first objected to the surveying teams crossing their land, followed by hordes of navvies laying tracks and digging deep cuttings, they were not slow in perceiving the advantages of the new method of travel.

The immediate reaction of most hunting men to the suggestion of having a railway driven across their country was that hunting simply could not continue. To many it seemed like the death-knell of foxhunting. No doubt there were some hunts which were adversely affected and gruesome stories of accidents to hounds straying on to the lines are not unheard of even today, but surprisingly enough the effect of the railways eventually proved to be diametrically opposed to the general expectations. It became possible, by judicious use of the railways, to hunt in countries where it had not previously been possible. By sending two hunters ahead to a railway station and picking them up in due course, hunting could be enjoyed with several packs many miles apart. To this extent hunting in the latter half of the century was to receive a stimulus from the railways which had not been anticipated.

There were other side-effects which were undoubtedly favourable to hunting. Those farmers who had previously concentrated on breeding horses for coach work now turned instead to breeding hunters. With the introduction of good coaching strains, such as the Cleveland Bay and others, an improved standard of heavy hunter inevitably followed. Furthermore, the vast numbers of ostlers, grooms and post-boys who had been attached to the various large coaching concerns, or inns, were available to work in the hunting field. From around 1835 onwards every hunt in the country can have had no difficulty in obtaining kennel staff or second horsemen. Finally, the roads which had once been comparatively crowded with coach traffic soon became grass-grown and empty save for occasional farm-carts and foot traffic. Hunting, which had already begun to achieve much better sport than in the previous century, was thus to achieve near perfection.

In practice the Newmarket and Thurlow country was never greatly affected by the railways and the first in that area was only completed in 1846. Throughout the period in question, therefore, the countryside remained entirely dependent on horse transport. There was unfortunately also a paucity of records at this time. In 1823, after Squire Osbaldeston had left the country as abruptly as he had arrived, it is not clear whether the Reverend Davers was still hunting his hounds from Rushbrooke. There is also a disparity of dates as to when his successor, Mr George Mure, took over the country, some records giving 1825 and others 1827.

Mr Mure (1797–1848) was, as his name suggests, of Scottish origin – his cousin, the owner of large estates at Herringswell Hoo, near Mildenhall, to whom he was heir, having been amongst the first of many Scots to settle in East Anglia. He himself had been gazetted into the Grenadier Guards and at the age of eighteen served at Waterloo. Like Colonel Cook, however, he preferred hunting to a military life.

It was almost certainly 1827 when he took over the kennels at Rushbrooke with a view to hunting the Suffolk country, but the scale of his establishment is not clear. The costs of hunting at this period are, however, well covered by

Colonel John Cook in his *Observations*. He noted that a friend had asked him his opinion on the costs of hunting twice a week with a pack of hounds. He answered accordingly:

At the present rate of taxes, supposing the price of corn, meal, hay &c to be what it is now, I should say for twice a week only, twenty five couple of *effective* hounds would be sufficient; and supposing you hunted your own hounds, and had only one whipper-in, five horses and a hack for yourself and servant would be quite enough. You must also have a groom, helper and feeder; making in the whole four men, five and twenty couple of hounds, five hunters and a hack. The earth-stopping expenses will depend upon the country. The calculation I have made is as follows:

The expenses for twice a week:	£
Six horses, including groom and helpers	300
Hounds' food for 25 couples	150
Firing	30
Taxes	80
Whipper-in and feeder	140
Earth-stopping	50
Sadlery	40
Farriery, shoeing, medicine, &c	50
Young hounds purchased and expenses at walks	60
Casualties	100
	1000
A second whipper-in and two horses in addition	170
	1170

Expenses for three times a week:	
Twelve horses, groom helpers, &c	600
Hounds food for forty couples	220
Firing	40
Taxes	100
Two whippers-in and feeder	210
Earth-stopping	65
Sadlery	80
Farriery, shoeing, medicine, &c	80
Young hounds purchased and expenses at walks	80
Casualties	150
	1625

Expenses for four times a week:	
Fourteen horses &c.	700
Hounds food for fifty couples	275
Firing	50

29

Taxes	120
Two whippers-in and feeder	210
Earth-stopping	80
Sadlery	100
Farriery, shoeing, medicines, &c	100
Casualties	200
	1935

A notable point in Colonel Cook's book, dated 1826, is that he listed only one pack still hunting in Suffolk, namely Mr Charles Newman's Essex Union, from which it would appear that the Reverend Davers had certainly given up his hounds by this time, while Mr Mure had not as yet started his pack at Rushbrooke. Of course, this does not allow for small private packs such as the Talents or the Invincibles, for the latter may well still have been hunting as indiscriminately as ever since their owner and Master Mr Andrews did not die until 1846. Squire Osbaldeston by this time, of course, was back with the Quorn, where indeed Cook lists him as hunting once again. It would seem therefore that for that year at least Mr Charles Newman's subscription pack was the only one hunting the Thurlow country until Mr Mure in the following year started hunting from Rushbrooke what was in essence the Suffolk country, including also the Newmarket and Thurlow territory. Whether he took over the Reverend Davers hounds or whether they had long been dispersed is another matter.

For the next seventeen years, with Will Rose as huntsman and Sam Hibbs as whip, Mr Mure was to hunt the country with considerable zest, taking in much the same area that had been hunted by the Dukes of Grafton. Like the Graftons before him, he seems to have covered a vast range of country, on one occasion even running a fox from Pakenham Fen almost to Colchester before giving up due to lack of scent. How many days a week he hunted is not clear, but he seems to have hunted the Thurlow country when it suited him and to have provided good sport for his followers.

It is significant that about this time, 1827, a Thurlow Hunt Club was formed, perhaps only with a view to preserving foxes, of which the country was clearly in short supply according to both Colonel Cook and Squire Osbaldeston, or perhaps with a view to starting up a subscription pack once again. Whatever their intentions, the Thurlow Hunt Club only appears to have survived a few years and left no records of its meetings. The conclusion must be that Mr Mure managed to show sufficient sport in the Thurlow country to satisfy those concerned.

No doubt in 1831 the hunt followers were surprised by the spectacle of their old Master, George Osbaldeston, riding over to Newmarket at regular intervals while preparing for his epic ride of two hundred miles in less than ten hours for a wager of one thousand guineas. During most of the cubhunting season of that year. while hunting the Pytchely, he used to ride once a week from Pitsford in Northamptonshire to Newmarket, a matter of sixty miles, to ride a further eighty miles at full gallop on the horses he had chosen for the wager. His routine was to start for Newmarket after cubhunting with the Pytchely on Wednesday, spend Thursday on Newmarket Heath and return that evening ready for cubhunting again on Friday with the Pytchely.

It must be this that gave rise to the enduring and often-repeated legend that for a season, or even longer, he hunted both the Newmarket and Thurlow and the Pytchely countries together, commuting regularly between them overnight. Apart from the sheer impossible physical strain involved in such a feat, which he would undoubtedly have chronicled with justifiable pride in his diaries, the costs would have been more than even such a free-spending wealthy sportsman as Osbaldeston could have afforded. It is perhaps possible that on one or more occasions when they were meeting near Newmarket he went out with Mr Mure's hounds over the Thurlow country, but it seems highly unlikely since he would clearly have preferred to hunt with his own hounds and he was obviously involved in an intensive training programme at this period.

As a feat of endurance his two-hundred-mile ride against the clock and his preparations for it were remarkable enough by any standards. He completed the distance in eight hours forty-two minutes 'in gallant style' and then 'kept it up till two o'clock next morning'. Almost certainly many of his old followers from his days with the Newmarket and Thurlow were amongst the spectators on the Heath when he won his wager on 5 November.

Although Mr Mure was perhaps not in quite the same class as the 'Squire of All England', he must have proved a popular enough Master of Hounds, for he continued to hunt the country without any overt opposition. In 1836 he inherited the family estates at Herringswell Hoo from his cousin, but by then he had already moved his hounds there from Rushbrooke. When he wished to hunt the Thurlow end of the country it seems to have been his habit to move down to stables at Fornham for a few nights.

It was not until March 1845 that Mr George Mure finally retired at the age of forty-eight, after hunting the country with the same huntsman and whip for seventeen seasons. The last entry in his hunting diary read: 'Stopped by frost, 17 days; hunted, 38; killed, 24 foxes; ran to ground, 5; blank days, 2.' From this it would appear that he was in the habit of hunting twice a week or thereabouts. It would also appear that the foxes justified the title of 'stout' generally applied to them, in the sense that they seem to have provided good sport.

The pack was then taken over by Mr John Josselyn (1816–1888), member of an old Suffolk family, who hunted them from his estate at St Edmund's Hill, Bury St Edmund's. No doubt the huntsman, Will Rose, had decided to retire at the same time as Mr Mure, for one of Mr Josselyn's first actions was to take on Will Jarvis as whip and promote Sam Hibbs to huntsman, a position he filled ably until his death in the saddle in 1864. An extremely popular Master, he was to show great sport in the Thurlow country, including a notable hunt in February 1846, when they found at 'The Lawn' and killed at Weston Colville, an eighteen-mile point.

There is little doubt that during the prolonged hiatus, while the Newmarket and Thurlow and Suffolk hunts were virtually one entity, the southern end of the country round Thurlow was frequently invaded by other hunts. The East Essex and the Puckeridge were only two which had occasional successful runs ending deep in Thurlow country. Clearly such a state of affairs was not entirely desirable, even if it was to continue to the end of Mr Josselyn's three separate periods as Master.

Of course, then as now, occasional invasions of neighbouring hunt territory were unavoidable. Ansty, that regular if highly inaccurate contributor to the *Sporting Magazine* on the subject of the Puckeridge hunt, wrote of a day on 24 December 1827 when Mr Hanbury's pack, as they were still known, found at Hadham Park and running by Dunmow finally lost their fox at Skreens in the Essex country. Not content with this remarkable thirteen-mile point he claimed that on the same day Mr Conyer's Essex hounds found at Skreens and after a five-hour hunt lost their fox at Hadham Park. According to his account some of the hounds and followers changed packs when crossing, although neither was aware of the fact until they found themselves back where they started. Were the story true the inference must have been that a strong drag had been laid, but the entire story is invention. Mr Nicholas Parry's hunting diaries, starting in 1827 and ending in 1874, indicate that 24 December was an uneventful day. Once again the *Sporting Magazine* has to be treated with reserve, if not suspicion.

Another example of Ansty's high-flown style in describing another hunt of the same season, however, merits quotation. After hounds had met at Rowney they found a fox which

went straight to the edge of Thaxted village, direct through the corner of Marks, and being severely pressed with a head a sheet might cover, never touched another wood. It took exactly one hour and ten minutes to conquer him and he died at the end of fourteen miles, after being viewed from field to field, within a short distance of Wethersfield . . . Gurney, Wyman, Pottrell and George . . . took the lead and were never headed . . . Barwick [the huntsman] got floored by a brook within the last mile; but without his cap and well plastered, he took the fox up in the middle of a field! . . . This is the run Mr. Gurney told me was one of the best he ever saw in his life!

Mr Dick Gurney, despite his very heavy weight, had been famed in the shires for the quality of his horses and his style of hunting before coming to live with his brother-in-law Mr Sampson Hanbury. It must have been a good hunt to merit his praise. From Rowney to Wethersfield is only a nine-mile point, but allowing for Ansty's inaccuracy it may have been this hunt which Mr Gurney was often quoted as claiming to be the best fourteen miles he had encountered in a long experience.

As well as being a heavy-weight Mr Gurney was obviously a character of notable eccentricity, always tying up his shoes with rope yarn. He also seems to have had an affinity for heavy-weights, for he was extremely fond of fatstock breeding. He fed and nurtured two enormous Scotch bullocks for three years and had a special van built to take them to Smithfield. The day before their departure the larger one died and he never sent the other.

On 20 March 1829, on the occasion of Mr Sampson Hanbury's thirtieth season as Master, a dinner was held at the town hall in Ware at which he was the guest of honour. With the Duke of Wellington's Beer Act of 1830 already in preparation it may well have been that he thought his days as Master were numbered, for this was intended to break the growing monopoly of the brewers. In that it gave a free licence to beer shops in fact it merely affected the already failing fortunes of the coaching inns. The brewers actually sold more beer than previously. Instead of giving up hunting and their masterships of hounds they appeared the following season mounted on blood horses of better quality than before.

In practice it was not long, notwithstanding the unexpected effects of the Duke of Wellington's Act, before Mr Sampson Hanbury felt compelled to give up the mastership. He retired in 1832 and in 1833 a similar dinner to the previous one was held to present him with 'a vase, value 350 guineas, surmounted by a dog fox in full chase'. On the front was a vixen and cubs and on the reverse a group of hounds. A copy of the list of subscribers and a sketch of the sides of the vase engraved on copper plate still exists at Brent Pelham Hall. Significantly, one name has been neatly scored through, possibly that of a would-be subscriber who failed to subscribe.

It must not be thought that there was any deterioration towards the end of Mr Hanbury's mastership for during all George Barwick's period as huntsman from 1823 to 1832 there had been memorable sport. Admittedly, in the season 1829–30 it was such a hard winter they were stopped from 19 December to 10

February, seven weeks and three days, the longest period in their history. Of the season 1830–1, however, Mr Nicholas Parry, himself subsequently to be Master for thirty-seven seasons, noted with approval: 'Foxes ran well, were well found, well hunted and well killed. Never recollect such sport in Herts.'

Unfortunately the 11th Lord Petre (1793–1850), who succeeded Mr Hanbury as Master of the Puckeridge Hounds – as they were now generally known – brought his own huntsman with him. George Barwick was forced to take a post as huntsman to Mr Mark Millbank in the Bedale country back in his native Yorkshire. The Puckeridge was soon to feel his loss badly.

Lord Petre was well accustomed to hunting his own family pack, having hunted the Essex Union country for the previous ten years with his own hounds. His contract now was to hunt a subscription pack three times a week for three years with a guarantee of £1500 for the first year and £1200 for each of the next two seasons. It is clear that hunting a subscription pack and thus laying himself open to the criticism of his subscribers, either verbally in the field or in print in the press, was not what he had been accustomed to at all. Neither his huntsman Hort, nor Lord Petre himself, escaped criticism. Indeed, they received little else. Some comments from well-informed quarters were as critical indeed Mr Nicholas Parry wrote in 1832, after his first season:

In consequence of Lord Petre's men being badly mounted and knowing nothing of the country, and none of them anything about hunting except the huntsman, who could not ride at all to his hounds, we lost all our best foxes that would have shown us runs. Never recollect so many foxes in Herts, nor so well found, and with proper management we must have had a capital season.

Of the season in 1833 he wrote, even more blightingly:

. . . the foxes were very abundant and ran particulary well and straight in Herts and had Lord Petre and his huntsman left the hounds alone, they must have had a capital season. As it was, by holloaing the hounds off the scent, and lifting them when they were on, they lost all their best runs and scarcely killed any foxes, except by mobbing them in the very hot weather at the end of the season.

Mr Delme Radcliffe of Hitchin Priory, Master of the neighbouring Hertfordshire, after his first day out with the Puckeridge under Lord Petre's mastership on 16 November 1833, noted that:

. . . Lord Petre's huntsman decidely the worst I ever saw attempt to hunt a pack, hurrying and lifting them when hounds should hunt and craning and losing no end of time when they should be lifted.

On 13 December 1834 in Lord Petre's last season, however, Delme Radcliffe wrote that:

St. John's. Found in St. John's, ran to Clothall Bury, then over the open to Baldock, through the river at Radwell on towards Stotfold, when he was headed by a sheep dog, came back and was killed near Norton. 1 hr and 2ms. Some part fast. Very pretty and altogether satisfactory. Very little fencing.

It seems that even Lord Petre did have some good days, but it is equally clear that they were few and far between. The criticism seems to have been general and he resigned his mastership at the end of his three-year contract in the spring of 1835. He then returned to the Essex Union – no doubt amid sighs of relief all round.

Unfortunately, from the viewpoint of the Puckeridge hunt his successor was not a great improvement. Mr John Dalyell of Lingo in Fife, for the previous four seasons Master of the Forfarshire Foxhounds, was a man of decided views. A Scotsman without experience of dealing with English farmers, he soon showed himself short of the major requirement of a subscription pack Master, namely tact. A heavy-weight but bold horseman, he was a keen if inexperienced huntsman unused to a plough country.

In May 1835 Mr Dalyell came to live at Hadham Lordship, having undertaken to hunt the country three days a week for three seasons with a guarantee of £1200 a year, a length of contract now rare. From Forfarshire he brought with him twenty-three couples of hounds, three horses and his first whipper-in, John Skinner. Also accompanying him was his wife, described as 'a good looker and good goer', who used to hunt regularly with him on horseback, the first lady to hunt with the Puckeridge.

Before the season had properly started, in the autumn of 1835, Mr Dalyell was tactless enough to inform some local farmers who had come out cubhunting that they would not be expected until the opening meet of the season. Matters soon went from bad to worse. The sporting journalist Charles James Apperley, writing under his famous pen-name Nimrod, praised Dalyell's record as a Master in Scotland, but claimed he was not successful with the Puckeridge due to the handicap

which I doubt not would put the temper of my worthy friend, Mr. Dalyell, to a severer test than its nature was able to submit to . . . in the shape of foxhunting farmers on galloping hackneys who taking advantage of the innumerable lanes with which the Puckeridge country is intersected, together with their knowledge of the same, are perpetually heading foxes, already very little disposed to run straight, although proverbially stout.

Apperley's rather florid prose ignores the fact that under Barwick there had been plenty of good hunts and no complaints about the farmers. Another article in the *Sporting Magazine* indicated that the farmers did require some discipline. Writing on 2 December 1835, the contributor noted that on his way to a meet at Stansted he had seen several farmers waiting at Birchanger, knowing this would be the first draw, a thing very unfair to any Master.

Mr Nicholas Parry's comments on the 1835 season, however, were as usual succinct:

... Plenty of foxes in Herts and they ran well all season, but Dalyell, owing to his not leaving hounds alone at first, got them out of blood and they could scarcely kill any foxes, although they had some good hunting runs ...

His summary of the second season was much more favourable:

It was a very wet winter with a great deal of snow and consequently a capital scenting one for Herts, and the foxes not having been killed for 2 or 3 years were nearly all old ones, and showed some famous sport, and the hounds from getting into blood and being left alone, kept well together, showed themselves tolerably stout, particularly the bitches, beat nearly all the horses and killed several times after famous runs. Never saw so much sport from home in my life.

In this third and final season Mr Dalyell had good reason for not showing much sport. Hunting was stopped by the extremely bad winter of 1837–8 for a matter of seven weeks and one day. Although they had previously been stopped in 1829–30 for seven weeks and three days the indications are that the weather all round was more atrocious this season and hunting accordingly much worse.

In his first season at least, having got across the farmers, Mr Dalyell had little chance of showing sport. On one occasion it seems, when he entered Scales Park, he was met at the entrance by two foxes hanging dead from the branches of trees. In ordinary circumstances such an insult to a Master would have entitled him to retire, but the three years' contract resulted in him staying two further years. It appears that he did his best, but although better than the three years of Lord Petre's mastership, Mr Dalyell's was not amongst the happiest the Puckeridge enjoyed.

Starting at Hadham Lordship in 1835 Mr Dalyell moved in his second season to Much Hadham, where he built 'temporary kennels' of which no traces remain. He used his whipper-in, Jack Skinner, as huntsman while hounds were in covert, claiming that his own fifteen stone made it impossible for him to work in covert. When hounds were in the open he again took over as huntsman, but such a plan was clearly fraught with disadvantages and incipient trouble. Furthermore, Skinner broke his leg early in the second season and his substitute was little use. Finally poor Skinner died in the third season, while bad weather and poor scent put a stop to sport for almost the whole of it and hard dry weather without scent produced poor sport thereafter. In short, although Mr Dalyell had more than his share of bad luck, he also asked for trouble and received it in full measure. The Fates seem to have been against him.

In the spring of 1838 a joint mastership was agreed between Mr Nicholas Parry of Little Hadham, Mr William Wigram of Bennington Park, a son of the founder of the famous Blackwall Line of sailing ships, and Mr John Archer Houblon of Hallingbury Place. The latter, scion of a wealthy landowning family, retired in 1842, having lent his name and influence to what was to become one of the most successful masterships of the Puckeridge in the nineteenth century. Mr William Wigram, a wealthy bachelor with shipbuilding as well as shipowning interests, was to remain Master until 1854, leaving little mark in the hunting field, being perfectly content to leave matters to Mr Parry's undoubted ability. Thus Mr Parry had two joint Masters who supported him ably until 1854 while leaving him with almost complete control.

In effect, Mr Nicholas Parry was the sole Master of the Puckeridge hounds from 1838 for the next thirty-seven years. Born in 1796 the son of Mr Segar Parry, High Sheriff of the county in 1814, he had previously hunted regularly in the midlands. A fine horseman and notable foxhunter, he had long been a leading light of the hunt. Farming at Little Hadham Place, previously Hull Farm, in 1838 he was at forty-two a landowner, farmer and fine horseman, as well as a keen foxhunter. He also had notable charm and tact and was a careful manager possessing considerable authority when required.

The hunt took over the pack from Mr Dalyell, which he in turn had taken over from Lord Petre, who had in the first place obtained it from the syndicate of local farmers in 1832. They also engaged Richard Simpson as huntsman. He had served as whipper-in and in other capacities with the Holderness, the York and Ainstey, the Bicester and the Surrey Union. Although the Puckeridge was his first post as huntsman, he proved an excellent choice. Even in his first season he was reported as a 'quiet rider, has a very quick eye for country and for hounds and a most astonishing perception of a fox's line'. Another pleasing Dickensian description of him in 1841 was: 'A right-built, neat little fellow, about five and thirty years of age, with a varmint expression of countenance and altogether the look of one who had come into the world with a horn in his mouth and a pair of top boots on his legs.'

The new management were clearly determined to spare no expense and for first whipper-in they employed Richard Morris, who in 1854 went on to the Cambridgeshire hunt. They also had a good stud of horses and much more local support than the previous Masters had enjoyed. Typical perhaps of the local enthusiasm are the entries in the diaries of Mr William Westwood Chafy of Conington House, near Cambridge. He wrote:

Saturday, November 3rd, 1838. Met the Puckeridge Hounds (Mr. Parry) Cumbelow Green. Found directly, ran him ten minutes and killed. Found again at Clothall Bury & had a racing ring of 20 minutes and back, did not hang a minute, but straightaway to the Bradfield Woods. Here we had a pull for a moment & away again thro' Buckland straight to Capons – up to this time one hour & five minutes. Here we had a check for ten minutes, when away we went again (I think with a fresh fox) over a heavy country to Rookywood, where we hardly checked a minute, but raced over the open as if for Nuselles Park. Before he reached it, however, he bore to the left, & was killed in a small plantation within a quarter of a mile of the Town of Royston. Time form Capons fifty minutes from point to point, i.e. from Clothall Bury where we first found to the kill 10 miles, but as we went certainly not less then twenty. This was a first rate thing. The new huntsman, Simpson, I like. He is wonderfully quick and seems bent on nothing but killing his fox. I think him a little too fond of his horn. The first whip, Joe, too is a clever fellow. The hounds hunted well. Mr. Parry is a first-rate Sportsman, & tho' fifteen stone, sails famously across country. Rode the Rusher, who carried me famously. I did not send him overnight so that he must have gone about seventy miles. Hacked over Pussy to Royston and back from there. Home ½ p.4.

At this time, of course, the Puckeridge country was almost at its best.There was no wire, still no railways, no artificial fertilizers, and even the Great North Road was only stone-covered, while all the rest of the roads were little more than tracks, grass-covered and if much used deeply rutted. There were also many more large woodlands and cover for foxes was not lacking. Many of the woods then existing have now vanished and others are now much smaller. Even this, however, does not fully account for the excellent sport shown by Mr Parry and Dick Simpson. They were clearly a formidable combination.

Bell's Life for 16 December 1838 provided a stirring account of one of the most famous hunts of Mr Parry's period as Master, the great Sandy Warren run which lasted for two hours and five minutes, covering an estimated twenty-three or -four miles with a point of between sixteen and seventeen miles.* After lauding the principals, Mr Parry and Dick Simpson, before describing the run, there was a further journalistic peroration which merits repetition:

The sport of the season has been brilliant, but Saturday was a day the like of which few look on twice in their lives, even though they live to the age of the veteran John Chapman, who, though upwards of seventy, was one of the few in at the death.

It concluded:

. . . out of a very fine field not more than twenty saw the finish . . . Simpson stuck to his hounds well and killed his fox mounted on his third nag . . . In returning home horses were to be seen in all directions and very many were left in the neighbourhood. We have since heard of the death of three, one of which we regret to say was Simpson's.

Mr Parry's own account of the hunt ended succinctly as usual: 'I should say it was the best run with one fox I ever saw in my life.'

The John Chapman mentioned in the above account was regarded at this

*See Appendix, page 157.

38

time as 'the father of the hunt'. A great character, born in 1763, his picture was painted by Francis Grant in 1840 in his seventy-eighth year. It is said that he dined too well the night before the sitting and had to borrow an oversize hat, having lost his own, and that Grant faithfully recorded the effect. It is possible, on the other hand, that the artist merely failed to get his proportions correct.

Another notable feature of the account is that it is happily one of the last to mention horses dying in the hunting field of exhaustion or overriding as the result of a long run. At the turn of the century it had almost been a matter of pride to record how many horses had died in the field in such instances. Realization that this was primarily due to bad management in preparing the horses for hunting and was no matter for boasting was already beginning to dawn.

One more of Mr Parry and Dick Simpson's famous hunts was that on 18 March 1840, when hounds killed near Blackmore End in the parish of Wethersfield after finding in Oak Wood, a point of some eleven miles. By some error the fox's mask was inscribed 'Killed at Brann End', which does not exist. When this discrepancy was noticed some fifty or sixty years later many ingenious explanations were put forward resulting in endless controversy. The puzzle was only finally solved by reference to Mr Parry's diaries when they were eventually discovered in 1950 after having disappeared for years.

On 27 March 1840, soon after the Oak Wood to Blackmore End hunt, hounds killed 'a mangey fox' in Plashes, which was the first recorded instance of the disease which was to affect hunting with the Puckeridge so badly in the early twentieth century. According to Colonel John Cook this was more often than not caused by bag-men or mangy foreign importations. The Puckeridge were certainly not accused of hunting bag-men at this time. Indeed in the *Sporting Magazine* for May 1842 an article entitled 'A Strong Hint to the Puckeridge' by 'John Plain' suggested the opposite:

> A fox is no sooner found and Simpson away at him, than forth go the Whips to the right and left flanks and Mr. Parry also, according to his best judgement, all bent on killing, and if the hounds cannot hunt him, the lifting system is brought into play in the most effectual manner that I ever witnessed. What Mr. Parry means to hunt next year I am at a loss to conjecture, unless there is to be an importation.

This rather snide piece of anonymous journalese suggesting that foxes were being ridden to death by four men working as a team without hounds playing any part in the proceedings was, of course, a travesty of the facts. In the previous four seasons Simpson had killed twenty-six, thirty-one, twenty-five and a half and twenty-four brace of foxes and in 1842–3 he killed thirty-one and a half brace, so that these extremely barbed comments had absolutely no foundation in fact. These figures were in themselves proof enough that the number of foxes available for the hunt depended almost entirely on the numbers killed by keepers and landowners convinced that the hunt was unlikely to do it for them. When foxes were seen to be killed effectively no one objected to preserving them.

In 1844 Mr Parry moved the hounds from Puckeridge to Albury End, which was nearer his home and more convenient for visiting. Here the hounds were to be kennelled until 1876, when Mr Parry finally gave up hounds. In the meantime they continued to provide excellent sport to the satisfaction of all concerned, except possibly the occasional visiting journalist.

Chapter 5

The Years from 1845 to 1875

BY this time communications had improved to such an extent that news of current affairs reached everyone in a few days without the cushioning time-lag of the previous century, which had largely blunted its impact. During the Crimean War from 1854 to 1856 the despatches of William Howard Russell, war correspondent of *The Times*, revealed the utter incompetence of the military high command in the persons of Lord Raglan and the Earls of Lucan and Cardigan, even if exact apportionment of blame may have been difficult. The full defects of the eighteenth-century system of promotion by purchase were plain to see at last and the nation's indignation was aroused. With the outbreak of the Indian Mutiny in 1857, the complacency of British rule in India was shaken and at home the effect was much the same. That everything was resolved by 1861 with the formation of a Legislative Council in India was almost by the way. The nation as a whole was becoming involved in current affairs overseas in a way that had never happened in the eighteenth century.

By 1850 the coach services had almost entirely vanished and the railways reigned supreme. From 1850 to 1875 they steadily improved. Intensive competition between rival railway companies led to cheaper rates, better time schedules and better service all round. It soon became possible for the hunting man to send his horses to meets too distant for consideration previously. Hunts which before had not seemed within reasonable reach of London suddenly found they had increasing numbers of subscribers. Long weekend shooting parties also became more common.

There were also immense advances in the manufacture and design of shotguns during this period. A breech-loading gun had been invented by the French gunmaker Pauly, but in 1851 a primitive form of pinfire cartridge was demonstrated at the Great Exhibition by the Paris gunmaker Lefaucheux. By 1852 Charles Lancaster had produced a much improved pinfire cartridge of his own, by 1861 the centre fire cartridge had been developed and by 1867 the Purdey bolt action heralded a new age of shooting. With W. W. Greener's intoduction of choke boring in 1874 the modern game gun had to all intents and purposes appeared. The natural result was an immense increase in the quantities of game reared and also in the numbers of people shooting, often to the detriment of foxhunting interests.

An important development for foxhunting was the formation in 1856 of the Masters of Foxhounds Committee, also known as the Foxhunting Committee of Boodle's, under the chairmanship of Lord Redesdale. Until then those Masters of Foxhounds who were also members of Boodle's Club had met in-formally to discuss any disputes, such as quarrels over boundary coverts, when these were referred to them. The formation of a Committee of six members, elected by some twenty-four Masters or past-Masters of Foxhounds who were members of Boodle's was intended to constitute a more formal tribunal, but its weakness remained that it had no real authority. It was, however, the forerunner of the Masters of Foxhounds Association formed in the later decades of the century.

Various significant changes in the hunting field since 1800 had also begun by this time to gain general acceptance. The old-fashioned treatment of horses was for the most part giving way to more humane standards. At one time it had almost been a matter of pride to dwell on the number of horses killed in the course of a prolonged hunt, although this was frequently due largely to lack of proper preparation and general unfitness. More careful preparation and training for the hunting season as well as the use of second horses by heavy-weight hunting men began to reduce such needless casualties to a minimum. By this time also Beckford's comments of 1780 that no hunt should last more than two hours had finally began to take effect, since both hounds and horses were being bred for speed and the average hunt, now carefully timed, seldom lasted longer.

As a result of the increased speed of hounds and horses, the simple snaffle bit of the eighteenth century, which was all that had been required at that time, had perforce, in the faster hunting shires, given way to the double-bridle by the early part of the century. By mid-century there was still considerable argument on this score elsewhere. The question of martingales and whether they should be used or not was also a vexed one, then as now. Some held that a horse needing one should not be hunted and others that more were fitted with them than required them. Some maintained they were a handicap to a horse in recovering itself and yet others that a head-tossing horse jumped better with one.

The cruel and unnecessary fashion of cropping a horse's ears had been generally dropped in the early nineteenth century, but the fashion of docking tails needlessly short in a 'cock-tail', common in the early part of the nineteenth century as seen in Alken's prints, was longer in disappearing. By the mid eighteenth century the switch or long tail was more generally accepted fashion. By then, however, the custom of clipping horses originally introduced by veterans of the Peninsular Campaign around 1815, or the alternative of singeing them, had been widely introduced. While this led to greater fitness for hunting, the objection to it was the danger of the horse catching a chill, especially in the often badly ventilated stables of the time.

Throughout the greater part of the nineteenth century horses were still generally kept in stalls, although it was widely accepted that boxes were preferable. There were also regrettably many horse-owners who believed firmly in bleeding, purging and physicking their horses long after these had been given up as sound treatment for humans. Such treatment, taking pints of blood from a tired horse, or purging, or dosing with physick before hunting, must often have had more fatal effects than overriding. In general, horse management still left a great deal to be desired and veterinary surgery and diagnosis were still extremely primitive.

Fashions in hunting clothes underwent considerable change between the Georgian and Victorian periods. The old heavy coat of the eighteenth century gave way during the Regency period to a tight double-breasted tail-coat with a roll collar and narrow lapels showing a high coloured cravat. Breeches became impossibly tight and often of leather. Latterly more comfortable wear returned, with breeches looser above the knee and more sensible single-breasted coats suitable for doing up at the neck to keep out the weather.

Gradually, red came to be regarded as the only acceptable colour for the coat; it was generally termed scarlet, or pink, and first referred to as the latter in print by Colonel Cook in his *Observations*. It also for a while around the 1840s and 1850s became the custom to wear with the coat a hunting cap, which had previously distinguished the hunt staff and Master of hounds. The generally accepted hunting boots, originally known as Napoleons, were worn with mahogany or coloured tops. Variations in the colour of the tops from hunt to hunt were not uncommon, as was the habit of wearing contrasting coloured collars signifying membership of a particular hunt, although this was worn by invitation only, as were hunt buttons. In the early part of the century parsons sometimes wore purple coats, but by around 1850 the only acceptable variant on scarlet, or hunting pink, was black.

The only exception to this in the hunting field was the colour of habit worn by ladies, which varied from black to green or snuff colour. The customary hat varied from a beaver to a low-crowned hat with plumes. Although ladies in the hunting field had been known occasionally, prior to the 1850s they were a rarity. The invention of the extra hunting horn crutch on the side-saddle about this time, along with the tight skirt, made jumping easier and safer. Between 1850 and 1875, with increasing emancipation, the number of ladies out hunting multiplied steadily.

Initially there were two principal types of ladies to be seen in the hunting field. The daughters of aristocratic families, who knew what they were about and were well mounted, were generally in the lead. The 'pretty horse-breakers' of Rotten Row – epitomized by the immortal 'Skittles', the leading courtesan of the Victorian period, who hunted regularly in the shires and was credited with introducing the top-hat and veil as feminine hunting headgear in the 1870s – were generally not far behind them. Following their example as the emancipation of women developed there were increasingly those who simply enjoyed hunting and whose husbands, brothers or fathers, were subscribers to the hunt.

Despite the steady emancipation of women, the Victorians were not long in introducing a certain rigidity of etiquette into the hunting field. Even the language of the chase altered somewhat. Whereas the eighteenth-century hunting man rode after hounds, it became customary to refer to riding to hounds. Leaping hedges, ditches and gates changed to jumping fences and timber. For no apparent reason the old word 'cover' was changed by gradual usage to 'covert', although either was acceptable until three parts of the way through the century. More understandably, the fox himself, formerly known as Reynard, was nicknamed Charles James Fox after the famous politician. Charley, not unreasonably, became a favourite shortened version.

In the 1850s Mr John Josselyn, Master of the Suffolk, recorded a special fox, 'a sort of phantom creature', which always defeated him. This remarkable phenomenon lived in the Hitcham Wood on the Bildeston side of the country and at the first sound of the hunt's approach, the crack of a whip, or thud of a horse's hoof, was away, always making in the same direction. Sam Hibbs, the huntsman, aware of his habits, one day got hounds away with him almost in view. According to report the pace was a cracking one. They ran him through Thorpe Monk Park, Raw Hall Wood and nearly to the Links, where he doubled back through Thorpe, eventually beating hounds near Woolpit Wood. On the way home one of the hunt followers remarked to Hibbs: 'Well, Sam, if you couldn't beat him today you never will.' To which Sam duly replied, 'No, sir, I don't think I ever will.' Nor apparently did he. The phantom duly lived and died unbeaten.

On one occasion in their enormous country they started three foxes at Blackwater and finally ran the one they settled on seventeen miles and a half, killing him at last at Attleborough in one hour and fifty-five minutes. In his own view this was one of Mr Josselyn's finest hunts. Already it was noticeable that they were hunting faster and covering a lot of ground. If they were hunting less often on the Thurlow side of the country at this time it was presumably due to lack of foxes in that direction, for there was certainly no shortage of keen foxhunters, as events soon proved.

In April 1858 a meeting was held at the Crown Inn, Great Thurlow, with a view to restarting the old Thurlow Hunt Club. The preliminaries clearly showed there was sufficient interest and no lack of support. On 21 May in the following year another meeting was held in the Rutland Arms at Newmarket. As a result of this meeting a list of Rules was duly drawn up, from which the following have been extracted:*

1st. – That the Club called the Thurlow Hunt Club be revived and re-established.

2nd. – That the object of the club shall be the preservation of foxes in the district known as the 'Thurlow Country' which extends on the Suffolk side as far as Dalham, Denham Thicks, Barrow Wood, Easty Wood, Denston Groves and Cavendish Covers; and on the Essex and Cambridgeshire sides as far as the Suffolk Hounds Hunt.

From this it is clear that, whereas the country had been hunted since the time of Osbaldeston by what amounted to a neighbouring hunt, the main bulk of the hunt supporters remained loyal to their own country, which they still regarded as a separate entity, even if somewhat short of foxes.

Other points of interest included:

7th. – That Cubs shall be purchased, and turned down at such parts if the Thurlow Country and in such covers as the Committee may determine.

8th. – That one sovereign shall be given to any keeper, woodman, or servant, who shall take care and rear any of the purchased Cubs.

9th. – That the sum of £2 shall be given to any keeper, or woodman, on whose woods or covers a litter of foxes shall be bred and reared.

10th. – That a donation of a sovereign shall be given to every keeper, or woodman, in whose woods or covers there shall be a 'find' and more than one 'find' on the same day shall not entitle the same keeper or woodman to more than one donation.

After deciding that an Annual General Meeting should be held in 'The Crown Inn, Great Thurlow, or such place as the Committee may at any time determine' there came a further interesting point:

*For full list see page 183.

12th. That if any complaint of the loss of fowls, &c, by any person not being a member of the club, be laid before such meeting, such complaint be considered by the members present, who shall have the power, if they think proper, to award compensation out of the funds of the club.

There then followed a list of subscribers, mostly local farmers, including two Gardners, four Frosts, four Webbs, and five Kings, all names to be conjured with in the annals of the Newmarket and Thurlow hunt, even if this particular committee was wound up in 1868. Yet, even if the Thurlow Hunt Club ceased to exist after a decade – presumably because it was felt they had fulfilled their main function of repopulating the country with foxes – the local farmers regularly continued to present a 'Thurlow Farmers' Purse' to the hunt each year.

In the 1850s the idea of making good losses of poultry was comparatively advanced. It was unusual, to say the least, before this for the hunt to consider claims for damages of this nature. When, however, it was decided to set about breeding foxes deliberately, it must have been felt that some form of compensation must be made to those who had suffered by it. With the advent of the farming slump in the 1870s, caused by the free importation of corn from the Middle West, it says a great deal for the Thurlow farmers that they still continued not only to support the hunt but to present their annual 'Purse'. With such keenness behind them it is not surprising that the formation of the Newmarket and Thurlow in its own right as a hunt was not long delayed. It speaks volumes for the sport provided by Mr John Josselyn that it did not arise until after his retirement in 1880.

Mr Josselyn and his first huntsman, Sam Hibbs, were an immensely popular combination. Sam Hibbs used to ride a remarkable chestnut horse called Cock Tail which had been fired twice all round, an almost unheard-of thing, but he only gave Hibbs one fall in thirteen years. On 16 February, as hounds were killing their fox at Whipstead, Sam Hibbs had a fit and fell dead from the saddle. His funeral was attended by the entire Suffolk hunt in pink and black, the old chestnut following behind the coffin with saddle, horn and boots reversed. It was no doubt the death Hibbs would have chosen, but as the end of the season Mr Josselyn retired, handing over to Mr John Ord of Fordham.

In 1867, to everyone's delight, Mr Josselyn took over once again following Mr Ord's resignation. After a further four years Mr Josselyn again resigned in 1871. From 1871 until 1875 Mr Edward Greene, M.P. for the Stowmarket division of Suffolk for twenty-five years, and his son, afterwards Sir Walter Greene, M.P. for Bury St Edmunds, hunted the country as joint Masters. It was reported that they had some particularly good sport during this period on the Thurlow side of the country, by this time of course freshly stocked with foxes.

In 1874 the young Mr Walter Greene had an unfortunate coaching accident and was severely injured. Although his father continued as sole Master for a year, he appears to have been happy to resign in favour of Mr Josselyn once again, when it was apparent that his son would not be recovered sufficiently to help him for some time. Thus in 1875, riding at twenty stone, Mr Josselyn entered his third and final term as Master of the Suffolk. He continued to show good sport on the Thurlow side of the country and seemingly to satisfy everyone over a vast area, from the Duke of Grafton at Euston to those in the south, providing the Thurlow Farmers' Purse each year, for all appear to have been keen fox preservers and sport generally continued to be very good. Rather than the great landlords such as the Duke of Grafton, however, it was the farmers who were the mainstay of the hunt.

During most of the thirty-seven years of Mr Nicholas Parry's long mastership of the Puckeridge from 1829 to 1875 much the same could be said of the farmers in that country. They too, under his careful and tactful direction and leadership, were keen sportsmen and preservers of foxes. Throughout his mastership, with several different huntsmen, he continued to show good sport and kept enthusiasm for hunting at a high pitch. Much of this spirit of mutual co-operation between the farmers and the hunt was fostered during the period from 1838 to 1851 covering Dick Simpsons' tenure as huntsman, when there was some truly excellent sport with many outstanding hunts.

Notable as perhaps the finest season of all during this period was that of 1845–6. Hounds hunted one hundred and eight days of which five were blank and they were stopped on three. Seven brace of cubs were killed and twenty-one and a half brace of old foxes, while another ten were marked to ground. In this magnificent hunting year the sum total was that hounds made at least six points of five miles, seven of six miles, one of seven, one of nine (a twelve mile point in all), one of ten, one of twelve and one of thirteen. Understandably the season was the finest in Mr Parry's memory and much was due to the work of Dick Simpson as huntsman.

Good as the sport must have been that season, it may be inferred from the length of the points that foxes were not as plentiful as they were even two decades later. They were no doubt strong and active. well able to cover their ground, but hounds were less likely to be checked by the scent of a fresh fox. Nor, as yet, was there any wire to worry about, so that hunting conditions were as close to perfection as could be expected.

Given such circumstances, combined with an experienced Master and huntsman, good whippers-in and a fine pack of hounds, some excellent hunts were to be expected and were duly recorded. Dick Simpson's own records and Mr Nicholas Parry's diary entries are brief and somewhat laconic, although an excellent cross-check on others. The reports in *Bell's Life* and similar journals provide a clearer picture of the more outstanding hunts, but perhaps the liveliest account of any day was provided by Mr William Westwood Chafy of Conington House, near Cambridge, whose account of a hunt in 1838 at the start of Mr Parry and Dick Simpson's partnership has already been quoted.

Mr William Chafy was born in 1814 and educated at Eton and Cambridge, where he was a first-class classical scholar. While in his early twenties he crossed China from end to end, with only Chinese companions, the first white man to do so and return to England alive. Back at Cambridge once more, he settled down to the life of a country sportsman and scholar. From 1837 to 1867 he filled four large ledgers with accounts of 2822 days' hunting in his lively detailed style. From 1837 to 1847 he lived at Conington House, from 1855 to 1867 he was at Bowes, House, Ongar, but continued to hunt with the Puckeridge. In 1867, aged fifty-three, increasing weight, the cares of a large family, and 'gouty bronchitis' appear to have brought his hunting career to an end.

As an example of a mid-Victorian scholar and hunting man's keenness for the chase, prepared to hunt in highly improbable circumstances, making light of accidents which would have daunted lesser beings, Mr Chafy's account if the historic Puckeridge hunt of 14 February 1846 deserves inclusion in any event. He wrote:

Saturday 14th February, Valentine Day: and a memorable day indeed to me; one that can never be erased from my memory till the latest moment of my life. Dear Annette was taken ill during the night & $\frac{1}{4}$ to 5 I started on Claybrook & rode him to Cambridge in 50 ms. Got Fichlin up & off in $\frac{1}{4}$ hour, & rode back still faster, but even with all this dispatch dear Nette had presented me with a little girl 3 ms before our return. Never dreaming of being able to hunt I dispatched Isaac on Pussy to Royston to bring back Cole with Artist and Giraffe, but the child being born 20 ms to 7, & dear Nette & it doing both so well, after breakfasting with Fichlin, I started at $\frac{1}{4}$ to 9 on the Rusher to Royston (having galloped him at an awful pace the whole way), there mounted Artist & Cole Giraffe, & met the Puckeridge, Cumbelowe– Found Clothal Bury & such a fox, went thro' one of the Wallington Springs, then turned back as if for Clothal Bury, but kept straight over the finest line I ever crossed in Hertfordshire, great large fields of 80 & 90 acres, by Cumbelowe nearly straight to St. Johns, just skirted it to the right, & went between it and Moor Hall Springs a great pace up to Green Munden thence to & thro' Hamels Park up to the Roman Catholic College at Old Hall Green, over the road & left Plashes on the right, down to Standon where he beat us, 12 to 14 miles straight – a wonderful fine run, wanting nothing but a kill to render it ne plus ultra. They are certainly a first rate pack of hounds & did their work to perfection on this day – Time one hour & 40 ms.

Drew several springs in the Hadham country blank, left off close to Hadham. Rode Giraffe, who carried me splendidly – I never was better carried; Cole rode Artist & I rode him back after hunting thro' Standon to Puckeridge, thence to Royston, about 16 miles – Dined with Thurnall – Then got on Rusher to come home & all things went well & he gallopped along with me a great pace, till we reached Knapwell drift, to me ever ill-fated Knapwell drift – Riding the hedge (pitch dark) Rusher slipped into a newly made deep narrow bottomed ditch, & lay with all his four legs in the air, & me under him, all but my head & shoulders. I could not by any possibility extricate myself; & at first called out lustily for help, & called Murder till I was exhausted, but no one appreaed to hear me, though I could hear all the market carts passing on the St. Neots road, & was only 500 yards from the farm house in the drift. Thus I lay in this perilous state for above an hour, without a prospect of help – at last Rusher made a desperate struggle, & as good luck would have it, instead of getting my head under him, he enabled me to extricate myself during the 10 seconds of his momentary struggle, & slip onto the bank more dead than alive – for I never expected to come out alive; & nothing but the most miraculous interposition of Providence, I am convinced, saved me. Having lost my hunting cap, neck cloth, etc etc in this sad plight I crawled down to the farm house in the drift & at last got some men with lanterns to come & try to get poor Rusher up. This we succeeded in doing at last with some little trouble, & with the aid of these men Rusher and I got to Knapwell village to Mr. Whitehead's, who kindly sent me home in his gig, with his son to drive me & the men brought home good dear old Rusher. Never did I come home before in such a plight or such a deplorable condition, but oh! my thanks to Providence were unbounded, as indeed they ought, for my preservation. Poor Annette of course was sadly frightened – Did not get home till past 10 – Therefore I say, what with my good fortune in the morning & bad in the evening Valentine Day of 1846 will never be forgotten by me.

If 1845 was outstanding for the number of good hunts, the following season was notable for the fact that on 13 November the Puckeridge killed a fox at Waltham Abbey, only fourteen miles from London Bridge. They thus found themselves closer to London than at any time since that date, a physical impossibility today. In 1847 there was another exceptional hunt which, despite the report of a fourteen- or fifteen-mile point in *Bell's Life* of 5 December,* was nearer eleven miles.

One of the rare occasions when Mr Parry successfully hunted hounds himself, a task he normally left to his huntsman, was on 25 January 1851, in Dick Simpson's last season. This hunt, on 10 February was well described in the issue of *Bell's Life* for 16 February 1851*, ending: the superior horsemanship of Mr Parry and the judgement displayed by him in hunting the hounds (having no assistance from his own men) was beyond all praise. . . .

Dick Simpson's abbreviated account of the day ran:

Met at Hazelend found in Burchanger run one to ground at Stanstead Park away with the other over the Forest up to Harlow to Manwood and kild him a very good day's Sport one of the best scenting Days I ever saw in My Life . . .

*See Appendix, page 158.

As this was one of the very rare occasions when Dick Simpson had got left behind there may have been a touch of sour grapes in his comment that it was such a good scenting day. Be that as it may, Mr Parry had killed successfully after a nine-mile point, hunting hounds single-handed and not without some difficulties. This was no mean feat for a man of fifty-five, who was accustomed to leave hounds to his huntsman to handle.

During the following month the Puckeridge ran a fox northwards to Newton, where they lost him, the most northerly point reached in Mr Parry's period as Master. The furthest south was Monkhams on 13 November 1846, the furthest west Kimpton Hoo on 28 March 1846 and the furthest east Gosfield Park, 18 March 1840. The distance covered was thus thirty miles from north to south and forty miles from east to west, or an area of 120 square miles. Significantly, perhaps, all these exceptional distances were covered during the period when Dick Simpson was huntsman.

On 16 April 1851 Dick Simpson hunted the Puckeridge hounds for the last time before retiring to farm at High Wych. He recorded: 'Met at Peverils found in Peverils wood a very good Fox a very good run and Lost him at Scales Park.' Thus with an eight-mile point he ended his career with the Puckeridge, although persuaded to come out of retirement for short periods to act as substitute huntsman in cases of sickness for hunts which included the Grafton, Burton, Bramham Moor and Hertfordshire. Apart from these brief exceptions, while he continued hunting until the age of eighty, he remained in retirement at High Wych until his death in 1888.

Another notable hunt servant of this period was Abraham Firr, the kennel-man. Born about 1800, he was first engaged as kennel boy to Mr Hanbury's hounds in 1814. He remained in the kennels at Puckeridge for eighteen seasons under Mr Hanbury, also under the masterships of Lord Petre and Mr Dalyell. He removed to the Essex kennels until 1855 when he returned to the Puckeridge at Albury End in 1855, remaining with them until 1876. His son, Tom Firr, was subsequently huntsman to the Quorn from 1872 to 1899, one of the greatest huntsmen of his day.

Perhaps the best-known character of Mr Parry's establishment, however, was his second horseman, 'Old Brewer'. He is well described in a letter written by Mr Edward Taylor to Mr Edward Barclay on 14 June 1904:

The photograph is an admirable likeness of 'Old Brewer' who was for so many years Mr. Parry's second horseman, and a marvellous man he was! Always on the spot when wanted – never seen during a run - he knew every gate, gap, lane and 'earth' in the country and at the finish turned up at once with his horse *quite fresh*. John Leech was very fond of introducing him to 'Punch' notably the picture where 'the Squire's second horseman is showing a short cut home over a line of gates.' He showed him wearing a *cap*, but this he *never* did – always a tall hat – and such a hat! rusty brown brushed the wrong way – a ten season hunter!

John Leech (1818–1864) was the famous sporting illustrator of *Punch*, who hunted regularly with the Puckeridge and was familiar with Mr Parry and many of the leading characters of the hunt, particularly Mr Charles Adams of Barkway to whom he addressed a delightful sketch with the accompanying message:

Tuesday, Dec. 14th 1852.
My dear Charley Boy,
Hip! Hip! Hurrah
The Almanack is finished and now for a day with the Puckeridge.

As late as 1897 a keen Puckeridge supporter wrote:

Many students of John Leech and his art will recollect the picture of the nervous gentleman in the dog-cart. 'Don't you think Robert, going so fast down-hill is very likely to make the horse fall? and the groom's reply, 'Lor' bless yer – no sir! I never throwed a 'oss down in my left, 'xcept once, and that was one frosty moonlight night (just such a night as this it was) as I was a-drivin' a gent (as might be you) from the station, when I throwed down this werry oss in this werry identical place.' The nervous gentleman was John Leech himself on his way from Royston station to Barkway, and he told the joke at the dinner table that evening where he was staying with his old friend Adams.

Clearly Leech must have enjoyed good sport with the Puckeridge under Dick Simpson, also under his successor John Dinnicombe, who had hunted the V.W.H. since 1848. During 1852 and 1853 the Puckeridge seems to have had some good sport, even if not quite up to the high standards set by Dick Simpson. In 1852 there was at least one nine-mile point and in 1853 two eight-mile points, but on each occasion the hounds failed to kill.

On 11 February 1854 the hunted fox was shot in front of the hounds, a regrettable occurrence over which historians appear to have drawn a veil, perhaps advisedly. In practice historians seem to have drawn a blank over much of this period, since Mr Parry's diary is as usual laconic and if Dinnicombe kept one, as he was probably made to do, it has not survived. There is an account of a seven-mile point in *The Field* on 10 March 1855, but perhaps today the hunt on 17 March, the following week, is of greater interest. Although this was only a four-mile point, they crossed the Great North Road and the railway, 'The Great Northern Railroad', twice each in a hunt of two hours, close to Stevenage.

In 1856 Dinnicombe was succeeded by Joseph Orbell, who had been huntsman of the H.H. He had also been second whipper-in to Dick Simpson from 1841 to 1842 and first whipper-in from 1842 to 1849. Unfortunately, he seems to have been less than good as a huntsman. Mr William Chafy thought little of him, writing after a moderate day's sport on 5 November 1856:

They ran well *out* of covert, but not a bit *in* covert. We were not half a minute behind this fox into Hasty Wood & yet they could never speak to it after the first 20 yards in covert. The Hounds were very high in flesh. Orbell fat & I thought slow, very slow in drawing. He bundled along better when they went over country. Mr. Parry thinner than ever, but looked the picture of health & rode as hard as ever.

Although Mr Chafy recorded a few good days, the standard of sport gradually decreased with Orbell as huntsman and in 1859 he retired, officially due to ill-health. On 23 February 1859 Mr Chafy wrote: 'Orbell was ill with rheumatism. Alfred Hedges hunted them; Parry had given notice to resign. They had had a bad season'. Despite this statement by Mr Chafy there appears to be no other suggestion that Mr Parry thought of resigning. However, it is clear that the 1858–9 season was a bad one and Orbell's resignation overdue.

In 1959 Alfred Hedges, who had been first whipper-in, took over as huntsman and for the next sixteen years, until Mr Parry's retirement in 1875, he remained in office. He appears to have been a model, hard-working, pleasant and reliable hunt servant, but without the distinctive fire and ability of Dick Simpson. Unlike his predecessors, however, he kept a very good diary. Amongst the entries in 1861 is the first mention of a hazard that was to become all too familiar in the years ahead, namely wire fencing – presumably sheep netting, in this instance fatal to the fox rather than to horse and rider: 'February 20th. Hockrill. Found a Fox . . . in attempting to jump the wire fence he got beat and the Hounds killed him. . . .'

In the season of 1862–3 Mr Chafy recorded a notable incursion deep into the Essex country, which was also his first mention of the use of the railway when hunting. In the same year, 1863, the hunt supporters presented Mr Parry with his portrait by Sir Francis Grant to commemorate his twenty-fifth season as Master. With his huntsman, Alfred Hedges, Mr Parry is shown holloaing a fox across a ride in the Warren with the famous dog hound Gulliver (1859) in the lead, a foundation sire of the Puckeridge pack today.

In the following season, 1863–4, Mr Chafy again recorded a good hunt with an eight-mile point on 2 March, once more noting his use of the railway to get him back home by ten in the evening. During the 1864–5 season another March hunt, on the 6th, was recorded in *The Field*, which claimed it as a nine-mile point. Mr Chafy's last recorded hunt with the Puckeridge, however, is well worth quoting in full:

Monday April 3rd, 1865. Met the Puckeridge Pye Corner & had a capital day's sport, killing a brace of foxes & hounds going home at $\frac{1}{4}$ to 2. Drew Gilston blank. Found in a beautiful little copse close to Allen's Green. Unfortunately killed in covert, a dog fox. Found again in Golden Grove, away through Eastwick to Great Hadham village, Culver, Littley, & pointed for Maddam & a wide ring back to Eastwick, on thro' Golden Grove & pulled him down, one hour & quarter. Capital hunting run & never saw a huntsman do better than Hedges on this day. I was charmed with my day's sport. I actually saw a brace of foxes killed & hounds going home before two & I caught the 2.30 train from Harlow & was back in London by $\frac{1}{2}$ p. 3. – almost incredible. Rode Free Trade, Lenton, The Cardinal. Came down from Town by 8 train to Harlow & back from Harlow by 2.30 train. In Brunswick Square $\frac{1}{4}$ p. 4.

30 miles to covert, 34 home=64; hunting 26=90 (including rail)

While the hunting may be as good today, the train service has certainly not improved and Mr Chafy would no doubt have much to say on that score. However, although Mr Chafy may no longer have recorded hunting with the Puckeridge, the following year was within living memory of Mr J. W. Sworder, another famous Puckeridge supporter, who only died in 1933. As late as 1910 he wrote his own account of a famous hunt in the 1865–6 season recorded briefly by Hedges as follows:

February 26th, 1866 Angel Hadham. Found at Ringsbury lost him at Throcking. After the hounds went he was picked up in a dieing state in Adams garden at Throcking. A good day. Scent good.

This was a good point of eight miles and tradition adds that when Mr Parry was informed on his way home that the fox was in Mr Adam's garden he refused to return to find him. The fox was then stuffed and according to one account ended a victim to moth and was thrown away.

Despite the absence of the long points of Dick Simpson's day, it is notable that the seasons now seldom recorded blank days. The inference is clear that, due largely to Mr Parry's long period as Master and his outstanding influence in the country, there were more foxes and less chance of the old long points as a direct result. The sport was brisk and even on poor scenting days there was less chance of a blank day. Hedges seldom had more than one blank day a season as opposed to Simpson's average of nearly four. His total kill during the season varied from eighteen and a half brace to forty and a half brace as against Simpson's twenty-six-brace average. The sport may not have been as brilliant, but it was more reliable.

There were also still occasional long points. During the 1869–70 season on 19 January hounds ran for two hours and five minutes and made a seven-mile point, killing their fox. An earlier hunt on 29 December 1869, and an even finer hunt the following season on 27 January 1871, which has been regarded as amongst Mr Parry's six famous hunts, were both recorded in *The Field*.

To such a keen foxhunter as Mr Parry lawn meets were anathema. On 15

November 1872 there was one of the few lawn meets he suffered, at Youngsbury, when Mr Arthur Giles-Puller assembled a vast concourse of friends and neighbours. He added a brass band and three cheers for the Queen, which caused hounds to bolt. Hedges and his whippers-in were forced to gallop round the park to collect them. Both on this and another lawn meet in the same year Mr Parry pointedly made the only bye-days of the season. The hunt which ensued was predictably a poor one.

The season 1873–4 saw at least one outstanding hunt noted in full in W. Lucas's *Hunting in Herts & Beds*. This hunt, on 18 January, ended in an eight-mile point and a good kill in the Cambridgeshire country. Unfortunately, the following season of 1874–5 was a poor scenting one and, with the exception of one six-mile point when the fox was lost, contained no outstanding days. Since it was both Mr Nicholas Parry's and Alfred Hedges' last season this seems a pity, but it is indicative of the standard of sport they provided that even so the average days were good notwithstanding. At the age of seventy-nine no doubt Mr Parry felt he had earned his retirement after thirty-seven years imbuing the love of hunting throughout the Puckeridge country and breeding a first-rate pack of hounds. He died in December 1879, aged eight-three. Hedges, who retired at the same time, developed a lung infection and died in 1877 at the age of fifty.

Chapter 6

The Years from 1875 to 1900

THE last quarter of the nineteenth century was the period when outwardly Britain had achieved the zenith of her power and greatness. This was the period that saw Queen Victoria declared Empress of India (1876) and in the two ensuing decades her Jubilee (1887) and her Diamond Jubilee (1897). The little dumpy figure swathed in shawls was the Queen Empress ruling over subjects scattered all round the world and wherever the British ruled their trade prospered. The industrial products of the midlands, of Manchester and Birmingham, were sent to the farthest corners of the globe and accordingly the vastly increased population, centred principally in the manufacturing towns and in London itself, should have prospered. Many did, but there was also considerable, grinding poverty, and in the country, with the steady flood of cheap grain from the Western States of America, the farmers suffered increasing hardship. The development of frozen beef imports from the Argentine and mutton from Australia in the 1880s and 1890s completed the farming slump and agriculture was not to recover until the Great War of 1914–18.

Various innovations in farming which had been introduced during the first seventy-five years of the century had by this time begun to have their effects on farming. The steam engine on the farm, used to power machinery such as threshing mills, was an asset, but the steam plough was merely a fresh hazard in the hunting field. It was, however, not nearly so disastrous or far-reaching as the use of new fertilizers, the sowing of winter wheat or – even more restrictive – the sowing of clover or new grass. Chemical fertilizers, guano and nitrates, or fish manure, even pig dung, all tended to destroy scent, nor did they improve hunting clothes. Whereas winter wheat could be ridden over without damage if not too wet, young clover or new grass was liable to be severely damaged. The result was a general shortening of the hunting season to the beginning of April.

Wire, which had appeared in the 1850s and 1860s, had begun to be something

55

of a problem in places by the 1870s, but the introduction of barbed wire in 1882 was a much more serious matter. Here was a cheap method of fencing stock which farmers, forced by their circumstances to economize, simply had to use, whether they themselves approved of it or not. In their prosperous years they might have preferred post and rails, or hedges, but during a time of deep recession they had virtually no alternative. Fortunately both the Puckeridge and Newmarket and Thurlow countries were 'unfashionable' plough country with deep ditches and hedges for the most part, hence they were never greatly troubled by this problem which affected many other hunts very badly.

The self-binding reaper, invented in 1884, was only one example of new farming methods increasing the drain of men from the land. It enabled one man to do the work in the harvest field of ten men with scythes and sickles. Yet as long as there were only horses available to plough and harrow, or for draught work around the farm, there remained a nucleus of skilled horsemen throughout the country who appreciated the sight of the hunt and whose sons often made excellent hunt servants with an intrinsic understanding of their work. Furthermore, while ploughing was dependent on horses the stubble remained unploughed often until well into the spring, providing good galloping ground in the plough countries. Although it might often be irksome to find men at work draining the fields and heading the fox, it meant better drained land and hence easier going another year.

On the other hand many of the new coverts which had been eagerly planted in the early part of the century were badly planned, or were by this time overgrown and impenetrable. Too many patches of thick gorse close together proved as much a handicap as a help to hunting. The increase in rabbits also tended to prevent foxes requiring to hunt far for their food, hence making them less prepared – or able – to run far. With a general tendency for there to be more foxes than earlier in the century, points generally became shorter as a result.

Perhaps the most important development for foxhunting during this period was the formation of the Masters of Foxhounds Association in 1881. In 1880 the foxhunting members of Boodle's had quarrelled with the management of the club and withdrawn in a body. The result was a temporary hiatus in foxhunting management. The Duke of Beaufort therefore circularized all Masters of Foxhounds, asking them to meet and form a new governing body. Since it was far more representative than the old committee, the M.F.H.A. was able to enforce its decisions more effectively. Furthermore, in 1886 they took over the *Foxhound Kennel Stud Book* from 'Cecil' (Cornelius Tongue), thus controlling foxhound pedigrees as well as the hunts. The F.K.S.B., with records going back to the turn of the century in some cases, was of immense benefit to foxhunting in that it

The Layston meet of the Puckeridge hounds, 12 February 1859

ABOVE: *The Newmarket and Thurlow at Six Mile Bottom,* by J. F. Herring Senior

BELOW: Captain Charles Barclay

The joint Masters of the Puckéridge hunt for the season 1947–8, Mr E. E. Barclay, Major
M. E. Barclay and Captain C. G. E. Barclay, a portrait presented to the Masters in 1956 'by
their many friends in the country as a token of their gratitude to the Barclay family for
the sixty consecutive years since 1896 during which its members had been masters'.

ABOVE: Mr J. D. Webb, a portrait presented by members of the Newmarket and Thurlow hunt on his retirement as chairman of the hunt committee, 1967

BELOW: Mr and Mrs E. H. Vestey, joint Masters, with Tony Champion, huntsman, of the Newmarket and Thurlow hunt

enabled M.F.H.s to register their breeding and improve hounds systematically.

The railways had already proved their worth to the foxhunter, who could now start early from London in time to arrive at a meet and return that evening in time for dinner. This was a service which was to be still further improved with the introduction of hunt specials and by the end of the century had attained considerable importance. By then, of course, the appearance of the motor-car had also begun to have its effect. There were already some who used these newfangled devices instead of covert hacks, to the general displeasure of their friends. The very appearance of a motor-car was enough to startle most horses and to cause endless trouble at a meet.

The vast increase in wealth and the numbers of new rich resulted, among other side-effects, in an enormous impetus for game-rearing and shooting, which closed many coverts to the hunts for much of the season, if not completely. On the other hand it also led to an increase in the numbers of those hunting. Those hunts within easy reach of London benefited to a considerable extent by the support of rich industrialists, stockbrokers, business and professional men, who settled in the country and sent their sons to the new public schools which had proliferated during the century to learn to behave like gentlemen. The process had been happening for centuries, but the scale, especially during the last quarter of the nineteenth century, was far greater than ever before.

Although there had always been a certain anti-hunting element, originating in the dislike of the dispossessed Saxons for the Forest Laws enforced by their Norman conquerors, this now began to evince itself more clearly as a social issue. The Victorian era was immensely class conscious. Those who could not afford to hunt were jealous of those who could. The answer to the question 'Do you hunt?' had a clear social significance in some eyes. Such attitudes, of course, merely intensified the dislike and opposition of those ready to take offence. For the first time a definite anti-hunting element based on class-consciousness was apparent, but it was essentially an early manifestation of the growing split between town and country, for in the country itself the hunt was generally supported by all classes without considerations of this nature.

Already the prophets of doom were sounding the death-knell of foxhunting. William Dixon, the sporting journalist, who wrote under the pen-name 'Druid' and was reputed never to have hunted in his life, although an inveterate gossiper with hunt servants, as might be expected in such circumstances, harked back to the past glories of foxhunting. In the 1860s he referred nostalgically to the earlier days of the century:

Never was a period more propitious for the chase ... The country was not grid-ironed by railways, nor did the steam-engines impregnate the air with noxious gas. There were not two or three men draining in every field. Hunting was then at its culminating point. Modern science has doubtless filled the pockets of the jobber and speculator, but it has gone far to destroy the noblest pursuit which the Gods ever bestowed on mortals.

Delme Radcliffe, much more experienced in hunting practice, wrote more realistically as late as 1880: 'Railways *in being* are hateful and sport-spoiling enough; but railways in progress are to a hunting country as the Colorado beetle to the potato.' The fact of the matter was that every hunting man tended to look back on the previous era as being better than the present, harking back to the famous hunts of his youth and contrasting them with indifferent sport in the present. Such is human nature. Yet, despite all the apparent handicaps, hunting continued to be amongst the foremost sports of the countryside. In a class-conscious age there might be a growing split between 'fashionable' and 'unfashionable' hunting countries. The shires with their racing grass pastures provided great sport, it is true, but the ploughland hunting countries could also provide sport of great interest to those understanding and appreciating good houndwork. The latter were the hunts primarily supported by the farmers themselves, attracting little support from outside in most cases.

The Newmarket and Thurlow hunt lay in just such a backward pocket of countryside, neither fashionable, nor highly populated, with a mainly mixed agriculture, part heavy ploughland, never very attractive to the visiting foxhunter, but providing good sport to those who knew their country. Although affected by the changes in agriculture, many of these had proved advantageous rather than otherwise, Many of those parts of the country which had been boggy were by this time well drained, or in the process of being drained. The plough might still be sticky enough in all conscience, but foxes were no longer as scarce as they had been in Osbaldeston's day. The work of the short-lived Thurlow Hunt Club had seen to that at least.

Mr John Josselyn's final term as Master of the Suffolk lasted from 1875 to 1880, with Tom Enever as kennel huntsman. Although riding at twenty stone and never a hard rider, Mr Josselyn generally seems to have been in at the finish or thereabouts. He also seems to have shown very good sport, especially on the Thurlow side of the country. At the end of the 1880 season he finally retired, aged sixty-four, and died four years later in 1884. He was succeeded by Mr Greene, later to be Sir E. Walter Greene, by this time fully recovered from his coaching accident and once again prepared to take over as Master.

Fortunately at this stage we have available for reference the detailed hunting diaries of Mr Thomas Purkis of Barham Hall, Linton, which extend with few gaps from 1880 until his death in 1932. Born in 1854 he went to school at Bishops Stortford Grammar School at the same time as Cecil Rhodes. When he started his diaries in 1888 he was already at the age of twenty-six, farming under the direction of his father at Barham. His keenness on hunting, shooting and coursing was already apparent, but gradually foxhunting became his consuming passion in life, to the exclusion of all else. From 1898 until 1926 he was to be the honorary secretary of the Newmarket and Thurlow hunt. He did not, however, restrict himself to hunting with only one pack. At various times he also hunted with, amongst others, the Suffolk, the Essex, the East Essex, the Cambridgeshire and the Puckeridge. He was indeed particularly fond of hunting with the Puckeridge, next to the Newmarket and Thurlow, and thus provides a useful link between the two hunts. In his crabbed handwriting he undoubtedly left an extremely valuable record of sport over the years for which he deserves our thanks.

Nor was he afraid to criticize whenever he felt it justified. Even Mr John Josselyn did not escape entirely. An early entry in 1880, during Mr Josselyn's final season, read:

Thursday, 12th February. Met Suffolk Hounds at Thurlow Crown. Found a brace of foxes at Trundley. Made a muddle of them and then 1 at Carlton Wood, but soon lost him, then went on to Widghams found a fox and ran him about the Woodlands for 1 hour and a half and killed.

One of the principal objections of the Thurlow supporters to hunting with the Suffolk was apparent from the entry for 19 February 1881, during Mr Greene's first season as Master:

Met the Suffolk at Saxham White Horse. Rode to Mr. R. King's to breakfast and then drove up and found at Ickworth Park and ran him a ring for 40 minutes round by Whepstead, very pretty. Could not stop to see him killed as I had twenty five miles home.

During his early seasons young Thomas Purkis noted shooting both partridges and pheasants with his father and friends, as well as coursing hares with the family greyhounds, but even in his first season he recorded forty-six days' hunting. He also noted days when hounds had to be whipped off various coverts in November because they had not yet been shot. Mention of foxes seen caught in traps, or with only three legs, or killed with snares on them, also indicated the continued conflict of interests between hunting and shooting.

He was somewhat critical of young Mr E. Walter Greene as Master, recording on 30 November 1882: ' . . . got no sport as Mr Greene will lift the Hounds . . .'

It was not all criticism, however. He also noted some good days as well,* although in general sport under Mr Greene does not seem to have approached the standard of his predecessor Mr Josselyn. In any event, at the end of the season Mr Greene resigned.

The start of the 1883–4 season saw a major change. Mr Edward Browne took over as Master of the Suffolk and was content to let the Newmarket and Thurlow country go to Mr Jesse Coope, Master of the East Essex. Mr Coope thus took on an area almost as large as the old combined Suffolk and Newmarket and Thurlow country had been. From the Newmarket and Thurlow supporters' viewpoint it was not really a change for the better, merely a variant on an old theme. Mr Purkis was initially somewhat scathing. He wrote:

> Nov 19. Met the East Essex (late Suffolk) at Linton Station. Bad Day's sport. Found a brace of foxes. One only had three legs, which the hounds killed.
> Nov. 27. Met Mr. Coope at Baythorne End. Drew all the country blank till we got to Sturmer Hall Groves where we found a fox and soon lost him again. One of the worst managed days I was ever out.

He did, however, record some good hunts as the season progressed and there was one notable day with the Suffolk on the boundaries of the present Newmarket and Thurlow country.* By this time, of course, hunting men were using the railways freely, even chartering 'hunt specials' to transport pack and huntsman to distant parts of a large country. This was the method occasionally used by Mr Coope, for on 4 February 1884 Mr Purkis noted: 'Mr Coope had to whip off to catch the train.' The following day, while out with the Suffolk, he himself was forced 'to come home by train, as we left off 7 miles the wrong side of Bury'.

Despite the fact that Mr Purkis recorded it as 'the best season I ever remember', Mr Coope must have found hunting such a vast area regularly somewhat wearing. It also seems likely that he was not particualarly popular on the Thurlow side of the country. By this time they were no doubt getting tired of simply being an appendage to another hunt's territory. In any event it is clear that the Thurlow Farmers must have got together, for the following season Mr Coope was content merely to hunt the East Essex country, while the Newmarket and Thurlow hunt was once again reconstituted as a separate entity. For the first time since the days of Osbaldeston the Newmarket and Thurlow country was hunted by its own pack of hounds.

The moving spirit behind this successful and well-timed revival was Mr James Gardner of Saxon Hall, on the Duke of Rutland's estate at Cheveley. With the Duke's backing and congratulations Mr Gardner took over as Master of the

*See Appendix, page 123.

re-formed Newmarket and Thurlow hunt. An extremely popular tenant farmer in the district, it is plain that Mr Gardner also had the backing of his fellow farmers. The new hunt and the new Master soon showed some good sport.

It is certainly clear where Mr Purkis's sympathies lay. His first entry for the 1884-5 season was: 'October 9. Met Jim Gardner (Thurlow hounds 1st time ever out) at Brinkley . . .' That first season Mr Purkis's diary abounds with phrases such as 'hunted very prettily'; 'Hard day for hounds and horses'; first forty five minutes very good' and so on. Of particular note was a hunt of 19 January which he noted as 'a clipping day'. on 16 April, after a 'Very good day's sport', he recorded: 'Hunt dinner at the Rutland Arms in the evening where I went.' Of the season itself he simply recorded: 'Been out 58 times.' Clearly, however he thought it had been a good one and that the Newmarket and Thurlow hunt had begun well.

Almost predictably, the following season of 1885-6 was not so good, as scenting conditions were generally poor. After the final day on 15 April Mr Purkis recorded: 'Last time. A very poor season. Been out 57 times.' The season of 1886-7 started with the note on 11 November: 'Thurlow Hounds did not meet on account of F. Archer's death.' It is a reminder of the hunt's closeness to Newmarket that hunting was thus stopped as a mark of respect for the passing of a great jockey, who must have been a familiar figure in the hunting field and well known to the hunt followers.

In December of that season the diary was enlivened by mention of a kill close to Ditton Church 'when a crazy Parson took our names to draw a summons for killing the fox in his meadow'. The two finest hunts of the season were in December when scent was good and there was another notable day when a fox was killed in a dense fog in February in Six Mile Bottom. Otherwise sport must have been poor as he ended: 'Very poor season. Been out 53 times.'

With the exception of a couple of good hunts in December* when hard weather set in early there was little of note in Mr Purkis's diary for the 1887-8 season. On 19 December, however, he noted the first hunt breakfast:

Met the Thurlow at Babraham freezing hard all day. Did not begin to draw until 12.0 after a grand breakfast at Lord Cadogan's. Found a good fox in his covers but lost him directly. Then drew Balsham and went home as it was too hard. Rode Lancer and sold him to a Mr Sanders. 60 guineas.

Hunting was then postponed due to the icy conditions until 5 January and thereafter the weather was never very favourable, justifying the sour comment at the end of the season: 'Worst season I ever had. Had 42 days.'

*See Appendix, page 124.

The 1888–9 season was another poor one, with a significantly large number of blank days chronicled. One of the better days on 27 December started: 'Met the Thurlow at Horseheath Mill. Found a fox in my cabbages . . .' In January, however, there were several blank days in succession and on 28 February Mr Purkis's suspicions were aroused. He noted: 'Met the Thurlow at Brinkley. Found a fox . . . ran through the Severals by Wratting Park and Rands Wood and killed just before he got to Lophams. I think it was a drag up to Rands Wood.' Altogether foxes seem to have been scarce and scent poor. Not surprisingly, he ended his entries bleakly: Very bad season. Only been out 44 times.'

There was a good opening to the 1889–90 season with 'a very pretty 30 minutes', but thereafter came significant blank days in some of the best coverts. Then unfortunately Mr Purkis's diary suffers a hiatus for the rest of the season and the next. This was Mr James Gardner's final season as Master and in the 1890–1 season he was succeeded by Captain J. Gordon Miller, who lived and 'kennelled' at Little Thurlow. Apart from one or two quite good days' sport in March 1892 there is little record of Captain Gordon Miller's period as Master. Reading between the lines it would appear that Mr Purkis did not think much of him and it is interesting to note that the only reference to him in *British Hunts and Huntsmen* is a cryptic if tantalizing comment on 'the meteoric career as M.F.H. of the notorious Captain J. Gordon Miller'. It would appear that he was of a similar mould to Surtee's Soapy Sponge, or Facey Romford, departing overnight and leaving his creditors gnashing their teeth.

The successor to the dashing Captain was Mr E. Molyneux of Steeple Bumpstead, who according to Mr Purkis was quite the opposite, being far too slow. On 28 December 1892 he wrote scathingly:

Mr Molyneux would put the hounds into the cover instead of holding them forward and lost quite fifteen minutes before he hit him off again . . . when we lost him. The Master did not find again as he was afraid of hurting his horses. Might have been a good day as there was a ripping scent. . . .

One of the hazards of hunting near Newmarket, which was to become an increasing drawback, was recorded on 29 January when 'the Paddocks and yearlings baffled the hounds and we lost him'. Due to the steadily increasing number of studs near Newmarket quite a large area of country was to become barred to the hunt over the years. This, however, had little to do with Mr Molyneux's style of hunting, which did not please Mr Purkis. Comments such as 'Mr Molyneux left a great many of the most likely covers undrawn, very slow' – or even more simply 'Mr Molyneux made a muddle of it' – speak for themselves.

For all that Mr Molyneux does not seem to have been a very inspired Master, he built the hunt kennels at Thurlow, and sold them to the hunt at less than half their cost on his retirement. For this if nothing else the hunt owed him a debt of thanks. In practice it would appear that the hunt was having some difficulty in finding a Master at this time, for, according to Mr R. W. King's notes when he was chairman of the hunt committee in 1894, 'A letter was read from the Master to the Hon. Sec. giving notice of his intention to resign the Mastership of the Newmarket & Thurlow Hunt at the end of the present season.' It was then proposed by Colonel Goodchild and seconded by Mr R. King that he be asked to reconsider his 'determination' and withdraw his resignation, but Mr Molyneux was not to be persuaded.

He was succeeded for the 1894-5 season by Mr George Bowen, a man of great charm, who was later to be joint Honorary Secretary of the Puckeridge hunt from 1904 to 1915, further cementing the links between the two hunts. Unfortunately he was even less of a success than Mr Molyneux. A the end of the season Mr Purkis noted succinctly: 'Been out 41 times, killed six brace of foxes. Bad season. Worst I ever had.' At the end of the season, quietly but firmly, Mr Bowen resigned. In desperation the hunt committee then turned back to Mr Molyneux and persuaded him to take over the task once more.

Unfortunately, once again Mr Molyneux failed to provide a very high standard of sport, although some phrases in Mr Purkis's diary for the season are happily descriptive. On 11 November 1895 he described the hunted fox as 'grounded in the Railway Cutting'. Even better was his glorious use of the Suffolk word 'puggle', meaning to poke with a stick. On 30 December he recorded of the fox: 'He got in a hole, puggled him out and killed him.' The meet on 2 January was not without interest, for in the middle of what seemed a promising hunt at Cheveley Green 'our Master lost his temper and had the hounds whipped off and taken home as somebody from Newmarket tried to hunt them'. The only day of the season which warranted the description good was 6 January* and at the end of the season Mr Purkis summed up: 'Been out 60 times; killed 10 brace of foxes and ran 5 brace to ground. A very open season but not a good scent.'

At the end of this season Mr Molyneux once again quietly but firmly resigned and was succeeded by Mr W. H. Pemberton-Barnes. Mr Reginald S. Hicks, himself subsequently Master and a keen supporter of the hunt, described the new Master thus:

A queer little character with an even queerer wife. He never buttoned his Pink Coat up and as he had an enormous moustache he resembled when he was galloping and one was riding behind him, nothing so much as a yacht in full sail with his moustaches representing jib and foresail and his hunt coat flying out at both sides looking like a mainsail and spinnaker. Old Mrs Barnes had a rough old tongue and I remember hearing the 2nd Whip

*See Appendix, page 125.

complaining that he'd never been sworn at so by a lady before, to which she retorted, 'Oh, well you damned soon will be if you stay with me long.'

Mrs Pemberton-Barnes apparently also insisted on feeding the hounds loaves of wholemeal bread, but Mr Pemberton-Barnes, 'queer little character' or not, started to show some good sport once more and Mr Thomas Purkis's diaries, as well as those of Mr Hicks himself, detail several good hunts* over the next two seasons. Mr Purkis's summary of the 1897–8 season may have been coloured by the fact that on the last day, 24 March, they ran into a blizzard and had to go home. He recorded: 'A very bad finish to a very poor season; has always been too dry for this country.' Despite this he had been out on no less than sixty-seven occasions.

On 17 March of that year the hunt held what Mr Hicks described as

the very last old fashioned Pt. to Pt. race ever held in England. We started in a field close to Little Thurlow Church and were told to ride the nearest way we could to a Flagstaff set up somewhere close to what was then Mr. Hick's farm between Hundon and Stradishall, without going more than twenty yards down any road . . . Great fun, after which lunch at Stradishall the home of the Bower family, and a bit of foxhunting to top up with.

Unfortunately there is another hiatus in Mr Purkis's diaries with the season 1898–9 missing, although Mr Hicks's diary for the season, while nothing like so comprehensive, does not detail much sport. One of the better days was retailed by Mr Hicks in his general recollections of the hunt written many years later. He wrote:

On February 10th we had a very fast gallop indeed from Trundley Wood to ground near Hundon Church. This I think was the last day old Dick Ellis of Lucy ever went out hunting. He was over eighty years old and having got away right on Hounds Backs, so to speak, no one ever caught him, try as hard as we would. Pretty well 5 miles as hounds ran and over a nice bit of country. The old man drove home in his old 4 Wheel Buggy from Bradley Fox but caught pneumonia from which he never recovered.

Mr Purkis's diary is available again as reference for the 1899–1900 season when he noted on 5 November that one of his neighbours 'Mr Binney showed he was foolish enough to turn a bagman down, which the hounds killed and would not look at.' Nevertheless, they went on to kill three more foxes and with one or two exceptions this was the best day of the season.† There was heavy frost, snow and occasional heavy fog, a regular local hazard two or three times each season. Throughout Mr Purkis's diaries indeed there is a comment every season about whipping off because of fog, or killing a fox in dense fog, with consistent

*See Appendix, page 125.
†See Appendix, page 126.

64

regularity. His final comment on the season was the entry 'Been out 55 times; ten blank days, very poor season.'

It is a noticeable feature of Mr Purkis's diaries that he regularly refers simply to 'The Thurlow', whereas Mr Hicks from the 1896 season onwards refers always to 'The Newmarket and Thurlow'. He himself subsequently suggested that the Newmarket addition was adopted when Mr James Gardner gave up the Newmarket Drag Hunt, which he had apparently started on giving up the foxhounds. However, Mr Hicks gives no date for this and it is clear that by the 1890s the hunt was generally known as the Newmarket and Thurlow and was once again well established after the years of merger with the Suffolk.

If the Newmarket and Thurlow had undergone various vicissitudes over the years they were now well established once again. During the same period, however, which saw the Newmarket and Thurlow's fortunes re-established, the Puckeridge suffered some of the worst years in their history. It is only fair to add that these years were the ones coinciding with the great farming slump of the 1870s and 1880s caused by the import of cheap grain and frozen beef from abroad. The farmers of Hertforshire, mainly arable land, who relied to a large extent on the London market were harder hit than many.

On Mr Parry's retirement in 1875 he was succeeded by Mr Robert Gosling of Hassobury, near Bishops Stortford, the head of the well-known family of private bankers, eventually to be merged with Barclays. Mr Gosling agreed to hunt the country three days a week, with a guarantee of £1750 to include earth-stopping expenses. As huntsman, to replace Alfred Hedges, he brought in Robert Allen, who had whipped in to the Rufford and the Essex.

Initially the hounds remained the property of Mr Parry and continued to be kennelled at Albury End. Perhaps not altogether surprisingly, the first season does not seem to have been a good one, but in the following year, 1876, Mr Gosling bought the hounds (forty-nine couple) from Mr Parry for 2000 guineas and kennelled them at Manuden. This move seems to have been a successful one, for Mr Gosling's second season of 1876–7 provided a number of good days, of which the best was noted in his diary for 20 December as: 'Elmdon Lee; Found at the How, ran by Triplow and Newton to ground near Harston in the Cambridgeshire country. 1 hr. ½.' This was a point of eight miles and took the Puckeridge farther north than at any time in their history.

The 1878–9 season was a poor one, but there was some improvement in the 1879–80 season, despite bad weather. On 23 February Mr Gosling recorded a seven-mile point well into the Essex country.* However, foxes were becoming

*See Appendix, page 159.

F 65

scarce and money was becoming even scarcer. There had already been a threatened deficit of some £600–700 in the 1876–7 season, which had only just been raised, and despite a lower guarantee of only £1400 there was another prospective deficit of £248 in 1878. This was paid off, but was followed in the year 1879 by a deficiency of £200 and it was found that only £1000 could be raised as subscription for 1880–1. Crisis point had been reached.

Mr J. P. Judd for the hunt committee was given the unenviable task of explaining to Mr Gosling that little more than £800 could be guaranteed, but that 'If you give up the country it will not be hunted in 1880–1'. Mr Gosling's reply was,

> As I do not hear of any other gentleman mentioned as ready to take my place, on the following conditions I am willing to go on hunting the country for another season. That there be no by-days, the by-day coverts to be hunted on regular hunting days, and I will not undertake to draw the neutral coverts to the west, from Aston to Bush Wood, unless I wish to do so; of course I reserve to myself the right to do so at any time.

This seemingly sensible solution was greeted with applause and the ensuing season of 1880–1 showed some good sport with at least one outstanding eight-mile point.* The following season of 1881–2, however, was very disappointing and a clue to the reason for this may be found in Mr Thomas Purkis's diary:

> February 16. Met Mr. Gosling's Hounds at Elsenham, drew all covers blank up to Widdington High Wood. Found a brace of foxes there but no sport as Allen made a muddle as usual. Found second fox at Quendon Park and lost him the same. Beautiful hunting day. Rode Duchess.

At the end of the 1881–2 season Robert Allen left and was succeeded as huntsman by William Wells, who had been whipper-in to the Belvoir. The difference was at once noticeable. The 1882–3 season was much more successful and the 1883–4 season even better, with some excellent hunts. Mr Thomas Purkis, with his usual knack of choosing a good day to be with hounds, chronicled some very good hunts and there was a point of ten miles on 9 January 1884. Sport in the 1884–5 season was not quite so good, but still well up to standard.

In 1885 Mr Robert Gosling announced his resignation as Master. He was admittedly only receiving about half of the original guarantee of £1500, but the real reason was not financial. He was obviously aware of dissatisfaction amongst the supporters of the hunt on the western, or Saturday, side of the country. This was not really his fault. When the country had defaulted in its guarantee he had resigned. When pressed to remain he had suggested a perfectly fair solution, namely omitting the bye-day and not necessarily hunting the neutrals, which could be hunted by the Hertfordshire, and this proposal had been accepted unanimously.

*See Appendix, page 159.

Of course, Mr Gosling's kennels at Manuden were on the Monday and Wednesday side of the country. The hunt supporters on the west side of the country, led by Mr Felix Calvert of Furneux Pelham Hall (1847–1909) and Mr J. W. Leader of Buntingford, and backed by the powerful Sworder family, large farmers, who were intermarried with the Chapmans, Coopers, Rolfes, Sales, Seabrooks, Smyths, Wallers, Wymans and other old-established farming families, felt that they were not getting the same sport they had enjoyed under Mr Parry. The fact that Mr Gosling provided both hounds and kennels and had to hack from nine to sixteen miles to meets on their side of the country does not seem to have weighed unduly with them.

On receiving his resignation the hunt committee asked him to reconsider his decision. Mr Gosling suggested that he might arrange some of the furthest Saturday meets for 11.30 or 12 o'clock. This was rejected at a meeting where the Saturday country were strongly represented and Mr Gosling confirmed his resignation and put his hounds up for sale. A committee was appointed to find a new Master, but lacking kennels were unable to do so. They then set about building new kennels at Braughing in the centre of the country.

Meanwhile the Monday and Wednesday supporters, neighbours of Mr Gosling's in the east, formed a deputation to inform the committee that they wished Mr Gosling to hunt that side of the country. The committee replied that their powers were merely to find a Master for the whole country. Thereupon the deputation took the law into their own hands and asked Mr Gosling to accept this proposal, which he duly did. The Saturday contingent claimed the deputation had acted unconstitutionally and in July held another committee meeting.

It was recorded that 'the proceedings commenced with the reading of correspondence between Captain W. H. Patten Saunders, equerry to His Imperial Highness Nicholas of Russia, Duke de Leuchtenberg, Mr F. C. Swindell, of Chesterfield Lodge, Lichfield, and Royal Crescent, Brighton, Mr Felix Calvert and Mr J. W. Leader. Captain Patten Saunders recommended Mr Swindell as Master in these terms:

He is under thirty, very enthusiastic in the cause of hunting, practically one of the best huntsmen in England, has always had some hounds or harriers himself and has hunted some of the big packs in the absence of some of the Masters or accidents to huntsmen. He has never been mixed up with anything prejudicial to the position of an M.F.H. and in fact I should say would be a very eligible and popular Master. Many M.F.H.s, Peers and Commoners would, I know, gladly endorse everything I say, and Coutts would be his financial reference if required.

Since Mr Gosling was already in possession of his part of the country it was agreed at this meeting that Mr Swindell should hunt the vacant part of the country for two days a week in the 1885–6 season and the entire country the following season. Despite the absurd style of Captain Patten Saunders' recommendation Mr Swindell turned out a surprisingly good choice in the circumstances. The only point not mentioned was that he was the son of a bookmaker. Since he had been a highly successful bookmaker, this enabled his son to accept the mastership of the Puckeridge with a guarantee of only £500.

In August Mr Swindell set up in Layston House, Buntingford, and built himself temporary kennels there. In October a compromise was reached between his supporters and Mr Gosling that a line from Ware through Puckeridge, Hare Street, Anstey, Langley Lower Green, Arkesden, Saffron Walden and the Chesterfords should separate Mr Gosling's hounds on the east from the Puckeridge on the west. Mr Gosling himself agreed to resign in May 1886 in favour of a Master 'acceptable to the whole country'. Unfortunately, in January a deputation of landowners in Mr Gosling's country held a private meeting and requested him to continue hunting their part. Assuming – not unnaturally in these circumstances – that Mr Swindell was not acceptable to the whole country, Mr Gosling announced his intention in 1886 of continuing to hunt as before.

The country was now split into factions and the dispute grew extremely bitter.

In 1889 the dispute was referred to the M.F.H. Association who decreed that

1. The Puckeridge country must be hunted by only one Master and one Pack.
2. Mr. Gosling was not entitled to hunt any portion of the country.
3. Mr. Swindell had never properly been elected Master.
4. Therefore the arrangment made in October 1885 should continue until May 1st 1890, when a general meeting should be called and a Master elected to hunt the country as a whole.

In 1890 a meeting was held and Mr Swindell stood and was elected. Mr Gosling's supporters were incensed and feelings ran even higher. Mr Gosling himself resigned, but sold his hounds to a committee of his supporters, who changed their name to the Herts and Essex and continued to kennel them in the Manuden kennels with Mr Gosling as their elected Master. Of course, feelings then reached a state of near civil war. Challenges, free fights, interference with neighbouring coverts, lawsuits and utter chaos ensued.

In 1893 the M.F.H. Association was asked to intervene and wisely decreed that on 1 May 1894 the authorities of both hunts must resign and a Master unconnected with either should be brought in to hunt the country. Despite the urgings of his supporters Mr Swindell wisely accepted this decision and withdrew to hunt the Old Berkshire, where he was extremely popular. The Hon. L. J.

Bathurst, who had hunted the Exmoor Foxhounds, was elected sole Master and the Puckeridge was itself again.

During this period of at times extreme disturbance, bad for sport and bad for the hunt, Mr Thomas Purkis had as usual distributed his favours impartially, hunting with the Puckeridge (Mr Swindell's) and Mr Gosling's hounds, or latterly the Herts and Essex, each in turn. It is apparent from his records how the hunting was adversely affected, but he also included some accounts of good sport. There were indeed some very good hunts recorded both with Mr Gosling in the east and Mr Swindell in the west during this period.

The new Master who now took over the Puckeridge, the Hon. Lancelot J. Bathurst (1868–1928), brother of the 7th Earl Bathurst, was an excellent choice. With youth and charm on his side, as well as energy and experience, he threw himself into his task of reuniting the country and showing good sport. He bought Mr Swindell's hounds for £1200 and also took on his huntsman James Budd. By so doing he lost the splendid pack of hounds built up by Mr Parry and continued by Mr Gosling, for this was now dispersed. If nothing else the hunt had lost in this respect, for these hounds represented years of study and experience in hound breeding.

Mr Bathurst's stay with the Puckeridge was short, only two years, from 1894 to 1896, but it was what the country required. His first season he killed forty-five brace of foxes, hunting on a hundred and two days, even with snow on the ground. The record stated: 'Sport up to the end of December very good and altogether a most satisfactory season.' There was one seven-mile point on 21 December, but the second season was not quite so good. The summary of the season 1895–6 was: 'Scent fairly good up to Christmas. Very bad remainder of the season.' As usual Mr Purkis managed to see some sport in both years and appeared to think well of the new management.

In 1896 Mr Edward E. Barclay was appointed Master on the retirement of Mr Bathurst back to his beloved West Country as Master of the Eggesford Hounds in Devon. With a guarantee of £2000 a year Mr Barclay agreed to hunt hounds four times a week. A member of the well-known banking family of Scottish origin, famous throughout East Anglia, Mr Barclay had hunted harriers and beagles for eighteen years before taking on the Puckeridge.

Moving to Brent Pelham, he selected as his huntsman James Cockayne, who hunted the bitch pack, while he himself hunted the dog pack. Breeding his own hunters and his own hounds was part of his nature. His principal worry in his early years with the Puckeridge was a scarcity of foxes. During the first dozen years of his mastership this was to remain one of his greatest headaches. In the season of 1900–1 a quarter of the hunting days were blank or produced only one fox. There were, however, some good days in the interval and as usual Mr Purkis managed to see some sport. The main point with Mr Barclay's election as Master was that the Puckeridge unbeknownst to themselves were ensuring a continuity and security in the next eighty years which any hunt might envy and no other hunt could equal.

Chapter 7

The Years from 1900 to 1920

THE turn of the century saw the military might of the great British Empire still locked in a humiliatingly unequal but long-drawn-out and bloody struggle with a comparative handful of sharp-shooting Boer farmers. Like the American woodsmen in the War of Independence more than a century before, they confronted a highly trained British Army and by their superior knowledge and understanding of the terrain, as well as by their irregular tactics and utter determination, confounded them. Between 1899 and 1902 volunteers from all parts of Britain went out to South Africa and many of them failed to return.

The yeomanry regiments were principally officered by keen hunting men with many others in the ranks. Nor were their womenfolk lacking in spirit. Countess Howe, herself a dedicated foxhunter, turned her energies instead to organized fund-raising for charity and in 1900 opened a field hospital in Deelfontein with six hundred beds. One ward was named the Hunt Ward, in which beds were named after the individual hunts which had subscribed for them.

Names like Mafeking, Magersfontein and Spion Kop became familiar in every household. Communications had reached the stage where this was almost inevitable. The Boer War saw the countryside more deeply involved than in any previous war with familiar faces missing from the hunting field, often never to be seen again. It was a mild preparation for the long-drawn-out holocaust that was to come during the years from 1914 to 1918. With the Peace Treaty of Vereeniging in 1902, however, the British relapsed happily into the serenity of the Edwardian era.

The spacious Edwardian era, short interlude though it may have been before the world cataclysm of 1914 – after which nothing was to be ever quite the same again – was a glorious period. Old huntsmen might hark back to the golden days of the mid-nineteenth century when wire was unknown and mange in foxes unheard of except amongst bag-men from France. Yet there were numerous gains to offset the losses. The M.F.H.A. (Master of Foxhounds Association), formed in 1881, could rigidly enforce foxhunting's unwritten rules. The F.K.S.B. (*Foxhound Kennel Stud Book*), taken over by the M.F.H.A. in 1886, was the final arbiter of hound breeding, ensuring ever better standards.

Railways might bisect many parts of the countryside, but their advantages for hunting in most cases outweighed their disadvantages. It is true that the spread of industry in some places had already rendered parts of the countryside un-huntable, but this was counterbalanced by the ease of transport to other hunts. The introduction of motorized hound vans was a product of the Edwardian period, while frequently cars were used to reach meets in place of the old covert hack, to the consternation of many.

There was a general increase in hunt followers, especially in the numbers of women in the field. Some enthusiasts even started to follow hounds by car, anathema to Masters even then. Cyclists were commonplace and foot followers – especially in holiday times – often headed foxes, while popular meets were often extremely crowded, necessitating the widespread introduction of field Masters to control hunt followers. Even though the farming slump continued, few hunts could afford unnecessary claims for damages to crops or hedges.

It would be idle to deny that there was a considerable increase in wire in many districts, for the cheapness of this method of fencing made it almost a necessity in a time of farming depression. The introduction of hunt jumps during the Edwardian period in some hunts close to London, although an indifferent solution requiring much zigzagging and queuing, at least allowed hunting to continue after a fashion rather than stopping altogether. In other areas it was successfully kept to a minimum or warning signs were posted.

If wire was one hazard of the period, like rabies in hounds – already not un-known – foot-and-mouth disease in cattle and mange in foxes were yet others encountered by many hunts during these years. The first was not then considered quite the menace it is today and the second was not as extensive then as later, or possibly merely not always recognized as such. Mange in foxes, how-ever, was very widespread during the early years of the century, caused either by introducing infected strains, by inbreeding, or by poisons.

The deep division between hunting and shooting interests in many areas continued to cause problems. Trapping, snaring and poisoning of foxes re-grettably continued in many places, despite such panaceas as annual keepers' dinners and monetary rewards for litters reared or finds in coverts. High shoot-ing rents and the earnings accruing from driving birds, or acting as beaters, brought much-needed money into the pockets of countrymen, while all too often the hunt appeared uninterested and the hunt followers aloof. If not aloof,

Mr Thomas Purkis

OPPOSITE FAR LEFT: Mr George Bowen,
Master of the Newmarket and Thurlow 1894–5

OPPOSITE LEFT: Mr Robert Gosling, Master of the
Puckeridge 1875–85

OPPOSITE BOTTOM: Mr Frederick C. Swindell,
Master of the Puckeridge 1885–94, *centre*, with hunt servants

RIGHT: The Hon. Lancelot J. Bathurst, Master of the
Puckeridge 1894–6

BELOW: Mr Edward Barclay, Master of the Puckeridge 1896–1948

The Revd Sir William Hyde-Parker, Bt., Master of the Newmarket and Thurlow 1902–6

Mr Richard Bower, Master of the Newmarket and Thurlow 1906–10

Mr Herbert Jones

ABOVE: Mr Walter K. Cannon

LEFT: Mr Robert W. King

OPPOSITE TOP: Major Maurice E. Barclay, joint Master of the Puckeridge 1910–62

OPPOSITE BOTTOM: Robert Gardiner, huntsman to the Puckeridge 1911–37, on Silver Grill

Miss G. Cotton-Browne, with her harriers and hunt servants

Mr Robert C. Gosling

they might equally regrettably appear flushed and arrogant, the result of recourse to the spirit flask, generally at this period containing whisky rather than the brandy of a decade or so earlier, which was no longer readily obtainable due to the devastation of the vineyards in France by the phylloxera beetle.

The sources for the history of the Newmarket and Thurlow hunt during this period include, of course, the really excellent hunting diaries of that regular supporter since 1880 and ardent hunting enthusiast Mr Thomas Purkis of Barham Hall, Linton. Often joined during this period by his wife and sons, Claude and Anthony, his must have been a familiar figure indeed on his excellent old horse Reindeer, which during eighteen years of hunting with various packs in the area, including the Puckeridge, Suffolk, Essex, East Essex, Cambridgeshire and Fitzwilliam, only fell twice. Reading his accounts of the ordinary hunts, the bye-days and the blank days, as well as the more famous hunts which are included in the Appendix, it is easy to appreciate why hunting is so essentially the sport of the countryside.

Comparing most interestingly, and at times revealingly, with these diaries are those of Mr Reginald S. Hicks of Wilbraham Temple, near Cambridge, from 1896 to 1912, also a keen supporter of the Newmarket and Thurlow hunt. After following the Eton Beagles in the late 1880s he graduated to become Master of the Trinity Foot Beagles in 1892. After a spell as a farm pupil in West Norfolk he then started farming on his own account at Wilbraham and from 1896 hunted with the Newmarket and Thurlow, eventually becoming Master for a brief period, until illness abruptly terminated his spell in office. Described by one who hunted with him at the time as 'a great big fat feller', like many other Newmarket and Thurlow hunt followers, it would appear that Mr Hicks rode as a heavy-weight.

If Mr Hicks's hunting diaries are to be taken at their face value the 1900–1 season was not on the whole a very inspiring one. According to these a fox was killed with a snare on his foot on 6 December and on the 10th he noted: 'Chopped a bagged fox? at Rings Wood.' On the 24th there was 'thick fog, quite dense', a common hazard in that country. On 31 December he recorded rather self-consciously: 'Wore pink for the first time'. Then on 14 January without equivocation he wrote: 'Killed a *Bagman* in Ditton Wood. A hound got caught in a trap in Little Widgham. *Bravo Ellesmere* . . . Committee Meeting Brinkley. Pemberton-Barnes resigned.'

It would appear from these entries that things were getting rather slack in

73

Mr Pemberton-Barnes last season. On the other hand, quite a different impression is conveyed in Mr Purkis's diaries for the same period and it becomes evident that Mr Hicks was a stern critic, or perhaps his indifferent health, which even then caused him to miss some of the best runs, inclined him to harsher judgements. An interesting entry in Mr Purkis's diary, missing from Mr Hicks's notes, reads:

Feb. 11th. After Hounds being kept to Kennel a fortnight on account of Her Majesty The Queen's Death and then a sharp frost and snow for another week I met The Thurlow at Hawkedon Green. . . .

There followed an account of a good hunt of 1 hour 10 minutes and on 1 March an even better one of 1 hour 30 minutes.*

On 18 March 1901 Mr Hicks was elected M.F.H. '*pro tem*, for the Committee', which possibly explains the considerable difference between his entry for 8 April and that of Mr Purkis. Mr Hicks's entry read:

April 8th. Newmarket and Thurlow, Master P. Barnes. Bye Day. Found in Borley, but could do no good. Picked up a poisoned vixen with cubs in Balsham and went to interview Mr. Mann on the subject, but he was very rude and offhand. Mr. King hunted the hounds.

Due to the lack of mention of him it would be easy to assume that Mr Pemberton-Barnes had already given up the hounds, but Mr Purkis gives a very different picture of the day:

April 8th. Met The Thurlow at Woodman Spare the Tree for a bye day. Mr. Barnes had hurt his leg so he could not ride. Mr. King hunted the hounds. Drew Rands blank, found an outlier on Mr. Webb's land which the hounds soon ran into. Drew Balsham blank, found a suckling vixen dead thanks to Mr. Mann. Found at Borley but just as we found a thunderstorm came on and we could do nothing. Then drew Crafts [?], Northy, Hare, Lawn, Over Wood, North and Cadges blank. Rode Molly.

It is clear from these two entries alone what very different types these two men were. The one, a substantial farmer of good yeoman farming stock, had been born and bred in the country and educated at the grammar school in Bishops Stortford. The other, an old-Etonian gentleman farmer and son of a successful lawyer, had been brought up in Berkshire. It is evident that Mr Hicks on occasions lacked the tact and understanding required for dealing with the Suffolk countrymen, including some of his fellow farmers, although his health – which was undoubtedly bad – may have had something to do with this. Each, however, sheds invaluable light on the sport of the Newmarket and Thurlow over this period.

Following Mr Pemberton-Barnes Captain Charles Brook took over the mastership and it was Mr Hicks' task to introduce him to the country and to the

*See Appendix, page 126.

hunt followers. In the latter's view he was a very great improvement on Mr Pemberton-Barnes and his abrasive-tongued wife. He certainly seems to have introduced a good bitch pack, new hunt servants and better horses, generally tightening everything up somewhat, which had probably been required.

The hunting season of 1902–3, however, was a bad scenting one and on the whole there seems to have been only one outstanding day, on 9 January, when Mr Hicks – in a characteristic aside – noted that he was riding a horse on trial from a well-known dealer named Jack Duschene, which carried him extra-ordinarily well, so 'Naturally I bought him for 40 guineas. I named him Ashdon and he always carried me very well in spite of rather bad corns.'

At the end of the season Captain Brook announced his resignation, going on eventually to the Badsworth but leaving his pack of bitch hounds on loan to the Newmarket and Thurlow in the meantime. The committee then offered the mastership to Mr C. F. Ryder of Thurlow Park, who refused it, after which it was offered to the Reverend Sir William Hyde-Parker, J.P., C.A. (1863–1921) of Long Melford Hall, who accepted it. Although it was a journey of some twenty miles from Long Melford to the kennels for the new M.F.H., he proved a con-siderable asset to the hunt, as with the help of his friend and fellow cleric, the Reverend Jack Milne, M.F.H. of the Cattistock, he began to breed hounds specifically for the country, improving the pack considerably during the four years of his mastership.

Mr Reginald Hicks noted that, although considerably junior to them, he shared with both Sir William Hyde-Parker and the Reverend Jack Milne the fact that each had at one time been Master of the Trinity Foot Beagles. He was invited frequently to join them at the Peterborough Hound Show and similar events and confessed that he learned a great deal which was later to be useful to him when it came to his term as Master. This did not stop him occasionally being critical of Sir William's methods of hunting hounds.

The first clergyman to hunt hounds in the Thurlow country since the Rever-end Davers a hundred years previously, Sir William Hyde-Parker seems to have been a fairly formidable, if popular, character. Mr Hicks recorded that his 'sniffs' were devastating and renowned throughout the countryside. Writing candidly of his period as Master, Mr Hick's view was that

He had done us an awful lot of good by Breeding us a very good Pack of hounds. I think he had got more foxes in the country. I should not call him a *good* huntsman. He seemed to dislike Holloa's *so* much that sometimes he deliberately took no notice of them, and thus spoilt his chance of getting away on Top of his fox.

This failing apart, Sir William seems to have provided some good hunts. In his first season of 1902–3 there were several such, including one extremely

75

interesting occasion on 1 December when the Newmarket and Thurlow and Puckeridge hunts met head on, both in full cry, and combined forces to hunt the same fox, killing in the schoolyard at Linton to the great enjoyment of the youngsters there.* As the junior Master, Sir William very sportingly passed control in these circumstances to Mr Edward Barclay, then M.F.H. of the Puckeridge.

Mr Hicks's explanation of how this unusual occasion arose is probably the correct one. He wrote:

> The Puckeridge met at Chesterford Park and found a fox and ran him down towards Pampisford. The Newmarket and Thurlow met at Pampisford and having drawn all round there and Sawston blank, were on their way to try Cattley Drain and Hildersham Wood, when suddenly close to the London Road there was a fox. This I think must have been the Puckeridge fox for he turned right back and raced with us after him towards Chesterford when suddenly he found himself face to face again with the Puckeridge and not knowing what to do turned left handed as he was then facing and finally lost himself in Linton, where we killed him in the school yard with Both Packs. I think that when the Puckeridge originally found him he tried for Cattley Drain, but finding that stopped went on towards Pampisford which was his undoing . . . It was nothing of a day in the way of galloping and jumping being all over the light land.

The 1903 season was not quite so good, although there were some good days,* but the hunt benefited by the generous present of the pack of hounds previously loaned by Captain Charles Brook. With the addition of sound selective breeding by Sir William this bitch pack soon became a very considerable asset to the hunt. Unfortunately the 1904–5 season was an extremely bad scenting year, with a lot of frost and snow, but in his final season of 1905–6 Sir William again managed to show some good sport and by then his hound breeding measure were beginning to show effect.†

It was significant that at Sir William's final meet on 29 March, when a presentation was made to him of a piece of inscribed silver plate and a silver hunting horn, mention was made of the conflict of interests between hunting and shooting in the Newmarket and Thurlow country. Mr Reginald Hicks, making the presentation on behalf of the hunt followers, raised this thorny question and the difficulties besetting a Master. In the paper reporting the presentation there was also a letter underlining the opposition of the shooting interests. Significantly the editor prefaced the letter with a disclaimer in heavy type, reading: 'It must be distinctly understood that we do not identify ourselves with the opinions expressed by our correspondents.' The timing of such a letter can,

*See Appendix, page 127.
†See Appendix, page 128.

however, have been no accident and it certainly put its viewpoint forward forcibly:

Foxhunting versus Partridge Shooting.

Sir. Babraham, Pampisford, Hildersham, Abington and Balsham are situated in the heart of the best natural partridge shooting in England. In late years a pack of foxhounds, called the Newmarket and Thurlow Hounds have been located nearby and foxes highly preserved by the followers of these hounds, which have played havoc with the partridges in these districts. The destruction of game this year has been such that it has become a question of which sport has to go. If it is the partridge shooting it will be a loss of from 3s to 5s per acre on the agricultural land and agriculture is not so good just now as to enable it to lose the shooting rents and the working men can ill afford to lose the pay that partridge driving brings them. Some thousands a year are spent by the shooting tenants. It has been suggested that the farmers, farm workmen and shooting tenants should take immediate steps to kill down the foxes. Then a howl of indignation would arise from the followers of the Newmarket and Thurlow Hounds, a body that spends very little in this district compared with the shooting sportsmen. This is not a fox-hunting country but purely a shooting one, and it is felt that it is a big injustice that so much mischief should be done and no steps taken by the hunt to remedy it. When told about it, they only jeer. It is hoped they will now take the hint. Yours etc.

One of the Injured.

Such attacks in the press between the rival sports were, of course, not uncommon, but this very clearly underlined the feelings of many in the countryside who were more interested in the money to be made out of shooting in times of agricultural depression than in the sport to be had from either hunting or shooting. It is clear also from the tenor of the letter that the writer had aired his grievances and found scant sympathy from the hunting interests. It was this lack of understanding which led on occasion to the hunt unnecessarily making enemies, to poisoned foxes, or to the hunt being warned off land. It required an exceedingly tactful Master and representative hunt committee to prevent such conflict of interests.

Mr Richard Bower of Stradishall Place, Sir William's successor, who also was Master for four years from 1906 to 1910, seems to have been just the man for the job. Like Sir William, he bred his own hunters and continued to take an active interest in hound breeding, but he had the advantage of living in the country. Furthermore, he hunted hounds himself, although he engaged Sam Stobbert as first whip and continued with Pearce as second whip. According to both Mr Thomas Purkis and Mr Reginald Hicks, whose hunting diaries cover this period, he provided good sport* and seems to have killed more foxes than this predecessors. As far as foxhound breeding is concerned, however, it must be borne

*See Appendix, pages 128-30.

in mind that he had the benefit of Sir William's groundwork and the advantage of a sound basis on which to build.

During his first season of 1906–7 Mr Richard Bower showed his ability to get away fast on his foxes, but on the whole it was a poor season. The following season of 1907–8 was much better and in the 1908–9 season, despite eleven blank days, they killed ten and a half brace of foxes. The 1909–10 season, his last, was excellent with numerous outstanding days and they killed twelve brace of foxes, well above the average. His hunt followers, grateful for all he had done for the hunt as well as for the sport he had provided, presented him with a silver centre-piece on his departure.

Mr Hicks, one of his successors as M.F.H., wrote of him: 'He was one of the most fearless and brilliant men across country and I think the secret of his success was his speed in getting his hounds away on top of their fox.' At the end of the 1910 season he left to take on the Avon Vale where within six months he had met a tragic end. After a brilliant hunt early in the season, when he had left the field well behind, he was close up on hounds as they killed in the open. He threw himself off his horse and caught up the fox which still had strength enough to bite him on the wrist. As a result he contracted rabies and died soon afterwards in the Pasteur Clinic in Paris in October 1911.

The next Master of the Newmarket and Thurlow from 1910 to 1912 was Captain Edmund Deacon (1877–1915) of Sloe House, Halstead, late adjutant of the King's Dragoon Guards and a major in the Essex Yeomanry, who had been Master of the East Essex from 1899, hunting them himself from 1903 to 1909. Naturally a fine rider, who preferred his hunters as nearly as possible thoroughbred, he proved an excellent choice, providing some first-rate hunting during his two years as Master, more especially in his second season.* His death as Colonel of the Essex Yeomanry at Ypres in 1915 when he was last seen leading his men over the top blowing a hunting horn was one more tragedy of the 1914–18 War, but one which impinged deeply on many in the Newmarket and Thurlow country, who had warm memories of him in happier days.

During this Edwardian heyday, the prelude to the 1914–18 holocaust, there were several hazards, old and new, which presented themselves. An increasing hazard during the Christmas period seems to have been the large number of foot followers who headed the fox with monotonous regularity. Mr Richard Bower on one occasion also found his hunt held up by an express train on the line, but an entirely novel hazard presented itself in 1910 when his fox was headed by golfers on the links. Major Deacon, as he then was, also introduced a new hazard when he failed to turn up at a meet on 2 December 1910 because his

*See Appendix, pages 130–1.

78

'motor had been held up by the flooded roads'. Foxes in traps, or snares, still appeared occasionally and now and then poison was also mentioned, affecting either foxes or hounds, while mange was increasing amongst foxes, possibly due to this factor. Mr Hicks, now and then, also felt impelled to note possible 'bagmen' or 'suspicious' foxes, more commonly termed 'wrong uns' by Mr Purkis.

When Colonel Deacon resigned in 1912 Mr Reginald S. Hicks, who had meanwhile been Master of the Cambridgeshire Harriers for two years, was unanimously elected Master with a guarantee of £500 in return for hunting two days a week. Fortunately, as well as his detailed hunting diaries, Mr Hicks also kept a letter book, in which many extremely revealing details of the background to his period as Master are recorded. Extremely short though it was, abruptly curtailed by illness, his brief period as Master was certainly not without incident.

In one of his letters Mr Hicks recounted how he became Master of the Newmarket and Thurlow. It had been his ambition to become a Master of Hounds since hunting the Trinity Foot Beagles in 1892. While shooting in Kenya in 1909 he received a letter from an old friend, Mr George Foster, then joint M.F.H. of the Cambridgeshire, also 'secretly' joint Master of the Cambridgeshire Harriers with Mr R. Archdale, an arrangement transgressing the rules of the M.F.H. Association. The latter wished to resign and Mr Foster offered the vacancy as Master of the Harriers to Mr Hicks if he would provide the horses and their expenses, while being guaranteed the rest. This arrangement was accepted and for two seasons Mr Hicks hunted the harriers. On Colonel Deacon's resignation Mr Foster wrote to Mr Hicks: 'If you'd like to take on the Newmarket and Thurlow on the same basis as the Harriers you can, provided no one else knows.'

Despite the fact that he cannot have been a fit man at the time Mr Hicks accepted this offer with alacrity and took over as Master of the Newmarket and Thurlow. By April 1912 he had already hired Lawrence as first whip and kennel huntsman 'at 30s per week, house free and ordinary perks'. Others employed as hunt servants were 'Deacon's 2nd Whip at 21s per week'. 'April 6th. Hired Fred Bull as my 2nd horseman to be down here. 18s per week until Hunting Season after that 20s. Hired Harry Greene as Lawrence's 2nd horseman to begin on 21st June quarterly at 16s per week to live up at the Kennels.'

He was soon busy writing to all the estate owners in the district and the farmers throughout his country. A considerable number of these letters ran on similar lines:

Dear . . .

I have just accepted the Mastership of the Newmarket and Thurlow for next Season. Of course I know that this side of the country is more adapted for shooting than hunting, still if the natural animal does come along your way any help you or your keeper can give to-wards preserving him I shall be most grateful for and I need hardly say that I shall not attempt any turning down or anything of that sort . . . R.S.H.

This particular attitude does not seem to have met with everyone's approval, for he also noted a visit from Mr Thomas Purkis, then acting as honorary secretary to the hunt committee: 'May 20th. Purkis came down with an offer of some cubs from Bailey the Essex huntsman, which I refused, telegram and letter.'

His letter book is full of visits to farmers, keepers, letter writing, checking hounds and horses, visits to the Peterborough Hound Show and countless incidents of a Master's life behind the scenes. On 11 October he was forced to send a plea for help to his old friend the Reverend Jack Milne: 'Oct. 11th Wrote to Jack Milne asking him to lend me 3 or 4 couple of old hounds and take 3 or 4 couple of my young ones for a couple of months or so. Oct 13th. Heard from J. M. saying he would do so. *Good chap.*'

Despite George Foster's backing, it is clear that finance was always a nagging problem. Nor was he a fit man and the strain soon began to take its toll. Due to illness he was unable to attend the opening meet and after this unpropitious start it was not very long before he was forced to give up completely with duodenal ulcers. It was all just too much for him and the writing in his letter book steadily deteriorates as the months pass. The following extracts speak for themselves:

April 12th [1912] Saw Collins in Cambridge Market and told him quite straightforwardly that money absolutely prohibited my hiring his shooting or paying him £5 for a find as Deacon had been doing. Suggested that he should let the shooting in the ordinary way to someone and that I would do my best to fit in with his arrangements. Suggested Ryder and promised to let him know at once if I heard of a likely man to hire it. He said. *He didn't think that would suit very well*, but we parted amicably.

Sept 20th: Wrote to Purkis, Collins, Frost, Martin-Slater Junior, Gerald Slater, Col. Mercer, Goodchild and Lacey about Cubbing fixtures:

Oct 3rd. Received letter from Collins in reply to mine Sept 20th dated Oct. 1st asking me to pay £30 down and £5 a find for the right to draw Over Wood, Ley's Wood and Cadges. Wrote in reply under date Oct. 4th pointing out that Deacon had done that last year because owing to a misunderstanding they had insinuated that he had spoilt their chance of a let. That this was not so in my case because early in the summer I had told him perfectly openly that any such payment was impossible in my case and again asking whether I might draw the coverts on either the 10th or 21st of this month.

Oct 16th. Wrote to Collins saying that my letter of Oct 4th remained unanswered that I was drawing North Wood on the 25th and wanted to know if he wished me to stop hounds should they run across his farm.

Oct 19th. Heard from Collins requesting me to keep off his land for the present. Saw him again in Cambridge and said I presumed he would let me on later, but could get nothing definite from him.

Nov. 19th. Letter from Collins saying he would *not* let me into his coverts unless I paid £30 and £5 a find.

Dec 6th. Angry letter from Collins warning hounds off his land.

Dec. 10th. Copy of a letter to Collins:
Dear Sir I have your letter of the 5th instant and note its contents. I cannot admit however that any apology is due to you from me, as my hunt servants acting under my instructions headed the fox away from your land. Unfortunately he was headed back again by some ploughmen and as they were running well I could not stop them. I got to them just as they were entering your wood and immediately blew them off and lifted them round the other side and by so doing spoilt our chance of killing him as hounds were never able to settle again on the line properly. R.S.H.

Dec 31st Received a solicitor's letter from Collins warning us off his land.

Jan 1st Ordered to bed for a month by my specialist.

It was all over before it had properly begun. By 22 January his doctors had told him he was in for a long illness and he had sent in his resignation. Meanwhile, appeals for help to both Colonel Deacon and Sir William Hyde-Parker to take over the hounds for him had met with polite but negative responses. Things went from bad to worse and the final entry for 3 March was a sad one:

March 3rd 8 couple of hounds down with distemper including Harriet and Handsome. Dick the 2nd Whip ill with Flu or distemper also and killed a Vixen with 5 cubs inside her at Borley. A most disastrous time.

With this final shaky entry the letter book closes on poor Hicks's period as Master. As his correspondence shows, he did not have an easy time and he did his best for the hunt, even managing to show at least two consecutive days of good sport* during his brief mastership. In later years he was remembered by one old sportsman as 'a great big fat feller called Hicks', but his outward appearance undoubtedly belied the inner man, for he was not stout physically. After his one interrupted season as Master, the shortest in the history of the hunt, he had to give up hunting for good.

It is interesting to note from Mr Purkis's diaries that while he chronicled Mr Hicks's absences 'unwell', he did not unduly criticize the sport provided. Indeed,

*See Appendix, page 132.

from his diaries it does not seem to have been nearly such a disastrous season as Mr Hicks appears to have feared. It is noticeable, however, that under the ensuing Masters there is no mention of hounds being barred from Cadges, so that Collins appears to have come to some form of settlement with the hunt after Mr Hicks's departure from the scene.

The next Master, for the 1913–14 season, was Major A. C. Jaffe, who appointed Will Woodward as his huntsman. On 30 September 1913 Mr Purkis noted 'Mr Jaffe's first time out as Master.' In this final season before the 1914–18 War the sport shown was better than average. Hounds were out on fifty-four days, being stopped by frost only twice and having only two blank days. It was, however, a very dry and extremely poor cubhunting season and until Christmas scent was poor. Thereafter there were some good hunting days and one on particular on 16 February, with a nine-and-a-half-mile point in sixty-three minutes.*

Notable among the hunt followers during this pre-war period, many of whom were not to be seen again, was Mr Robert W. King, D.L., of Brinkley Hall, born in 1845, and chairman of the hunt committee for many years. With exeprience of thirty packs throughout the country, he was undoubtedly an excellent man for that sometimes difficult position as well as hunting regularly with the Newmarket and Thurlow he was a keen follower of the Devon and Somerset Staghounds.

Another keen hunt supporter was Mr Henry Webb of Streetly Hall, West Wickham, son of Mr Jonas Webb of Babraham, both of them original founder members of the Thurlow Hunt Club of 1858. Born in 1830, he first started hunting with Mr George Mure and continued hunting regularly until 1907. Like Mr Purkis, he also hunted occasionally with the Puckeridge, Essex, East Essex and Cambridgeshire. Amongst the leading Southdown sheep breeders, he was also well known locally for the excellent earth in a chalk pit on his land.

Amongst the Newmarket supporters perhaps the most prominent at the time were Mr Herbert Jones, jockey to H.M. King Edward VII, and the trainers Mr Walter Cannon, and Mr Thomas Leader of Wroughton House. Mr Cannon was the Master of the Newmarket Drag, which he had revived in 1906. While principal jockey to Mr Leopold de Rothschild he had won the Derby, the Guineas and the St Leger amongst many other stakes, both on the flat and over sticks.

The 1914–15 season, Major Jaffe's second and final year as Master before being mobilized, was a good one with some fine days' hunting,† although Mr Purkis noted that Woodward was over-fond of blowing his horn loudly and spoiling

*See Appendix, page 132.
†See Appendix, page 133.

sport as a result. No doubt he made his view plain, for he did not repeat the complaint more than once as the following season, when Mr C. F. Ryder had finally been persuaded to take over as Master, the sport was very good.* The combination of Mr C. F. Ryder as Master and Will Woodward as huntsman seems to have been a very good one indeed.

It was principally due to this combination, aided by the hunt committee under the chairmanship of Mr R. W. King of Brinkley Hall, with Mr Thomas Purkis as the honorary secretary, that the hunt weathered the war years successfully. Will Woodward, latterly with his sons Joe and Frank as whippers-in, was probably one of the best huntsmen the Newmarket and Thurlow ever had. He was to remain as huntsman for fifteen years under successive Masters, providing both a welcome sense of continuity and some outstanding sport.

Mr C. F. Ryder, a Yorkshireman by birth but as owner of Thurlow Park one of the principal landowners in the area, was to remain the mainstay of the hunt until his death during the Second World War. A good landlord and a strict fox preserver, he left his own testimonials that he was also a good employer. Albert Williams, son of his head groom, who started working for him at the age of twelve, graduating to second horseman during the war years and later marrying Will Woodward's daughter, was to remain with him for the rest of his life.

Although Mr Purkis's diaries indicate that the war had a severe impact on hunting, clearly the effects were not as disastrous as those of the Second World War. Foxhunting continued – if on a much-reduced scale. Proud father that he was, he noted with satisfaction that when Will Woodward was temporarily out of action with a dislocated shoulder from a fall out hunting his son Claude hunted hounds successfully. 29 January 1916 was indeed a great day when Claude not only hunted hounds well but killed his first fox, having 'pulled him down in the open'.† The 1916–17 season also saw some good hunts, one of the best being a ten-mile point in two hours,‡ but several others being rated very good.§

By the following year the strains of war had begun to tell very considerably. Mr Purkis noted fields of four or five on horseback and many more on foot. He noted bleakly at one point: '12 on horseback a big field for the times.' Yet, despite this and despite the difficulties of feeding horses and hounds, there were some very fine hunts. The last hunt of the season, however, was on 2 March, when the first fox of the day was killed after a brisk hunt. Then Mr Purkis

*See Appendix, page 133.
†See Appendix, page 134.
‡See Appendix, page 135.
§See Appendix, pages 134–5.

added the note: 'This finished the season of 1917–18 as the M.F.H. Association has asked all hunting to stop for this season on March 2nd on account of the cereal question for feeding horses.' The U-boat blockade had begun to have dire consequences and everyone was feeling the pinch badly.

The 1918–19 season's opening meet had two unusual entries. Mr Purkis noted:

Nov 11. Met The Thurlow at Thurlow Groves for Opening Meet. Drew Trundley (Engines working close by) . . . a miserable foggy drizzling rain all day. Heard the Armistice was signed. Church bells going all round the county.

The hunting season was quite a good one, although not particularly out-standing. There were some notable hunts,* but on the whole sport was average. At the end of the season Mr C. F. Ryder resigned and his place was taken by Lord Wilton (the 6th Earl), who wisely continued with Will Woodward as huntsman and showed good sport with some very good days.† At the end of the season, however, he notified the committee of his intention to resign and eventually it was decided to have a joint mastership shared between Colonel J. F. Ryder and Mr C. F. Tonge. This then was the arrangement as the Newmarket and Thurlow entered the 1920s.

Meanwhile, Mr Edward Barclay had been providing a much-needed sense of continuity with the Puckeridge. He was also busily engaged in trying to ensure a good supply of foxes, for this and mangy foxes were to be his greatest worry during his first decade or more in the country. James Cockayne, his huntsman, noted that in the last ten days of the season 1900–1 four were blank and four only produced one fox apiece. Over the whole season a quarter of the days were blank or produced only one fox. Scarcely surprisingly, Cockayne ended with the note: 'This ended the worst season I ever saw.'

Mr Purkis only seems to have had very indifferent days with the Puckeridge during this season and noted, unusually for him, on 17 December, 'bag-man I think', then, on 20 March, 'a wrong un' and 'another the same sort!' He appears to have missed for once the really historic run of the season on 4 March and also another on 23 March which must have been the last time the Puckeridge crossed not only the Great North Road but also the main railway line to the north.

In 1901 Mr Barclay moved from the Braughing kennels built for Mr Swindell to some he had built at Brent Pelham on his own estate, very nearly in the centre of the country. During the 1901–2 season there seems to have been little

*See Appendix, page 135.
†See Appendix, page 136.

in the way of outstanding sport. Mr Purkis merely noted that the Puckeridge were barred from Mr Fielden's coverts on 19 March and on 31 March, as was all too often the case, killed a mangy fox. It would seem that Mr Barclay was still experiencing the aftermath of the 'Row' while he was to suffer from mangy foxes until well into the next decade.

In the season 1902–3, on 1 December, came the historic day when the Puckeridge and Newmarket and Thurlow met and combined together to kill their fox in Linton schoolyard.* This was followed by at least two fine hunts, one on Christmas Eve and another on 4 February, both faithfully recorded in Mr Purkis's diaries. Unfortunately, in the season of 1903–4 Mr Purkis only recorded a mangy fox on 22 February and there seem to be few records of good sport this season. The 1904–5 season, Jim Cockayne's last before he went to the North Warwickshire, seems to have been a good one, as Mr Purkis reported two good days on 4th January and 7 February, climaxing with killing two mangy foxes on 1 March.

Cockayne's successor as huntsman was Ted Short, who had been whipper-in to James Bailey of the Essex. Short in name and physique, with tiny legs, he proved nevertheless to be a popular and successful character, although unfortunately he kept no record of events. Mr Purkis only noted one good 'slow but interesting' hunt on 2 December, but there appear to have been several good days. At the end of the season, however, Mr Barclay pointed out that there had been four blank days and twenty-five with only one fox. He offered his resignation if supplies of foxes did not improve. Fortunately they did, although it was another decade before mange finally disappeared.

According to *Horse and Hound* in 1906–7 'there were many good gallops, the longest being an eleven-mile point ending with a kill'. Unfortunately, Mr Thomas Purkis only recorded two good days† and it is clear there were many more, sadly lost to posterity. The 1907–8 season was noted as 'the best season during Mr E. E. Barclay's mastership of twelve seasons . . . the longest point was eleven miles'. Regrettably, Tom Purkis's diaries only record one or two indifferent days.

The 1907–8 season, however, was notable for the introduction of the first annual point-to-point in the Puckeridge country on a course laid out at Brent Pelham. The organizer of these successful meetings was Mr George Bowen of Ickleton, previously Master of the Newmarket and Thurlow from 1894 to 1895. From 1905 to 1915 he was to remain joint honorary secretary of the Puckeridge, providing yet another strong link between the two hunts.

*See Appendix, page 127.
†See Appendix, page 160.

85

On the same day as this first point-to-point Mr George Smyth of Quickwood, acting on behalf of the 272 Puckeridge hunting and non-hunting farmers, presented Mr Edward Barclay with a silver cup 'as a mark of their appreciation of the courtesy displayed and the consideration shown them during the thirteen seasons of his Mastership . . .' Already the scars of the 'Row' were beginning to heal and the country was once more becoming a united whole.

Bob Gardiner, who had been engaged as second horseman to Mr Barclay in 1896 and had graduated to second whipper-in to Cockayne – then first whipper-in to Mr Barclay – remembered a hunt in the season of 1909–10 when a fox was found at Blackditch, Watton and hunted by Aspenden Park into Buntingford. Here it vanished amongst some buildings, after climbing a heap of coal. Bob Gardiner dismounted and searching behind some faggots saw the brush just showing. It was quickly dislodged and killed, making a successful end to a seven-mile point.

In the following year, 1911, Ted Short left and Bob Gardiner was appointed huntsman in his place, a post he was to hold successfully for the next twenty-six seasons. His easy temper and charming smile concealed a high degree of efficiency. Horses and hounds went well for him and so did the foxes. In conjunction with Mr Edward Barclay he was to raise the standard of the Puckeridge to the highest levels. The Master had trained the man, but they made a wonderful combination between them. It is to this combination that the Puckeridge undoubtedly owed much of the splendid sport enjoyed during the 1930s and onwards.

In December 1911 Mr Edward Barclay had a bad fall and for six weeks thereafter Mr Maurice Barclay hunted the dog hounds. They had several good hunts, with one outstanding day on 26 January 1912, safely chronicled in Bob Gardiner's diary. This included a point of five miles and a hunt of an hour and fifty-five minutes. Hounds had twenty miles to cover to reach home and were out of their kennels for twelve and a half hours, almost all of it in the Hertfordshire country.

During the 1912–13 season Mr Thomas Purkis only chronicled one hunt – on 4 February – with the Puckeridge, when a mangy fox was killed in Quendon Park and another fox hunted sharply and then killed. Apparently the problem of mange was still prevalent. The following season of 1913–14, however, was to see hunting stopped due to an outbreak of foot-and-mouth, that scourge of the later decades of the century.

Amongst the more prominent followers of the Puckeridge in these pre-1914 days, many of whom were not to foregather after the war, the most notable sportswoman must certainly have been Miss G. Cotton-Browne, who was famed throughout Hertfordshire. The only daughter of the Reverend George Cotton-Browne, J.P., D.L., she first started hunting with the Puckeridge as a child. In 1905, not content with this, she formed her own pack of harriers and hunted three days a week with them, as well as continuing to hunt regularly with the Puckeridge.

Prominent amongst the hunt supporters, of course, was Mr Robert Cunliffe Gosling J.P., D.L., born in 1868, the eldest son of Mr Robert Gosling, Master of the Puckeridge during the famous 'Row'. On his father's death in 1895 he inherited the estate of Hassobury near Bishops Stortford and continued both to provide foxes and hunt with the Puckeridge.

Typical of many hunt supporters, perhaps, were two Scots. Major H. A. Anderson of Aspenden, Buntingford, who retired from the army in 1884, had been joint secretary since 1896. Dr James Cantile, born in 1851 in Dufftown, Banff-shire, one of the leading Harley Street specialists, was also a keen hunt supporter living near Buntingford.

Amongst the many sporting farmers supporting the hunt, the Smyth family of Quickswood, who had farmed eight hundred acres for over two hundred years, were particularly notable. Mr Hugh Smyth, who died in 1902 at the age of eighty-four, had hunted with the Puckeridge for seventy years. Twice married, he fathered sixteen children and was a keen shot as well as foxhunter. Mr George Smyth, born in 1863, his eldest son, first hunted with the Puckeridge in 1877 and was a keen member of the earth-stopping committee.

Another in the same mould was Mr Thomas Stubbing of Wareside, Ware, who farmed seven hundred acres there and a further eight hundred acres at Albury. Born in 1843 he first hunted with the Puckeridge at the age of ten, being blooded by Joe Orbell under Mr Nicholas Parry's mastership. He too was a keen member of the earth-stopping committee.

The outbreak of the 1914–18 War had an immediate and drastic effect on the Puckeridge. Mr Maurice Barclay departed at once to the expeditionary force with twenty-two of the hunt horses, while the number of hounds was greatly reduced. Subscriptions also fell off immediately, but the Masters willingly accepted a much-reduced guarantee and continued hunting four days a week with small separate dog and bitch packs until 1916. There was at least one outstanding hunt, on 5 February 1916, with the bitch pack making a six-mile point in twenty-five minutes, but by 1917, with the war entering its bitterest phase, hounds were still further reduced to a single small mixed pack, hunting only three days a week.

In the 1917–18 season, after hunting foxhounds for twenty-one seasons and harriers for eighteen seasons before that, Mr Edward Barclay passed over the hunting of this small mixed pack to Bob Gardiner, himself acting as Field Master. Arrangements were made to reduce hunting still further to only five days a fortnight, but the Armistice at the start of the season put an end to that and during the 1918 season there was some good sport with a historic nine-mile point on 22 March 1919.*

When the dog and bitch packs were finally restored in the 1919 season, Major Maurice Barclay took over as huntsman of the dog pack, a position he retained until the outbreak of the Second World War in 1939. Despite a serious outbreak of distemper, the 1919 season would also have seen a return to hunting four days a week but for an outbreak of rabies near the Brent Pelham kennels which completely disorganized everything. The resultant muzzling orders prevented hounds travelling to the west of the country. Fortunately, Colonel Page Croft, erstwhile Master of the Enfield Chace Staghounds from 1912, had just started a new pack of black-and-tan staghounds under the title of Colonel Croft's Staghounds at Fanham's in the western area. He agreed to turn over to hunting foxes and, hunting twenty-nine days, killed two brace of foxes and marked another brace to ground. On the only day during the season when the Puckeridge themselves had a good hunt, 26 January 1920, there was not enough scent to press their fox.

On 17 March 1920, at the annual hunt meeting, Mr John Sworder of Barkway, acting on behalf of three hundred and fifty subscribers, presented Mr Edward Barclay with his portrait by Mr H. G. Rivière showing him mounted on Huntsman with three couple of favourite hounds. He stated very justifiably that 'their gift was but a little thing in comparison with all that Mr Barclay had done for the hunt'. Truly, without him it could not have existed.

throughout Hertfordshire. The only daughter of the Reverend George Cotton-Browne, J.P., D.L., she first started hunting with the Puckeridge as a child. In 1905, not content with this, she formed her own pack of harriers and hunted three days a week with them, as well as continuing to hunt regularly with the Puckeridge.

Prominent amongst the hunt supporters, of course, was Mr Robert Cunliffe Gosling J.P., D.L., born in 1868, the eldest son of Mr Robert Gosling, Master of the Puckeridge during the famous 'Row'. On his father's death in 1895 he inherited the estate of Hassobury near Bishops Stortford and continued both to provide foxes and hunt with the Puckeridge.

Typical of many hunt supporters, perhaps, were two Scots. Major H. A. Anderson of Aspenden, Buntingford, who retired from the army in 1884, had been joint secretary since 1896. Dr James Cantile, born in 1851 in Dufftown, Banffshire, one of the leading Harley Street specialists, was also a keen hunt supporter living near Buntingford.

Amongst the many sporting farmers supporting the hunt, the Smyth family of Quickswood, who had farmed eight hundred acres for over two hundred years, were particularly notable. Mr Hugh Smyth, who died in 1902 at the age of eighty-four, had hunted with the Puckeridge for seventy years. Twice married, he fathered sixteen children and was a keen shot as well as foxhunter. Mr George Smyth, born in 1863, his eldest son, first hunted with the Puckeridge in 1877 and was a keen member of the earth-stopping committee.

Another in the same mould was Mr Thomas Stubbing of Wareside, Ware, who farmed seven hundred acres there and a further eight hundred acres at Albury. Born in 1843 he first hunted with the Puckeridge at the age of ten, being blooded by Joe Orbell under Mr Nicholas Parry's mastership. He too was a keen member of the earth-stopping committee.

The outbreak of the 1914–18 War had an immediate and drastic effect on the Puckeridge. Mr Maurice Barclay departed at once to the expeditionary force with twenty-two of the hunt horses, while the number of hounds was greatly reduced. Subscriptions also fell off immediately, but the Masters willingly accepted a much-reduced guarantee and continued hunting four days a week with small separate dog and bitch packs until 1916. There was at least one outstanding hunt, on 5 February 1916, with the bitch pack making a six-mile point in twenty-five minutes, but by 1917, with the war entering its bitterest phase, hounds were still further reduced to a single small mixed pack, hunting only three days a week.

In the 1917–18 season, after hunting foxhounds for twenty-one seasons and harriers for eighteen seasons before that, Mr Edward Barclay passed over the hunting of this small mixed pack to Bob Gardiner, himself acting as Field Master. Arrangements were made to reduce hunting still further to only five days a fortnight, but the Armistice at the start of the season put an end to that and during the 1918 season there was some good sport with a historic nine-mile point on 22 March 1919.*

When the dog and bitch packs were finally restored in the 1919 season, Major Maurice Barclay took over as huntsman of the dog pack, a position he retained until the outbreak of the Second World War in 1939. Despite a serious outbreak of distemper, the 1919 season would also have seen a return to hunting four days a week but for an outbreak of rabies near the Brent Pelham kennels which completely disorganized everything. The resultant muzzling orders prevented hounds travelling to the west of the country. Fortunately, Colonel Page Croft, erstwhile Master of the Enfield Chace Staghounds from 1912, had just started a new pack of black-and-tan staghounds under the title of Colonel Croft's Staghounds at Fanham's in the western area. He agreed to turn over to hunting foxes and, hunting twenty-nine days, killed two brace of foxes and marked another brace to ground. On the only day during the season when the Puckeridge themselves had a good hunt, 26 January 1920, there was not enough scent to press their fox.

On 17 March 1920, at the annual hunt meeting, Mr John Sworder of Barkway, acting on behalf of three hundred and fifty subscribers, presented Mr Edward Barclay with his portrait by Mr H. G. Rivière showing him mounted on Huntsman with three couple of favourite hounds. He stated very justifiably that 'their gift was but a little thing in comparison with all that Mr Barclay had done for the hunt'. Truly, without him it could not have existed.

Mr Frank Debenham, for many years secretary of the Puckeridge, and Mr Edward Barclay

Mr Edward Barclay on Epsom

Mr Frank Stacey, 1859–1932

Major Henry A. Anderson

Mr George Smyth

Mr Hugh Smyth

Mr Thomas Stubbing

Mr Colledge Leader

A group of the Newmarket and Thurlow hunt staff and supporters *circa* 1927. *Left to right*, Joby Watson, General Briggs, Mr Charles Tonge (Master), Basil Jarvis and Owen Webb

A day out with the Newmarket and Thurlow. A meet at Branches Park in 1925.
Included are, *extreme left*, Mr G. S. Poole on Drifter, *second left* Mr H. Leader on Jack Horner,
fourth from left Mr F. Archer on Double Chance, *fourth from right* Mr C. Tonge (Master), *third
from right* Mr G. Blackwell on Sargeant Murphy, *extreme right* Mr G. H. Tonge on Taffytus

Chapter 8

The Years from 1920 to 1945

THE years from 1920 to 1945 fall naturally into three distinct periods. From 1920 there was a hectic attempt at recovery from the war and a false boom, abruptly ended by the slump and recession of 1929 to 1931. This was followed by a period of slow growth in the 1930s, punctuated by crisis and threats of war and abruptly ended by the outbreak of the Second World War in 1939. The war years themselves were a period of grim determination to fight on 'for the duration' until final victory.

Although the 1914–18 War had ended the farming slump, which had lasted from the 1870s, and although farmers had been promised security in return for feeding the nation in its time of direst need, such promises barely lasted a decade. Faced with a slump and recession and a cry for 'Cheap food', they were promptly forgotten by successive governments and agriculture sank into a depression again from which there was to be no real recovery before the outbreak of the Second World War.

Throughout the three periods the mechanization of Britain was steadily increasing. It started with the slow spread of the motor-car on the roads. From 1920 onwards the roads were increasingly crowded with 'horseless carriages'. As speeds also increased, so the roads required improvement. Finally, in the later 1930s, came the period of traffic jams at weekends on the approaches to many large towns, particularly London. The roads were simply not adequate for the volume of traffic they were now being forced to carry.

The 1920s were a transitional period of slow change in the countryside, between the old Edwardian days of spacious living in an unmechanized land and the harsher, more mechanized, period from 1940 onwards. During the 1920s, and to quite a large extent during the 1930s, the countryside remained still in the age of the horse, with horse-drawn carts, binders and ploughs. Tractors were still expensive, largely untried innovations and combine harvesters, even in the late 1930s were rare and still regarded as being in the experimental stage. In a conservative countryside during a severe recession this was scarcely surprising.

Throughout the 1930s, however, necessity was the driving force and the more modern-minded farmers were turning to mechanization. When it was found that one machine could plough ten acres in a day which would have taken ten pairs of horses with ten skilled ploughmen, it was not long before the example was copied. The process was slow, but by 1939 the horse had already begun to give way to the tractor on the farm.

The realization that the day of the cavalry horse and the cavalry regiment was past, despite the introduction of the tank, was slow in coming. Throughout the 1920s the army remained largely unmechanized and even in the 1930s it was slow to adapt. The time when the argument that hunting provided a nucleus of horses available for the army in time of war, or good basic training for the cavalryman, was almost past as well. It remained true, however, that anyone who had learned to take a line across country was naturally better in charge of a tank in similar circumstances and it was thus that many of the tank commanders in the 1939–45 war received their soundest initial training.

In one respect the 1920s and 1930s saw a great change in hunting. The old hunt special trains became an almost forgotten feature. Motor-cars, motor horse boxes and trailers began to appear in the 1930s and meets were many a Master's mechanical nightmare. The hunt follower in motor-cars heading foxes was a commonplace of the 1920s and 1930s. So too was the hound van, or hound trailer, delivering the hounds to the meet.

Another feature of the 1920s and 1930s, a revulsion from the bloodletting of the war, an outlet for the hysteria which had been so long suppressed, an expression of 'class hatred', or simply a symptom of the mild lunacy of the times, was the formation of the anti-field-sport societies. By terming field sports 'blood' sports, they introduced a euphemistic element of sadism into their attacks, which no doubt rallied many who knew nothing about the matter to their cause. It had the beneficial effect of resulting in the formation of the British Field Sports Society, which rallied all field sports to fight the common enemy. Even if shooting and hunting had been largely by this time united, it was still a good move towards greater understanding and co-operation.

Yet another feature of the entire period was the enormous increase in the number of women in the hunting field. Whereas during the period from 1900 to 1920 they had greatly multiplied, now they began to outnumber the men on occasions. Nor were women Masters of Hounds, or joint Masters, so much of a rarity as they had been. Many women had helped to hunt hounds during the critical years of the 1914–18 War and no one saw anything out of the way in women acting as M.F.H.s in the hunting field thereafter. Furthermore, whereas they had previously ridden only side-saddle, with very rare exceptions, they now started to ride astride. Emancipation had finally arrived in the hunting field.

The vast increases in taxation after the 1914–18 War resulted in the splitting up of many large estates. It resulted also in increased feed bills for horses and hounds. Subscriptions had to be raised and guarantees were also of necessity larger. The slump and recession of the years 1929 to 1931 intensified these economic trends. Financiers and stockbrokers, who had previously hunted regularly, sold their horses and gave up their hunt subscriptions. Landowners who had lost heavily on the stock market found it necessary to reduce their stables, or sometimes even to sell their estates. Farmers, already living off their own produce and experienced in hard times, were not so greatly affected and to this extent hunting only suffered marginally, but inevitably in many areas wire proliferated as they sought the cheapest methods of fencing their fields available.

Ribbon development outside many industrial towns, and particularly outside London, uncontrolled and unplanned, led to a great deal of good hunting country being unnecessarily lost to the hunts. On the other hand, the trend of the 1930s towards weekend cottages in the country in many cases brought fresh support to the hunt, although in some it led to opposition from townspeople without any real understanding of country life or country ways. The division between town and country was beginning to be extremely marked.

During the 1930s new methods of agriculture, not always easily compatible with hunting, began to be introduced in places. The gyro-tiller and the deep plough hauled by crawler tractors turned the soil to a depth previously unknown, making deep land even deeper and providing a hazard not previously encountered. New chemicals on the land, spraying and manuring with artificial fertilizers, were more than merely ruinous to scent, – sometimes even proving dangerous to hounds and wildlife. Compared with more modern innovations, however, they were still in their infancy and since virtually no ploughing was started before Christmas there was still plenty of ground for good galloping hunts until then, even in plough countries such as the Newmarket and Thurlow and the Puckeridge. There was little real difficulty in providing good sport.

The introduction of the telephone over a large part of the country was another feature which affected hunting considerably. It was possible by this means to cancel meets, or make a last-minute arrangement regarding hunting, whereas previously matters had to go ahead as planned. Whether this was entirely an advantage may still be argued. There was a lot to be said for having to stand by fixed plans regardless of weather or other impediments. On the whole, however, this was advantageous and properly used, like the motor-car, could make for better sport. By 1939 it was fairly widespread, even in remote country districts, and messages could be passed to almost anyone required. Thus a last-minute change of plans could be catered for by a change of earth-stopping arrangements, or other details.

The wireless, or radio, also proved more of a boon than a handicap. By this means the weather forecast for the next few days ahead was disseminated throughout the country and by the late 1930s was achieving some sort of degree of accuracy on occasions. At least it was possibly some advantage to know that a thick fog was expected, even if all too often experienced local knowledge was very liable to be more correct. For those who were coming to a meet from a distance this may or may not have had advantages.

Tarmacadam on the roads, only introduced in many cases in the 1930s, was not an improvement, except for motor-cars. The lack of scent-carrying and the hardness for horses hooves, were the two prime disadvantages. The slipperiness in winter, when a sheet of ice formed readily on it, was another big disadvantage from the hunting viewpoint. It is really astonishing to realize that by the early 1930s the majority of by-roads and lanes in the area under consideration were still not tarred, but consisted of rough-surfaced gravel much more suitable for horses and for hunting.

The 1920–1 season, which had appeared to be full of promise with the appointment of Mr C. F. Tonge of Branches Park and Colonel J. F. Ryder, brother of Mr C. F. Ryder, as joint Masters, started instead very tragically for the Newmarket and Thurlow. The joint mastership was never to get beyond the cubbing season. On 8 November, the day of the opening meet, Colonel J. F. Ryder shot himself. When the news reached the honorary secretary, Mr Thomas Purkis, he immediately ordered hunting to stop and hounds to return to kennels. A delayed casualty of the bitter harvest of the 1914–18 War, Colonel Ryder's death cast a shadow over the start of the season, but in the way of things hunting was soon under way again. It was not in fact a particularly good season, although there were some good hunts* and at the end they had killed an average eight brace, with seven and a half brace marked to ground.

No doubt the presence of Will Woodward as kennel huntsman proved a continuing link, for he remained with Mr Tonge as Master for the next six seasons. The 1921–2 season was a good one, with some very good days indeed,† although Mr Purkis was to note on 30 March that 'some ill-advised fool had laid a drag, a most insulting thing to do'. Despite a bad scenting season they had a

*See Appendix, page 137.
†See Appendix, page 138.

total of fifteen and a half brace of foxes. The following season was even better,* with many good hunts and some quite outstanding ones, including a nine-mile point in one hour and fifteen minutes on 23 November† and another seven-mile point in one hour and forty-five minutes of 12 February.‡ The total number of foxes killed was seventeen and a half brace with eight and a half brace marked to ground.

The 1923–4 season started with even greater promise, but ended in disaster, with the entire country closed because of foot-and-mouth disease. Even so there was one six-mile point in an hour and fifteen minutes and some other good hunts.§ The 1924–5 season saw Mr Purkis first mentioning the now familiar problem of motor-cars lining the roads and heading the fox at the Boxing Day meet. Although there was one good eight-mile point in an hour and thirty minutes and some other good days,‖ Mr Purkis was noticeably rather critical at times. As he was getting older perhaps he found it more difficult to adjust to the hectic optimism and post-war boom years of the 1920s, or it may be that due to his almost excessive dedication to hunting he had neglected his farming and had been forced to sell his farm. At any rate whatever the reason, he certainly retired from farming and thereafter devoted himself entirely to foxhunting.

It was, however, during the 1920s that the hunt establishment attained greater heights than ever before. Mr Tonge was a keen hound breeder, introducing most effectively sires from the Berkely, Portman and Puckeridge. Apart from the huntsman Will Woodward, there were the first and second whips, a kennel-man and a boy, as well as a stud groom and two second horsemen to look after the nine horses for the hunt staff.

At this time the country was being hunted five days a fortnight and the old strife between hunting and shooting interests had entirely ceased. Everyone was dedicated to foxhunting and no one shot on hunting days any longer and keepers did not kill foxes. Poisoning and trapping were no longer hazards to be suffered in silence. Mr C. F. Ryder of Thurlow Hall was a keen fox preserver and General Sir Charles Briggs, ex-cavalry commander and successor to Mr R. W. King as chairman of the hunt committee, rented the shooting of several of the best coverts on the Wickhambrook side of the country as well as maintaining supplies of foxes in his own.

There was still plenty of grass at that time and the fields were generally much smaller, with accordingly more fences, while wire was even then comparatively

*See Appendix, pages 138–40.
†See Appendix, page 138.
‡See Appendix, page 140.
§See Appendix, pages 140–1.
‖See Appendix, pages 141–2.

rare. The arable land, still almost all horse-ploughed on a four- or five-course system, was sticky but quite rideable. At that time, also, the hunt had as part of their country on loan from the Essex the coverts of Langley, Bendysh and Hempstead. Despite the motor-car, the horse box and trailer were still unknown and hunt supporters were still principally local people. As always, there were many trainers, jockeys and others from Newmarket who followed the hunt.

Amongst the more prominent Newmarket trainers and other hunt supporters of the 1920s were such names as Fred Archer, George Blackwell, Bob Collins and his two sons, Walter Earl, Basil Jarvis, Harvey and College Leader and the Leaches. On one not easily forgotten day in December 1925 when the Newmarket and Thurlow met at Branches Park near Newmarket there were no less than five Grand National horses at the meet with owners, trainers or jockeys riding them. They were Fred Archer, the trainer, on Double Chance, winner in 1925; George Blackwell, the trainer, on Sergeant Murphy, winner in 1923, Harvey Leader, the trainer, on Jack Horner, a runner in the 1925 race; Mr G. S. Poole of the 20th Hussars on Drifter, second in 1922, and Mr M. Tonge on Taffytus, a frequent competitor. Fred Archer even brought out Double Chance at a meet at Sipsey Bridge just prior to his win in that year 'to freshen him up a bit'.

Otherwise, the 1925 season was more remarkable for a good deal of frost and for foot-and-mouth in the neighbouring areas. On the whole it was an extremely poor season, with few worthwhile hunting days. For Mr Purkis it was only enlivened by seeing a golden eagle on 3 February for the first time outside captivity. To such a keen foxhunter this was poor compensation for indifferent sport.

The 1926–7 season was one of mild crisis in the affairs of the hunt. No doubt, having had the hunt almost to himself during the war years, Mr Purkis found it hard to adjust to the now crowded fields. He certainly did not approve of steeple-chasers in the hunting field and noted at one point 'crazy thrusters' heading the fox. While he chronicled some good days' sport, including a hunt of one and a quarter hours, he was also once again incensed by the motor-cars at the Boxing Day meet. He was above all interested in hunting and clearly there were those, especially in Newmarket, who felt that he was old-fashioned and out of touch. Matters reached crisis point on 24 February when he recorded:

Met The Thurlow at Thurlow Crown after another Committee Meeting; a very stormy one in the Room and the weather was quite or even worse outside, as it rained pouring all the morning. I did not Hunt for obvious reasons and things said at the Meeting. They . . . found at Hart. Chopped a fox and killed another . . . without any sport.

The upshot of all this was that Mr Purkis resigned his post as honorary secre-

tary and his place was taken by Mr E. Cooper-Bland of Newmarket. Will Woodward retired at the end of the season and his place as huntsman was taken in
the following season by Jack Boore. For the 1927–8 season Mr Tonge hunted
hounds himself, but he also kept some horses in Leicestershire and hunted
there quite frequently. There were some good hunts during the season* but
no doubt sport could have been better had he been present more often. It can
have come as little surprise when at the end of the season he accepted the joint
mastership of the Belvoir.

The Newmarket and Thurlow hunt had benefited greatly during Mr Tonge's
seven years as Master. He had bred an excellent pack of hounds and produced
some splendid sport. With the wholehearted backing of Mr C. F. Ryder in the
background and the hunt committee under the able chairmanship of General
Sir Charles Briggs – aided by Mr Thomas Purkis as honorary secretary and Will
Woodward as huntsman – providing continuity and hard-won experience, he
had built the hunt up to a very high standard.

There followed something of a major change. Mr T. C. Eaton, a wealthy
young Canadian friend of Mr Henry L. Webb, agreed to take over as joint
Master with Mr E. Cooper-Bland, keeping on Jack Boore as kennel huntsman.
Mr H. L. Webb himself took on the post of honorary secretary and Mr Jack
D. Webb, his elder brother, then farming at Great Bradley, took over as point-
to-point secretary. Great-grandsons of Jonas Webb, an original founder member
of the Thurlow Hunt Club in 1858, they eptiomized the continuity of the
countryside. With the wholehearted backing of the hunt committee, this
team managed to show good sport during the three years the arrangment
continued.

A familiar figure still in the hunting field during this period was Mr Thomas
Purkis, who continued to hunt impartially with the Newmarket and Thurlow
and the Puckeridge until his death in 1932. Riding an old fat dun cob with a black
streak down its back, which he used for both riding and driving and which
always lasted the day, he was to be seen out in all but the worst of weathers.
It would be too much to say that he was uncritical of the new management
and when it came to hunting the Newmarket and Thurlow or any other
country he knew what he was talking about.

Despite Mr Purkis's occasional criticisms, although the sport shown may not
have been quite up to Mr Tonge's standards, there were some very good hunts
during this period. In Mr Cooper-Bland's first three years as joint Master
with Mr T. C. Eaton, the more notable hunts included a fox killed on Newmarket Heath in 1928 for the first time in living memory and on another oc-

*See Appendix, pages 142–3.

casion a fox killed in the Newmarket cemetery.* Throughout this period Jack Boore remained as huntsman with Sam Newman and E. Raper as first and second whips. The former was a particularly fine horseman, who was always given the difficult horses and for whom they always seemed to go well.

In 1931 there was another change. Mr T. C. Eaton resigned as joint Master and his place was taken by Mr A. M. Praed, of Ousden Hall, always a generous supporter of the hunt and a delightful man. Mr H. L. Webb also resigned and his place was filled jointly by Miss Tonge and Commander J. Gibbs, R.N. Jack Boore left that season as well and his place as kennel huntsman was filled by F. Wright. With this new team Mr Cooper-Bland continued as joint Master with Mr Praed for a further three seasons.

With the slump of 1929 and 1930 the farming boom ended abruptly and conditions, if possible, were worse than in the period between 1870 and 1914. Money, once again, was very short and subscriptions were not easily obtained from the farming community, although they generously continued to support the hunt in every way possible. The international situation was gloomy as crisis succeeded crisis, while wars – or fears of wars – were widespread. In the circumstances it is remarkable that hunting continued at all and without the loyal support of the countryside it could not have done so.

Despite these adverse circumstances there was some good sport during these years of joint mastership into the early thirties.† Whether Jack Boore or his successor Wright were as good huntsmen as Will Woodward is another matter, as is the question whether Mr Cooper-Bland and his joint Masters were of the same calibre as Mr Charles Tonge. It is indeed questionable whether a joint mastership can ever be quite as satisfactory as any good single Master and in any event comparisons are invidious. Mr Cooper-Bland was certainly not such an inspired hound breeder and though he rode hard to hounds perhaps not such a good huntsman, but he was a very good organizer and he steered the hunt through a difficult period for which he deserved the thanks of all concerned. In short, he was the right Master at the right time.

There were other reasons for the falling off in support for the hunt during this period. With the introduction of the horse-box trailer in the early 1930s, the Newmarket contingent, the young bloods and sporting socialites, turned readily to more fashionable hunts within easy motoring distance. The hunt thus lost a good deal of support at a time when it could ill-afford it.

Early in Mr Cooper-Bland's last season of 1933–4 the young Mr Robert Way of Borough Green noted in his diary the effects of gyro-tilling in the following terms:

*See Appendix, pages 144–5.
†See Appendix, pages 143–7.

Thursday. November 15th . . . We got in a lot of land which had been gyro-tilled. It is an absolute menace to hunting. It looks no different from ordinary ploughed land, but as the earth is stirred up for 20 inches if one accidentally jumps or gallops into a newly done field one sinks in about twelve inches. It is so heavy as to be almost impossible to ride across and leaves hardly any headland at the edge. . . .

At the end of the season Mr Cooper-Bland and Mr Praed resigned as joint Masters and were succeeded by Mr E. H. Deacon, the son of Colonel E. Deacon, who had been Master of the Newmarket and Thurlow from 1910 to 1912. Also retired from the K.D.G.s, like his father before him, and subsequently to gain the rank of lieutenant-colonel himself when recalled to active service on the outbreak of the war, he proved a good choice. Devoted entirely to foxhunting, a keen sportsman, a fine horseman and a charming man, his first action was to engage Harry Turner, from the Craven, as his huntsman.

Turner proved to be exceptionally able and the 1934–5 season was also an outstandingly good scenting year throughout. At the end Mr E. H. Deacon noted: 'Killed Cubbing, 14 brace. Hunting, 38 days, killed fourteen and a half brace, six brace over the record.' Whether in fact this was strictly accurate is almost by the way. The sport shown was consistently good and a good deal better than for many years. It was setting a high standard hard to beat and almost predictably the following seasons never quite measured up to this excellent beginning, even though there were some very good days.*

When Harry Turner left at the end of the 1936 season to become huntsman to the Blankney, Mr E. H. Deacon undertook hunting hounds himself, employing George Samways as first whip and kennel huntsman, assisted also by Mrs Deacon. With the backing of Mr C. F. Ryder – still a strong supporter of the hunt behind the scenes – and of the hunt committee, still with General Sir Charles Briggs as chairman, he continued to show sport up to the outbreak of war.

Just how considerable a fox preserver Mr C. F. Ryder had become may be a little hard to appreciate without outside evidence. In his first season Mr Deacon personally counted twenty-two litters of cubs within a two-mile radius of his house. He very soon appreciated, as he put it, that Mr Ryder 'treasured' his foxes. Whenever he went cubbing Mr Ryder would ask him how many he had killed, and if he said one, having killed three, he would be requested 'please' to go elsewhere as 'that was quite enough'.

On one occasion Albert Williams, by this time promoted to head groom in Mr Ryder's establishment, in succession to his father, was beside his employer when hounds checked and were at fault in Withersfield Green. Suddenly, Williams saw the hunted fox lying on top of the roof tree of the barn

*See Appendix, pages 147–8.

opposite Withersfield Hall and drew Mr Ryder's attention to it in the thatch.

'Don't tell 'em! Don't tell 'em!' Mr Ryder whispered. 'Let him stay there. Don't want to kill him. They've had a good run.'

On another notable occasion he was cross-questioning George Samways about whether a fox that had been killed in cover had been given a fair chance.

'Yes, sir,' replied Samways. 'He had a fair chance, but he didn't take it.'

Throughout the entire period of Mr Deacon's mastership, from 1934 to 1939, the threat of European war was ever present. Belatedly, Britain started to rearm and it was then that Stradishall airfield was built for the Royal Air Force as a base for Wellington bombers. It soon transpired that the pilots found it much more interesting to follow the progress of the hunt from the air than attend to endless bombing runs, or similar boring training flights. The results were disastrous, but fortunately the Commandant's wife was keen on hunting and the Commandant proved co-operative when approached. On being given a list of hunt dates no low flying was permitted on those days.

The storm clouds of Munich had presaged the outbreak of war in 1939 and in September reservists such as Mr Deacon were quick to return to the forces. Indeed they had no alternative. The press announcement concerning the Newmarket and Thurlow hunt read:

Mr. E. H. Deacon, Master of the Newmarket and Thurlow, has left to join his Regiment, and his wife has been elected joint-Master, and will carry on in his absence, with G. Samways as huntsman. Fifteen couple of hounds have been put down. As from Saturday, September 30th, no claims will be recognised or paid for damage done to poultry by foxes for the duration of the war.

After 3 September 1939 there was little hesitation about putting down large numbers of hounds and horses throughout the country. Newmarket especially suffered greatly on this score. Large numbers of thoroughbred horses were put down without hesitation, though with much heart-burning, when it was realized that another prolonged European war had been declared. Unless they were mares with high breeding potential, or stallions particularly prized for stud, there were few that survived.

Although Mrs Deacon continued to hunt hounds during a large part of the 1939–40 season, ably assisted by George Samways and by her husband on occasional leaves, during that period of 'the phoney war', it was a disastrous season, handicapped by nine weeks of frost and snow as well as outbreaks of foot-and-mouth disease. Coping with black-out restrictions, rationing of food, petrol and clothing, as well as with the housing of evacuees and with her own family, it was amazing that Mrs Deacon also managed somehow to cope with the hounds and hunting as well. Despite all this and a severe attack of measles, she success-fully completed the season without any major mishap, even showing some good sport on occasions, although noting matter of factly at one point:

Dec 18th. Nearly slaughtered on the way to the Meet by a searchlight lorry . . . .

It was unreasonable to expect anyone to continue such a heroic struggle without assistance and during the years from 1940–2 the hounds were not hun-ted. A greatly reduced pack was maintained with difficulty as a nucleus for the future, for in that period of toal war, after Dunkirk and the Battle of Britain, there seemed little time for anything not directly related to the war effort. Land that had never seen the plough before was put into use to provide food to prevent the nation starving. The countryside was fully occupied in growing as much as posisble to this end.

During this hiatus Mrs Deacon, assisted by anyone she could press in to help attended to all the needs of the hounds, except the actual slaughtering of the beasts brought in for flesh. Once they had been shot she would call in the aid of some anti-aircraft gunners close by and get them to help her to haul the beasts up to a beam, preparatory to skinning and butchering them. On one never-to-be-forgotten day she and her elderly governess together dealt with a cow, a horse and a donkey, which had all been brought in one after another.

In 1942 a hunt committee was formed to take over the responsibility for the hounds, since the majority of the old committee were either away in the forces, or, like General Sir Charles Briggs, had died in the early part of the war. Mr Bob Custerson, then farming at Great Bradley, became honorary secretary and with George Samways took out the hounds as often as possible. Mr Harvey Leader took over as chairman and Mrs E. Cooper-Bland arranged the meets and acted as Field Master. In 1945 Mr F. B. Taylor of Dullingham took over the chairman-ship of the committee and contributed largely to the upkeep of the hounds. Once again the farmers had taken charge of their own hunt. Thus it was that the Newmarket and Thurlow survived the war.

The Puckeridge in the meantime had a more settled history, almost entirely due to the Barclay family. Mr Edward Barclay and Major Maurice Barclay, the joint Masters, continued to hunt the country during the 1920–1 season and pro-vided excellent sport, including one particularly outstanding run of two hours and five minutes wth an eight-mile point. At the end of the season, however, they were forced to explain that they found themselves unable to continue in office with the existing guarantee of £3000, although prepared to continue for a further year for £3300. To ensure this sum a number of 'guarantors' agreed to subscribe a further sum, not exceeding £10 apiece, at the end of the season to ensure that there would be no deficit in the hunt accounts. This system of guarantors was to continue for over thirty years.

In 1922, however, both joint Masters tendered their resignations, as they found it impossible to bridge the gap between the sum subscribed and the liabilities of hunting the country four days a week. Eventually, after advertising in vain for a Master, the hunt formed a committee consisting of Mr Edward Barclay, Major Maurice Barclay, Mr Frank Debenham and Mr Frank Stacey to hunt the country. Major Maurice Barclay and Mr Edward Barclay were appointed joint Masters for the committee. Major Barclay was appointed to hunt the hounds on alternate days with Bob Gardiner, and Mr Edward Barclay was to be Field Master. The committee assumed full financial responsibility, but the Masters, on the other hand, as well as being the largest subscribers, also lent the kennels, kennel cottages – and, above all, the pack – to the hunt. This remarkable compromise continued until the hunt was eventually merged with the Newmarket and Thurlow.

Like all such loose arrangements, a great deal depended on the individuals involved and there the Puckeridge was extremely fortunate. In the Barclay family they had staunch supporters and in Mr Frank Debenham and Mr Frank Stacey another excellent partnership. A honorary secretary of the hunt from 1925 onwards, having been joint secretary since 1915, Mr Frank Debenham continued to do the work of some three men on a part-time basis until his death at the age of seventy in 1936. He was particularly talented in dealing with awkward characters and the story was often told of how he successfully enlisted the support of an extremely difficult newcomer, owner of one of the best coverts, who appeared on the farming scene shortly after the 1914–18 War.

After quarrelling with his neighbours, this particular farmer made it plain that he was not interested in anyone or anything except earning his living on his farm. Accordingly, everyone gave him a wide berth until Mr Frank Debenham and Mr Frank Stacey went to visit him in the middle of harvest. The farmer, sitting on his horse binder, busy cutting wheat, made it plain that he was too busy to talk about foxhunting.

'Look,' said Mr Debenham, with his usual charming, modest smile. 'My friend here, Mr Stacey, farms over a thousand acres and you're making him uneasy as he ought to be getting back to his harvest. Suppose you let him take over your place on the binder for a round or two while you tell me your plans for the farm. I'm a farmer myself and I've known this farm a long time. I'd be interested to hear how you're getting on.'

Unable to resist this approach, the newcomer smiled in return and handed over his team to Mr Stacey, who went off chuckling at the success of this manoeuvre. By the time he had shown his skill with a strange team for a quarter of an hour the ice had been broken and Mr Debenham and the stranger were talking like old friends. Within the space, of a year or two the Puckeridge hunt had no firmer, more loyal supporter. With a team like this the Puckeridge went from strength to strength.

Throughout the 1920s there were some historic hunts. The season 1923–4 produced some remarkably good days, of which the most outstanding was a seven-and-a-half-mile point in fifty-five minutes.* During the 1924–5 season the most noteworthy feature was the number of times that hounds ran into the neighbouring countries on unusual lines. The 1925–6 season also showed some very fine hunts, particularly one of an hour and fifty-five minutes with a nine-mile point.† 2 January of that season saw two hunts, one of seventy-five minutes with a five-mile, point and the other of ninety minutes with a six-mile point, fully fourteen miles as hounds ran with only ten of the field completing the day.*

Other noteworthy hunts of this period were a two and a half hour hunt with an eight-mile point crossing the London to Cambridge road in 1928 and a hunt of one-and-three-quarter hours with a four-and-three-quarter-mile point surmounting great difficulties and ending in a kill in January 1931.‡ An unusual hunt in April of the same year was with a mixed pack consisting of Weathergauge (1922) and fourteen couple of his sons and daughters. It would be pleasant to record that this splendid sire and his progeny killed, but in spite of a grand hunt they just failed to do so.

Perhaps the most outstanding hunt of the entire 1930s was one in January 1932 when the financial crisis was beginning to bite hard due to 'several good subscribers having either left the country or died'. This was a hunt of two hours and thirty minutes with an eight-mile point, some twenty-three as hounds travelled.§ The members of the hunt who finished this great day included Major Barclay, Bob Gardiner, Tom Kirkby (second whipper-in), Mrs Guiness of Westmill and Miss Linette Guiness, Miss Joan Fordham and Miss Barbara Fordham of Brent Pelham Hall; Miss Marriage of Aspenden; Miss Hannah Thwaites of Aspenden; Miss Jane Hickly of Much Hadham; Miss Turney of Hay Farm, Therfield; Mr Willie Sale and Miss Mollie Sale of Clothall Bury; Mr Norman Pryor of Manuden House; Mr Peter Pryor of Weston Lodge; Mr Sydney Smith of

*See Appendix, page 161.
†See Appendix, pages 161–2.
‡See Appendix, page 163.
§See Appendix, page 164.

IOI

Hole Farm, Stansted; Mr Russell Pigg of Chipping Hall; Mr W. Jackson of Fowlmere; and Mr Hanbury of Queenbury, Reed. It is noticeable that the women had already begun to equal, if not outnumber, the men.

From 1933 onwards the hunt establishment hunted four days a week, although without a second whipper-in, requiring harder work by the kennel staff to produce similar sport and outward appearances to the previous years. In spite of these handicaps the 1933–4 season saw two particularly fine hunts,* both in January and both on Saturdays. The first, on the 15th, produced a hunt of one hour and thirty minutes with an eight-mile point and a kill in the open. The second on the 20th resulted in a sensational kill after an hour and fifty-five minutes and a six-mile point in front of a line of guns, who 'took it very well'.

As with the Newmarket and Thurlow, the hot dry summer of 1934 resulted in an excellent hunting season. Major Barclay commented after the hounds had killed seventy brace of foxes in 131 days:

> This ends the best season by a long way that I ever remember. A record cubhunting, a poor scenting and dry November, but we got a lot of rain in December & sport was good right away on to the end. We had a wonderful fortnight's sport around Christmas time. Sport was fairly spread all over the country, but I think the feature of the season was perhaps the consistent sport shown in the woodlands in the north end of the country. Hounds killed 25 brace of foxes in this district alone, always a hard place to kill them in. The doghounds killed 82 foxes in 66 days.

In the 1935–6 season Major Barclay had completed his twenty-fifth season in office as joint Master and Mr Edward Barclay had completed his fortieth as Master or joint Master. They were accordingly presented with their portraits by Lionel Edwards as a token of the hunt's appreciation of their services and generosity. More than three hundred subscribers contributed to this presentation of their portraits and it was made by the chairman of the hunt committee, Major W. S. Gosling, son of the previous Master of that name.

The great hunt of the 1937 season was a three hour twenty minutes' hunt with a five-and-a-half-mile point by the dog pack on 1 March.† The season was somewhat shadowed by the announcement of Bob Gardiner's retirement, after forty-one years with Mr Barclay and twenty-six years as huntsman. He was presented with a cheque for £1000, subscribed by 450 of his friends, and, as he only retired as far as Bishops Stortford, he was often seen out with the hunt, returning to fill the gaps caused by the war from 1942 to 1944.

His successor as huntsman was the first whipper-in, Ben Wilkinson, whose service with the Puckeridge extended back to 1927. He proved to be a cheerful

*See Appendix, pages 164–5.
†See Appendix, pages 165–6.

and efficient huntsman and during the 1937-8 season showed excellent sport with the bitch pack, although the sport shown by the dog pack during this season was even more outstanding. From Christmas onwards they had some wonderful days, including eleven hunts with points varying from four miles to seven and a half.* Well might Major Barclay write:

This ends a very good season. The bitches had the best of the cubhunting & the doghounds of the regular hunting. It is the best season I have ever had with my doghounds. Out of 36 days hunting since the opening meet, 27 have been good days, 6 fair & 3 bad with them. There have been some very good foxes in the country & there have been 20 hunts with points of 4 miles & over, 12 of these have been with the doghounds. They have had the following good points; four 4-mile points, one 4½, one 5, two 5½ one 6, two 6½, one 7½. They, the doghounds, have not killed as many foxes as usual, but they they had an unlucky cubhunting – they hit all the unlucky mornings. They have marked a lot of foxes to ground. Many of their good hunts ended in this way. They are a great pack of hounds. We have killed our second largest number of foxes, viz. 57½ brace.

The general standard of sport in the 1938-9 season was higher than in the previous one, even if there were not so many spectacular hunts,† while the honours were evenly divided between dog and bitch packs. The bitch pack had one excellent seven-mile point on 25 February 1939, but the dog pack ended with a magnificent day on 1 April 1939. This was a fitting climax to the season for what was undoubtedly one of the finest packs in the country. It was noted by Major Barclay in his summing up as perhaps the most outstanding he remembered. He wrote:

This finishes one of the best seasons I ever remember. I have always thought the season 1934-5 was the best, but I am not sure this was not a better one. A very good cubhunting, followed by an exceptionally good November. This is generally a poor month for sport in this country. Scent was very useful throughout taking the season as a whole.

Again the doghounds have had the best of the regular hunting. Out of 38 days regular hunting with them, 28 have been good, 8 fair, 1 bad & 1 day (Boxing Day) on foot in the snow. They have killed 60 foxes in 61 days – a very good record. They killed 20 brace cubhunting & 15 brace regular hunting. We have had 21 hunts with points of 4 miles and over, of which 14 have been with the doghounds.

On 4 September 1939 Major Barclay hunted his doghounds for the last time and a few days later only seven couple were left alive of this fine doghound pack, then in its prime. For the first winter of 1939–40 Ben Wilkinson continued to hunt the much reduced mixed pack for three days a week, but in that hard winter hounds were not out for twenty-six days due to the weather. One of the notable records of the year was on Saturday, 21 October 1939, when cub-

*See Appendix, pages 166–7.
†See Appendix, page 168.

hunting in Broadfield Hall Wood a stallion hound of renown, Brigand (1934), hunted a fox away alone and killed him at Wood Farm at Friars. To hunt and kill single-handed is a rare feat indeed and it may be remembered that Mr Thomas Andrews was so proud when one of his famous 'Invincibles' named Chaunter performed a similar exploit in 1810 that he had his portrait painted in oils.

During the 1940–1 season Ben Wilkinson hunted hounds with Dick Bull the kennelman as his sole whipper-in. Captain Charles Barclay was home on leave in February and hunted hounds, ending a fine day with a hunt of one hour and twenty-five minutes and a five-mile point,* a very fine achievement for the first time of ever hunting hounds himself.

During the 1941–2 season Ben Wilkinson was fully employed manning the Observer post at Brent Pelhan as the Battle of Britain was fought overhead and Major Barclay managed to find time to hunt hounds on Saturdays, relieved by Bob Gardiner's return to help. In the 1942–3 season Dick Bull joined the R.A.F. and Ben Wilkinson was only able to spare time to feed hounds. Hounds were only out on nineteen days. During the 1944–5 season Major Barclay managed to hunt on Saturdays only with Ted Brown, another retired hunt servant, helping in the kennels and as whipper-in. In this way a nucleus of hounds was entered and the pack kept going until the end of the war.

*See Appendix, page 169.

Woodcock, 1942

President, 1948

Gravity, 1950, by Woodcock, ex Graphic, 1947

Poetry, 1951, by Woodcock, ex Picture, 1945, Champion Bitch at Peterborough, 1951

Charles Field, huntsman to the Newmarket and Thurlow, with hounds in Linton, 1955

Acting joint Master Mr J. D. Webb heading the Newmarket and Thurlow across country, 1956

OPPOSITE: Colonel D. R. B. Kaye, D.S.O., Master of the Newmarket and Thurlow 1958–9

RIGHT: The Newmarket and Thurlow, 1963. The Master, Mrs R. Riggall, and huntsman Tony Champion leading the pack

BELOW: The Newmarket and Thurlow, 1966. The Master, Mrs E. H. Vestey, and Tony Champion

OPPOSITE TOP: Mr and Mrs E. H. Vestey, Joint Masters of the Puckeridge and Thurlow, with, *from left to right*, Mr J. D. Webb (partly obscured), Mr John Beach, assistant secretary, Mr C. G. Hawkins and Mrs N. Streeter

OPPOSITE BELOW: Captain and Mrs Charles Barclay and Mr E. H. Vestey, joint Masters (with Mrs Vestey) of the newly formed Puckeridge and Thurlow, 1970–

RIGHT: Ned Paxton, kennel huntsman 1950–75

BELOW RIGHT: Captain Charles Barclay, joint Master of the Puckeridge 1947–70, and of the Puckeridge and Thurlow from 1970

Vestey Fox, by William Garfit.
The incident illustrated took place during a hunt on 8 January 1976 (Mr Edmund Vestey hunting hounds). A fox jumped up in the rough, ran through the covert and then doubled back to ground in a long land drain. After a noisy confrontation the fox popped out of the pipe, but instead of making a run for it sat down and calmly surveyed the scene

Chapter 9

The Years from 1945 to 1975

THE years from 1945 to 1975 can also be divided roughly into three periods, the flat austere post-war period extending into the later fifties, followed by the boom years of the sixties and the inflated start of the seventies. First, however, it is necessary to consider the effects of the 1939–45 war on the countryside. These years had seen vast changes not only in the countryside but in the way of life of the country people. Whole tracts of land had been flattened, bulldozed and turned into airfields, army camps, or ammunition dumps. Frequently tarmacadamed runways, or new roads, had been driven ruthlessly across erstwhile excellent coverts. Even when the Nissen huts and hangars had been removed after a decade or so, odd corners were likely to be found in unlikely places with concrete foundations and rusty rolls of barbed wire enmeshed in a tangle of undergrowth, invisible to the unwary eye.

The fifties saw tractors completely ousting the horse throughout the countryside and large combine harvesters began to appear on every harvest field. New fertilizers and sprays, dangerous to animals and man alike, were developed and used at times with startling lack of care and often disastrous results. The trend was to ever-larger fields with hedgerows being grubbed up to make room for new machinery and more efficient farming. New corn silos and storage bins, new methods of producing silage for feeding animals, and intensive fattening units for birds and beasts, transformed farming methods and the farmyards themselves. With the boom years of the sixties all these trends were intensified.

Inured to abrupt changes in the countryside by six years of war, the country people as a whole did not at first see the greater threats posed by the planners in the post-war decades. In the 1950s the concept of new towns to take the 'overspill' from London was put into practice. Stevenage, once a small, sleepy, posting village on the old coaching Great North Road, began its transformation into an industrialized mammoth development. Haverhill, once a weaving centre, then quietly stagnating, was later similarly transmogrified on a lesser scale. Only when it was almost too late and much of the damage had already been done was it appreciated that it was necessary to resist vocally and vigorously in order to survive.

The threat of a new airport at Stansted, which would have altered the face of the countryside as well as the lives of the inhabitants around about, was strenuously and lengthily resisted. The planning order decreeing a reservoir at Great Bradley, which would have drowned thousands of acres of good agricultural land and ruined much of the country for hunting, was also fought effectively. New motorways and similar 'planning concepts' constantly removed good farming land from use, turning it into sterile concrete unless resolutely opposed. During the 1960s, at least, the country people learned that they must resist and band together if they wished their way of life to survive.

The pressures on the countryside were not all from the government or the planners. With the vast increase in population in the post-war years and the urge for a country home inherent in so many people, the commuting belt stretched ever farther and farther into the country. Faster train services and new motorways encouraged the trend. Furthermore, every tumbledown cottage was bought and renovated for a weekend cottage, or for retired couples seeking a place in the country. Whole villages became sterilized in this way with the original inhabitants dispossessed. As was the case in the 1930s, this sometimes meant fresh support for hunting, but more often it meant opposition from someone unaccustomed to country life and convinced of the cruelty involved in a sport only dimly understood.

In 1949 a private member's bill was put forward to ban foxhunting. In the event it was withdrawn before being put to the vote, but another bill was introduced to make the hunting of deer, otter, or badger and the coursing of hare or rabbit illegal. It was defeated by 214 votes to 101, but the warning was plain. The immediate effect was to increase the support for the British Field Sports Society and make foxhunters, shooting men and other field sportsmen close their ranks. Further selective attacks by the League Against Cruel Sports and a vocal part of the membership of the R.S.P.C.A in the sixties and seventies have consistently been defeated and such bodies as the Game Conservancy have joined with the B.F.S.S. in defending the countryman's sport. In yet another sphere, however, the countryman has had to learn the lesson that to retain his way of life he had to unite to withstand outside political pressures, whether from planners or fanatics.

The picture has not been one of unrelieved gloom by any means. One of the most cheering features of the post-war period since 1945 from the hunting viewpoint has been the steady development of the pony clubs, the nursery for many budding young hunters, on an almost unbelievable nation-wide scale. Horse breeding with good blood available from premium stallions in the 1950s, and latterly in many small studs up and down the country, has provided excellent hunters. The introduction of dressage and cross-country events has led also to much improved horsemanship in the hunting field. The old hunting saddle and the backward seat of the 1930s and earlier has given way in many instances to forward-seat saddles. Whereas grooms of the male sex have become something of a rarity, girl grooms have made excellent substitutes since the 1950s. The preponderance of women in the hunting field was soon very clearly established and by the 1950s women Masters, no longer a rarity, were a well-established fact.

In 1945, however, the whole future of foxhunting seemed to be weighed in the balance. There were admittedly those hunts, such as the Puckeridge, which had managed to survive the war with a nucleus of hounds and strong support from the farming community. The same, to a lesser degree, could be said of the Newmarket and Thurlow. Here it was indeed entirely to the farmers that the hunt owed its survial, but no hounds had been bred during the war and they were not a very good nucleus to start from again. There were some hunts which failed to survive at all but, wherever they did, it was the farmers who proved the mainstay of foxhunting. The farming boom of the war and post-war years was paradoxically the principal reason that foxhunting itself survived.

In the 1945–6 season the Newmarket and Thurlow was still relying on Mr F. B. Taylor of Dullingham, who had taken over as chairman of the hunt committee from Mr Harvey Leader and contributed very largely to the upkeep of the re-maining hounds. With the assistance of Mrs E. Cooper-Bland arranging the meets and acting as Field Master, while also running a flourishing branch of the Pony Club, the hunt managed to show some sport. Sadly, however, many of the old regular pre-war supporters had ceased to follow hounds, or, like Mr. C. F. Ryder and General Sir Charles Briggs, had died during the war years. The out-look for the immediate future was not very encouraging.

A good example of those who were missed was the Reverend Stanley Austin, Rector of Withersfield for many years, who had been a familiar figure in the hunting field before the war in his black frock-coat and broad-brimmed hat, mounted on his old tubed horse appropriately named Rory. Whenever he ap-proached a ditch he was always heard to mutter loudly: 'Steady, Rory! We're all ready, Rory! Look out, Rory! Look out, Rory!', generally falling off on his head into the ditch thereafter when the horse abruptly refused.

A friend of Sir Alfred Munnings, he was well known for his eccentricity. When burying one of his old hunting friends at the end of the war on a freezing-hard morning with the ground like iron there was general consternation as the slings slipped and the coffin fell with a resounding crash into the grave. The Rector relieved the tension with a remark his friend would have delighted in, stepping forward to read the burial service, but prefacing it calmly with:

'Poor old Charles never took a toss like that out hunting.'

In the 1946–7 season Brigadier M. W. Selby-Lowndes took over as Master. Unfortunately, the weather was against hunting during that famous hard winter and foot-and-mouth restrictions also helped to make this one of the worst seasons on record. In all the circumstances it was scarcely surprisingly that Brigadier Selby-Lowndes only remained in office for the period of the one season.

Although Mr F. B. Taylor again took over as chairman of the hunt committee for a further season, he too then resigned. For the 1948–9 season it was thus necessary to make an almost entirely fresh start. A virtually new hunt committee was formed with Mr J. D. Webb, who had taken over his family farm of Streetly Hall just before the war, as chairman.

Mr Harvey Leader was persuaded to return as Master, agreeing to provide the horses, and Charlie Field was engaged as kennel huntsman at £5 a week. An old pensioner was put in to help him and an amateur whip, Bob Cowell, just out of the navy, went to live with him to gain experience. Mr Webb himself offered to provide fodder for the horses and the rest of the hunt committee agreed to work a rota system to provide food for the hounds, sending an agreed amount of oats to Linton Mill for oatmeal food. Only bran was required to be bought for the horses and the only expenses were Field's wages. The rest was provided by the farmers concerned from their farms.

The Newmarket and Thurlow, however, must always owe a considerable debt to the hard work put in at this time by Charlie Field as huntsman, for in this instance it was largely a question of the huntsman making the hunt. With only a scratch pack, since most of the old hounds were now past hunting and no puppies had been bred during the war period, he had a formidable task. He brought with him from the Chiddingfold one or two hounds and with these and one or two draft hounds from the Puckeridge, as well as one or two obtained by the Master, the nucleus of a fresh pack was formed.

The most outstanding import was a Cheshire bitch named Gravity, whose offspring have been notable throughout the post-war history of the hunt. Particularly good was a bitch Welcome, rated by Major Maurice Barclay as the best in the pack and equally good in her work. With such enthusiasm and backing from all concerned it was not surprising that the new hunt committee, Master and huntsman made a successful team, nor that a good pack was forth-coming by degrees.

There had at first been some fears locally that Mr R. A. Vestey, who had bought the Thurlow Hall estate on the death of Mr C. F. Ryder, might not be a hunt supporter. Fortunately these gloomy forebodings were entirely unfounded. Although personally more interested in shooting than hunting, he proved to be a good friend to the hunt. He also continued to employ most of the estate workers who wished to stay, including Albert Williams as head groom. It was largely due to the latter's tactful encouragement and enthusiasm as well as to the ready welcome and knowledgeable instruction on hounds and hunting imparted by Charlie Field whenever they visited the kennels, that Mr Vestey's children developed their liking for horses, hounds and hunting.

With the farmer members of the committee providing almost all that was required for the upkeep of horses and hounds the subscription was merely needed to cover the huntsman's wages. Thus for the 1949–50 season it was a mere £565 and the following season £566, rising to £912 in the 1951–52 season. By the 1952–53 season the hunt was well established once again and providing good sport. For that season C. Purvis was taken on as whipper-in to Charlie Field and two cottages were built for the hunt staff. Successful point-to-points and Hunt Balls helped to keep the hunt finances on an even keel each year, but, of course, the hunt finances were not great being largely borne by the individual farmers on the committee except for the wages concerned.

In the 1953–4 season the hunt was saddened by the sudden death of Mrs E. Cooper-Bland, who had been a keen and enthusiastic supporter of the hunt for over twenty-five years, more especially in the first difficult post-war years when a great deal of work devolved upon her. A new whipper-in, T. Coote, was employed and despite a bad scenting start to the season there was some good sport with an adequate supply of foxes. The hunt was extremely fortunate in having extremely little territory 'out of bounds' to them and the support from within the country continued to increase.

By the 1954–5 season with T. Pudney of the Essex Union now as whipper-in, the hunt could congratulate itself on having as good a pack of hounds as they had ever had and with plenty of foxes it looked like being a very good year. The weather, however, stopped hunting from 6 January almost continuously until 8 March. Nevertheless they killed nine and a half brace of foxes and ran five brace to ground, hunting for 34 days in all.

The following season was another disappointing one, starting with a very successful cubbing period, but followed by an abnormally dry spell with little scent. A prolonged cold spell then ensued allowing few good days. There was also something of a crisis when Mr Harvey Leader, after eight years as Master, announced that he could no longer spare the time to look after the hunt affairs and must now resign. Charlie Field, who also elected to go with him at the end of the season, was presented with a cheque for £270 by the members of the hunt in recognition of his services over his period as huntsman. It was decided to form a committee to hunt the country and Mr J. D. Webb, the chairman, agreed to become acting Master, while T. Kirkby, previously huntsman to the Tickham and Hertfordshire hunts, as well as whipper-in to the Puckeridge, was engaged in succession to Charlie Field. Mr R. A. Vestey generously undertook to provide the hunt horses, Mr Webb continuing to provide fodder for them, and various members of the committee feed for the hounds.

During their eight years together as Master and huntsman Mr Harvey Leader and Charlie Field had done a great deal for the hunt. During this period also the Pony Club had flourished and the future of the hunt was assured by encouraging the young entry, both hounds and humans. It was also during this period that the first one-day events were started at Denston Hall, only being discontinued due to the turf in the park being unable to stand up to the numbers of cars and horse boxes in wet weather.

The 1956–7 season proved an extremely mild one and scenting conditions were good. There were some good hunts* and seven brace of foxes were killed, while six brace were run to ground in forty days' hunting, with only one blank day. For the following season Mr J. D. Webb was joined by Colonel D. R. B. Kaye, D.S.O., late 10th Royal Hussars, a keen heavy-weight sportsman of similar noble mould to Mr John Josselyn, as joint acting Master with Tom Kirkby remaining as huntsman. With forty days' hunting and generally good scenting conditions this season was well up to average and eight brace of foxes were killed while eighteen and a half brace were run to ground. One good day's hunting, fortunately for Tom Kirkby, was on the occasion Ned Paxton and Bob Gardiner, huntsman and ex-huntsman of the Puckeridge, accompanied by Mr G. C. Newman of the same hunt, came over to see him perform with the Newmarket and Thurlow.

Unfortunately, both joint acting Masters signified their wish to resign, although Colonel D. R. B. Kaye offered to continue as Master with a guarantee of £1500. This offer was accepted by the committee and for the 1958–9 season he acted as Master with J. Deakin, previously huntsman to the South Pembrokeshire, as successor to Tom Kirkby. At the end of the season, however, Colonel D. R. B. Kaye resigned and the committee was forced to advertise the post of Master, selecting Mr J. P. N. Parker as Master and huntsman with a guarantee of £2500, employing D. Hargreaves as whipper-in.

Mr Neil Parker was unfortunate in that during his period of three seasons as

*See Appendix, page 154.

Master the country was hit by 'fox disease', resulting in a great dearth of foxes, thus making it extremely hard to show sport. Despite this, he managed to carry the hunt through this very difficult period successfully. He was greatly helped by Mr J. D. Webb as chairman of the hunt committee and from 1960 by Colonel D. R. B. Kaye, who took over as honorary secretary of the hunt on the resignation of Mr T. Hunter Blair. In the first year of Mr Parker's mastership a Hunt Supporters' Club was also formed, which soon proved a great asset.

In 1962 Mr Parker resigned to take over as Master of the Avon Vale and was succeeded by Mrs R. H. D. Riggall, with A. Champion as huntsman and A. Walker as whipper-in and the same guarantee of £2500. From 1962 to 1964 Mrs Riggall continued as sole Master, but in the 1964–5 season she was joined by Mrs E. H. Vestey as joint Master. At the end of this season Mrs Riggall resigned and Mrs E. H. Vestey carried on alone. Although Mrs Riggall had worked tirelessly for the hunt, it was becoming increasingly difficult to show sport as a two-day-a-week country with the changing pattern of the countryside. Increasingly early ploughing, so many studs near Newmarket barring a large part of the country in that direction, and the loss of a certain amount of country round Kedington and Haverhill, with other little pieces eaten away here and there, simply reduced the land available to hunt.

For the 1966–7 season Mrs E. H. Vestey was joined by her husband Mr Edmund Vestey as joint Master. At the end of the season, to everyone's great regret, Mr Jack Webb resigned as chairman of the hunt committee after nineteen years' tireless work on behalf of the hunt. Quite apart from such matters as supplying the hunt horses with fodder for sixteen years, his commonsense approach to matters and bluff good humour made him perfectly equipped to deal with everyone from ducal landlords to his fellow farmers. Furthermore, he not only provided a link going back to the days of Mr Charles Tonge's period as Master between the wars, but as far back as the Thurlow Farmers' Purse, and even to the formation of the Thurlow Hunt Club in 1858 when his great-grandfather was a founder member.

In recognition of his work on their behalf Mr Webb was presented by the hunt with his portrait in oils on his favourite hunter. His place as chairman of the hunt committee was filled by Mr Stephen Ryder of Great Bradley Hall, son of the late Mr C. F. Ryder, Master during the 1914–18 war and for long the staunchest supporter of the hunt. Here also is another example of the continuity which may be found in the history of almost any hunt and is the very lifeblood of the countryside.

It is also a good example of the pressures on the modern farmer and landowner, as well as on hunting, that much of Mr Stephen Ryder's land at Bradley Hall and a considerable acreage adjoining it had been designated as a reservoir for the Colchester area by the Water Authorities. In conjunction with the C.L.A. and other bodies he had fought this scheme and produced a most imaginative alternative, whereby water instead should be piped from the Denver sluice near King's Lynn to connect with the river Stour close to Haverhill. The effect in this instance was to prevent any further action on the part of bureaucracy. Similar decisive action and constant vigilance were required to prevent undue expansion of the 'new town' of Haverhill, which threatens to rival Stevenage on the borders of the Puckeridge country.

For the next three seasons Mr and Mrs E. H. Vestey continued as joint Masters. The following season of 1967–8 proved disastrous due to the widespread outbreak of foot-and-mouth disease, which almost brought hunting to a standstill. During the seasons of 1968–9 and 1969–70 there were some good days, but increasingly it was becoming obvious that with the pressures at work on the countryside there was simply no longer sufficient countryside available to provide the same sport.

At the hunt committee meeting at the end of the season it was proposed that a merger might be the answer and the Suffolk were at first considered, due to the erstwhile ties with that country. The equally strong ties with the Puckeridge, however, decided the committee to make an approach to them. Since they were suffering from precisely similar difficulties, it was felt sensible to amalgamate in the interests of both hunts. Over the centuries their histories had often been interwoven and they already had many hunt followers and supporters in common, so that in practice it meant little real change. It enabled both to provide better sport and also to reduce costs considerably. As individual hunts the Newmarket and Thurlow and the Puckeridge might cease at this point, but combined with each other as the Puckeridge and Thurlow they were to continue to show even better sport in the future.

To revert once more to the Puckeridge, the 1945–6 season saw the hunt still functioning after the war years. The list of subscribers had sunk parlously low, with only £872 subscribed at one point during the war. As life began to return to some form of peacetime normality, however, it had soon begun to rise and for this season it had risen to over £1500. Hounds hunted fifty-three days and killed ten brace of foxes, running nine and a half brace to ground. There were two hunts with four and a half-mile points and one with a four-mile point.*

*See Appendix, page 169.

On the whole everyone concerned was entitled to congratulate himself at the end of this first post-war season.

The notorious 1946-7 season, however, was appalling. Although the overall subscription had been raised to over £2100, everything including the weather seemed against hunting. The austerity of the post-war government seemed matched only by the general gloom at home. Hounds had a bad attack of distemper, despite inoculations, and four and a half couple were lost. This was the first outbreak of hard-pad, that vicious form of distemper – then comparatively new. Finally, after the weather had stopped hunting for twenty-two days, foot-and-mouth disease caused any question of further hunting to be forgotten. Hounds were out for thirty-two days and killed four and a half brace of foxes, marking a sinlge brace to ground. It was unquestionably the worst season on record, with snow lying six feet deep and more in places, while traffic on most roads was halted for long periods. Finally, a thaw was followed by floods and wet ground which made hunting impossible in view of the critical agricultural needs of the nation at the time. There were no hunts worth recording.

Fortunately the 1947-8 season was a different matter with the hunt really getting back into its old routine once more. Ned Paxton, second whipper-in during the 1936-7 season and first whipper-in from 1937-40, returned from war service on 1 May 1947 to succeed Ben Wilkinson as first whipper-in and kennel huntsman. The season was also a historic one in that Captain Charlie Barclay joined his father and grandfather as joint Master, a unique event in any hunt history. Three serving Masters, father, son and also grandson, was another proof of the Barclay support for the hunt, as well as a remarkable instance of family tradition carrying over three generations of the same family. Those whose memories stretch so far back may well remember with a chuckle hearing Major Maurice Barclay addressing such comments to Captain Charlie Barclay as: 'Blow yer horn, boy. Blow yer horn.' or more typically perhaps: 'This is the way the fox should go, whether he went that way or not I don't know, but that's the way I'm going.'

Sadly this great family triumvirate only survived for one year, for in March 1948 Mr E. E. Barclay died after all but fifty-two years as Master of the Puckeridge Hunt. It was his triumph that he took over a country still disunited after the epic 'Row' and with mange prevalent in the foxes, yet overcame both these handicaps. During his mastership he built up two great packs of hounds and his knowledge of hound breeding was unequalled in Britain. The standard of consistently good sport shown in the country under his mastership in itself indicated the degree of his success. His family, his son and grandson, continued the example he had set and the Puckeridge hunt owed them all a vast debt.

It is good to be able to record at least three fine hunts during Mr Barclay's final year. On the whole it had been quite a good average season without very good scenting conditions. Hounds hunted sixty-one days and killed twelve brace running nine brace to ground.

An account showing the costings involved in running the hunt at this time is of interest. Compared with before the war they had more than doubled and only the system of working guarantors could have kept the hunt going. The accounts read:

WORKING ACCOUNTS

Receipts:

To Subscriptions:		2,645 12 0
Interest in investments less Tax		65 5 6
Sale of Hides, Bones and Manure		298 16 5
Rents received:		
Maddam's Wood	12 0 0	
Meyers Gorse (less tax)	7 18 9	
Prior's Wood	10 0 0	29 18 9
Proceeds of 'Caps' donated per contra:		
Hunt Servants Benefit Society	43 16 9	
British Legion Appeal: Haig's Fund	25 1 1	
Royal Agricultural Benevolent Inst;	29 2 7	98 0 5
Sale of Underwood:		
Maddam's Wood	12 10 0	
Prior's Wood	6 0 0	18 10 0
Press Reports		2 10 0
Surplus from Subscriptions to Hunt through		
Point to Point		883 10 5
Surplus from Hunt Ball		257 0 0
		4,301 3 6

Season 1848–49 Expenditure:		
By Blacksmith		119 5 6
Chemist		45 11 10
Clothes for Hunt Servants		58 10 6
Fuel and Electricity		121 0 0
Forage		365 10 0
Hound Food		475 15 8
Gate and Bridges		63 16 6
Repairs: General	67 8 1	
Boiler	29 19 10	92 7 11
Haulage		106 13 0
Kennels, Renewals of Equipment etc		25 3 6
Stable and Saddle Room		38 0 6

Printing and Stationery	42	19	0		
Less Proceeds of Sales of Cards:	27	12	6	15 6 6	
Licences:				22 10 0	
Knackers:				27 15 6	
Poultry Claims, etc:					
Claims	294	2	2		
Finds & Litters	103	0	0		
Stopping	35	10	0	432 12 2	
Rates, Taxes and Insurance				152 2 6	
Taxes and Tithes: Maddam's Wood:	11	18	7		
Prior's Wood:	17	19	3	29 17 10	
Donations: British Field Sports Society:	105	0	0		
Proceeds of 'Caps' per contra:	98	0	5	203 0 5	
Depreciation: Horses				397 4 6	
Legal Charges				7 5 0	
Sundries and Huntsman's Telephone				18 12 8	
Veterinary Expenses				157 10 1	
Wages				1,309 16 6	
Surplus for the Season				15 14 11	
				4,301 3 6	

By the 1949–50 season the Puckeridge hunt was fully recovered from the war and post-war restrictions. Despite an extremely bad scenting season, they had some noteworthy hunts including two four-mile points and one of five miles.* The 1950–1 season also saw some good hunts,† but was primarily notable from the hunt's viewpoint as the year Major W. S. Gosling announced his retirement as chairman of the hunt committee after twenty-eight years. One of the largest landowners in the area, as well as a devoted hunt supporter, his retirement was greatly regretted. His successor, Brigadier Sir Edward Beddington, K.C.M.G., D.S.O., M.C., was faced with a hard task to keep down rising costs. By the 1951–2 season the working account had risen to £5596. The upward spiral continued steadily and inexorably and the following years saw it rise to £5894. Determined efforts to reduce costs, however, were successful and the 1953–4 season saw the account reduced to £5161.

The years from 1954 to 1956 saw some good sport* and costs maintained at a reasonable level. The 1956–7 season was a particularly good one, with sport much above average.† At the opening meet on 5 November the Masters, Major M. E. Barclay and Captain C. G. E. Barclay, were presented with a portrait by Mr Leigh Pemberton of themselves and the late Mr E. E. Barclay to commemor-

*See Appendix, page 171.
†See Appendix, pages 172–3.

ate the Barclay family's sixtieth year as Masters. Brigadier Sir Edward Bedding-ton, having announced his wish to retire as chairman of the hunt committee, was succeeded by Mr H. N. Sporborg, C.M.G.

The 1957-8 and 1958-9 seasons were both average, with some good hunts,* but they were notable as the last when the country was hunted three days a week. With the encroachments of the new towns, airfields and motorways it was felt there simply no longer remained sufficient country to continue hunting more than two days a week, with an occasional bye-day. The 1959-60 season saw good sport,† despite stoppage by foot-and-mouth disease and an outbreak of fox disease. Hunting sixty-two days, they killed twenty and a half brace of foxes and ran to ground twenty-four and a half brace. More important even than this was a complete revision of the system of guarantors and the introduction of a non-hunting subscription. The Hunt Supporters' Club started that season was to become a factor in the hunt's future, ending that year with four hundred members. For the first time, however, the working account reached £6300.

The seasons from 1960 to 1962 were average, with some good sport,‡ but the 1962-3 season was extremely disappointing, being one of the worst on record, with a few good hunts.§ Hunting was stopped by frost and snow for thirty-seven days, the longest period in the history of the hunt. During forty-one days hunting hounds killed only nine brace and ran a further eight brace to ground. The hunt was also greatly saddened by the death of Major M. E. Barclay soon after the start of his fifty-second year as Master. Like his father a brilliant hunts-man and judge of foxhounds, he had a wide circle of friends extending far beyond the confines of the Puckeridge country. Many neighbouring hunts and the Newmarket and Thurlow in particular owed him much for his help and encouragement in post-war years. His place as joint Master with Captain C. G. E. Barclay was taken by Mrs C. G. E. Barclay.

Two other sad losses to the hunt about the same time included the death of Bob Gardiner, who had served as huntsman for twenty-six years ending in 1937, although he had returned to help during the war years. Another familiar never-to-be forgotten figure whose death was also sadly recorded was that of Mr G. C. (Pino) Newman, the self-appointed terrier man for the Puckeridge hunt since the 1914-18 war. Considered delicate as a youth and educated at Magdalene College, Cambridge, where he followed the Trinity Foot Beagles, he remained dedicated to hunting on foot for the rest of his life, also to digging out foxes

*See Appendix, pages 174-5.
†See Appendix, page 175.
‡See Appendix, pages 175-6.
§See Appendix, page 176.

with terriers. Invariably wearing a stiff white collar, he was never seen to wear any form of raincoat or overcoat, regardless of rain or hail, a tribute to the effects of hunting on a delicate constitution. He was undoubtedly a unique character and the Puckeridge were fortunate to have his services for so long.

The 1963–4 season saw some good hunts* but it also saw the working account rising to £6943, and at the end of the year it was reluctantly decided that subscriptions would have to be raised to keep pace with rising costs. The effect of this was immediately noticeable in the following season which also saw some good sport,† when the accounts only showed a small deficit of £19. On the other hand, the 1965–6 season saw a rise in the working account to £7643.

It should be noticed here that the Hunt Supporters' Club was by this time proving itself a great help to the hunt in many ways, but mostly financially. By organizing raffles, dances and similar activities, money was raised for such things as a new hound van or similar equipment for the hunt. On occasion members' aid in the organization of activities such as point-to-points, hunter trials or similar events can be immensely useful.

The 1966–7 season was an extremely good one, with some excellent sport, but the effect of Selective Employment Tax proved an unexpected extra burden on the hunt, necessitating further rises in costs. The following season was ruined by the prolonged stoppage – due to foot-and-mouth disease – of thirty-six days, while the financial position of the hunt resulted in an Extraordinary General Meeting being called to discuss the problem of a working account of £8574. Despite all this, there were some good days, including one five-mile point.‡

The 1968–9 season was the last the Puckeridge were to have before their amalgamation with the Newmarket and Thurlow. Rising costs and the encroaching concrete of motorways, airfields and new towns has at last made it imperative that the hunt expand its ground in order to survive. Their long friendship and close ties made the amalgamation the perfect answer for both hunts, while their common problems were solved at one move.

The approach initially came from the Newmarket and Thurlow hunt committee, but the Puckeridge hunt committee were quick to appreciate the advantages offered on both sides. Under the chairmanship of Mr H. N. Sporborg and vice-charimanship of Mr R. S. Ryder, with Colonel D. R. B. Kaye, D.S.O., as honorary secretary and Mr M. G. Routledge as honorary secretary and treasurer, a new Puckeridge and Thurlow hunt committee was formed, amongst

*See Appendix, page 176.
†See Appendix, pages 176–7.
‡See Appendix, pages 177–8.

whom were names long familiar in the history of both hunts, including that of Mr J. D. Webb. The Masters of the old Puckeridge, Captain and Mrs C. G. E. Barclay, and the Masters of the old Newmarket and Thurlow, Mr and Mrs E. H. Vestey, became the joint Masters of the new Puckeridge and Thurlow hunt – probably the first double husband-and-wife joint mastership ever.

It was decided that the hounds should all be kennelled at Brent Pelham and the Newmarket and Thurlow kennels at Thurlow should be sold. Fifteen couple of the Newmarket and Thurlow hounds went to Brent Pelham and the other fifteen couple elsewhere. A similar reduction was made in the Puckeridge pack with the proviso that in the event of any separation at any future date fifteen couple of hounds should be returned by Captain Barclay to the Thurlow.

It was agreed that the new country be hunted four days a week. Prior to the amalgamation, the Puckeridge had normally hunted on Mondays, Wednesdays and Saturdays, while the Newmarket and Thurlow had hunted on Mondays and Thursdays. Under the new arrangements the Puckeridge end of the country was to be hunted on Wednesdays, Saturdays and alternate Mondays, and the Thurlow end on Thursdays and alternate Mondays. The hounds were to be hunted by Captain Barclay on three days a week and by Ned Paxton on one, with two packs hunting on Boxing Day. The guarantee was to be £10000.

It was a happy augury for the combined hunts that the first season of 1970–1 was an exceptionally good one. The number of days hunted was one hundred and two, with only eight stopped. Thirty brace of foxes were killed and twenty-nine and a half brace run to ground. In February there was one point of six and a half miles and another of eight and a half miles.* Altogether it was a very good beginning. With a working account of £10235 costs of the combined hunts, with much improved sport, were considerably reduced compared with the previous combined expenditure.

The 1971–2 season again produced some excellent sport.† Once more the combination of the two hunts proved itself to be a happy union. The season also saw an interesting exercise in public relations with an experiment directed by the Game Conservancy to check the effects of drawing a covert four days before shooting, instead of waiting until after it had been shot. The results were a triumph for those who claimed there would be no effect on the shooting.

On 20 November Captain Barclay drew Lophams Wood of thirty acres without finding a fox, but keeping hounds in the covert for the best part of an hour. Four days later he was one of the line of beaters driving pheasants over the guns and with Mr Terence Blank, scientist to the Game Conservancy, making a

*See Appendix, page 179.
†See Appendix, page 180.

test count. It was agreed that the effects seemed to be negligible. The guns shot within six of the previous year's bag and commented that they could see no difference, as did the head keeper. Furthermore, a fox which the keepers had confidently expected to see on the day of the hunt was driven out of the covert in the middle of the shoot. Small wonder that the hunt's annual gamekeepers' dinner is a well-attended event or that harmony prevails between the varied sports in the country, unlike the scene at the turn of the century.

With gathering inflation the guarantee was raised in the 1972–3 season to £12000, but even so it was soon to prove inadequate in the face of steadily spiralling costs. There was some good sport,* despite it being one of the driest years on record, but the whole season was shadowed by the tragic death in December of Mrs C. G. E. Barclay, joint Master with her husband since 1963. The entire hunt's sympathy went out to Captain C. G. E. Barclay and his family in their loss.

Although there was some good sport,† the 1973–4 season was a disappointing one owing to generally bad scenting conditions with only twenty-five brace of foxes killed and eighteen brace run to ground. The following season of 1974–5, however, was a good one,‡ with twenty-seven and a half brace killed and twenty-four and a half brace run to ground. Sadly, this was Ned Paxton's last season as kennel huntsman and he retired after fifty-one years in hunt service and thirty-nine years with the Puckeridge and the Puckeridge and Thurlow, save for his war service. N. Stubbings, the first whip, also left that season to go as huntsman to the Radnor and West Hereford. They were replaced by R. Quarmby from the Hampshire hunt as kennel huntsman and first whip and M. Ashton, also from the Hampshire hunt, as second whip.

During the 1975–6 season Captain C. G. E. Barclay hunted the bitch pack two days a week and Mr E. H. Vestey and R. Quarmby hunted the dog hounds. It is pleasant to record that there was some good sport§ with an outstanding nine-mile point on 4 December 1975;‡ as good a hunt as any in their history. For the 1976–7 season the Masters and hunt staff remain unchanged, but galloping inflation inevitably has had its effects. The hunting days are to be reduced to three days a week, Mondays, Thursdays and Saturdays, with as many Wednesdays as possible as bye-days. The guarantee has been raised to £15000.

Despite all the odds, despite fiercely spiralling inflation, enormously high costs of fodder, the looming threat of rabies in foxes, the enormous encroach-

*See Appendix, page 180.
†See Appendix, pages 180–1.
‡See Appendix, page 181.
§See Appendix, page 182.

ment of new towns, threats of airfields, motorways or reservoirs, somehow the Puckeridge and Thurlow have managed to survive and to show sport. There may be cause for much heart-burning and despondency amongst even their most ardent supporters at times, but in one form or another the hunt will continue to survive. It is a matter of pride that it should do so.

The sense of continuity in the countryside is too great to allow wars, revolutions, racing inflation, or other incidentals to interfere with it. The Webbs were founder members of the Thurlow Hunt Club in 1858 and almost certainly in 1827, or thereabouts, though no records now remain. There was probably a Barclay at Newmarket in 1605, newly arrived with King James I and VI. Yet more important even than the support of the farmers is the support of the ordinary country people. Those like Albert Williams, now friend and stud groom to Mr Edmund Vestey, whom he encouraged to ride and take an interest in horses and hunting as a boy, are the people on whom in the end the continuance of hunting depends. As long as they too are behind it, the Puckeridge and Thurlow will continue to gallop across the countryside to the sound of hounds and horn.

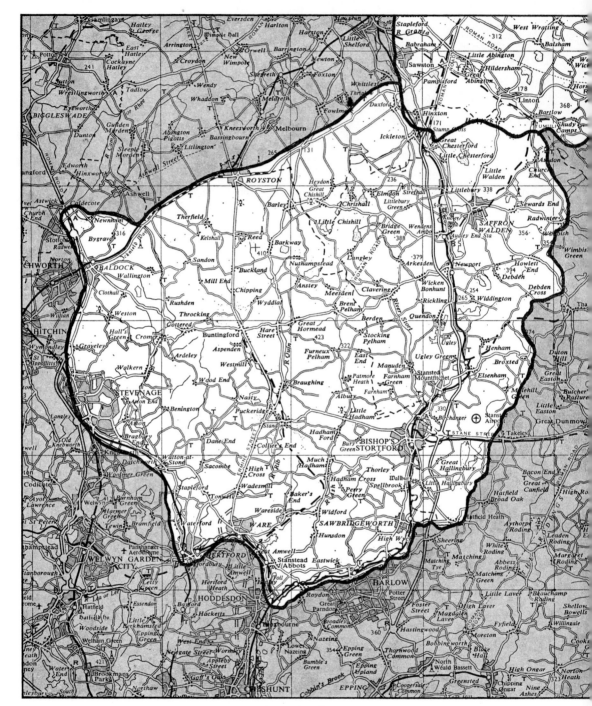

The Puckeridge country

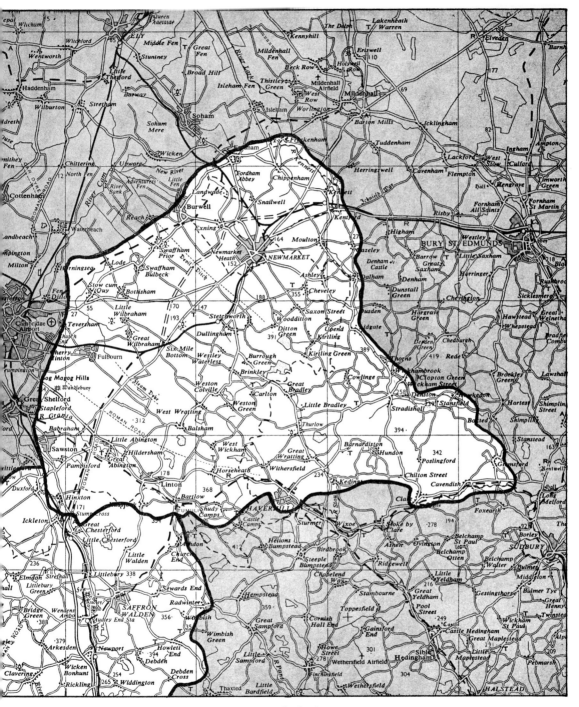

The Newmarket and Thurlow country

SCALE: ABOUT ONE INCH TO THREE AND A HALF MILES

Appendix

Extracts from the diaries of the Newmarket and Thurlow, Puckeridge, and Puckeridge and Thurlow hunts

1838–1975

The Newmarket and Thurlow Hunt Diaries

1875–80 season   *Master:* MR JOHN JOSSELYN
From *British Hunts and Huntsmen* (1908), an account of a meet with the
Suffolk hunt

Meet at Brinkley Hall, find at Weston Colville, close to the Mill, they ran to West Milton, then right handed to Westley Wood, through Brinkley, to Dullingham, on to Marmions and Boxfield, to Ditton Park, where he tried the 'earths' in vain, then on to Lucy Wood and back to Ditton Park. The pace up to this was extremely fast. They then went away for Pickmore Wood and Stetchworth to Devil's Ditch, the fox going to ground just in front of hounds and saving his brush by a few yards only. Time 1 hour 50 minutes, over a nine mile point, but as hounds ran fifteen miles.

1880–1 season   *Master:* SIR E. WALTER GREENE
From Mr Thomas Purkis's diary

Feb. 24th.   Met the Suffolk at Brinkley. Drew Weston's blank. Found at Allington Hill, had quick 25 minutes by Stechworth on the race course where we lost him. Found second Fox at Hare Park ran him up wind for 30 minutes by Stetchworth and killed him in the Devil's Ditch close to the race course. Rode Baroness. Very hard day.

1882–3 season   *Master:* SIR E. WALTER GREENE

March 1st.   Met the Suffolk at Bradley Oak. Found a fox at Trundley. Ran towards Lords Fields, when nearly there changed onto a vixen and she ran to ground in a drain. Found a second fox at Lophams. Ran very fast across Temple End up Abbacey when we checked for about three minutes and the pack divided, however three couple of hounds stuck to the hunted fox and took him a ring round to the Wratting to Thurlow road back again to Abbacey, dead beat when he stole out and we ran him nearly all the way in view across towards Haverhill where we killed him close to the back of the town. Time about 40 minutes without a check. Rode Duchess, who went wonderfully well.

1883–4 season   *Master:* MR BROWNE
From Mr Thomas Purkis's diary

Dec. 1st.   Met the Suffolk (Mr. Browne's) at Dalham Hall. Found a rare old fox there, who took us a ring a little over an hour to ground at Ousden but he was a very long way in front so the scent was not very good, however he was too hot to remain long undergound when the hounds got away close to him and ran very fast for another 1 hr $\frac{1}{2}$ when he could go no further and we ran into him close to Stansfield Church. Time from find to finish 2$\frac{1}{2}$ hours. Very good run.

1884–5 season   *Master:* MR JAMES GARDNER
From Mr Thomas Purkis's diary

Met the Thurlow at Brinkley. Found a fox then ran across to Weston and back round to Wratting where we lost him. Time 35 min. Found 2nd fox at Marmers Grove, ran through Widghams by Bradley Park nearly to Branches then bore to the right through Trundley right over to Kedington within a few fields of Lords Fields then round nearly to Hundon where we killed this grand fox. Time one hour and forty minutes. Rode Vixen. A clipping day.

1886–7 season   *Master:* MR JAMES GARDNER
From Mr Thomas Purkis's diary

Dec. 9.   Met The Thurlow at Brinkley. Found a good fox there which took us through Boro Green across to Marmers then on to Ditton Park, Ten Wood and Widghams where he beat us, time 50 minutes. Found 2nd fox close to Six Mile Bottom and raced him up to Willingham then round to Boro Green and rolled him over in the open. Time 35 minutes.

Dec. 16.   Met Thurlow at Withersfield. Found our first fox at Hall Wood. Ran very prettily across to Camps Park where he got to ground. 15 minutes. Drew Croats and Leys, Cadges blank. Found a good fox at North Wood, ran fast across to Hart Wood through Carlton on to Weston across to Brinkley nearly down to Six Mile Bottom then back to ground at Brinkley. We changed foxes at Weston. Time 1 hour and 20 minutes. Very good day. Rode Lancer went well.

1887–8 season   *Master:* MR JAMES GARDNER
From Mr Thomas Purkis's diary

Dec. 1.   Met The Thurlow at Cowlinge. Found a good fox at Trundley. Ran through Wadgells across to Ditton Park and then to ground at Lucy Wood. time 1 hour. Found 2nd fox at Cheveley Green. Ran a ring for 25 minutes and killed him where they found him. Rode Lancer.

Dec. 5.   Met The Thurlow at Brinkley. Found our first fox at Brinkley. Ran across to the Severals at Wratting where we lost him; found 2nd fox at Weston, ran fast up to Lophams across to Widghams and after running round the woodlands broke away for Brinkley where we ran into him just at dusk. Time 1 hour and 15 minutes. Rode Lancer.

1891–2 season   *Master:* CAPTAIN J. GORDON MILLER

March 17.   Met the Thurlow at Hawkedon. Found at King's Wood, ran across nearly up to Sparrow Grove in the Suffolk country and killed. Found 2nd fox at Appleacre, ran through Chipley then across the brook through Slaters Groves and killed him in Debden Rectory. Very good day. Rode Cracksman.

1895–6 season   *Master:* MR EDWARD MOLYNEUX

January 6.   Met The Thurlow at 'Hundon Plow'. Found at Clare Osiers, ran very fast to ground at Garrards Drain. Time 30 minutes. Bolted him and ran very quick back to Kings Wood where he doubled back by some buildings and we lost him. Drew Kings Wood, Long Wood and Chipley blank, found at Appleacre drain, ran very fast through Chipley and Hillybud through Denston Park when he doubled back through Hollybud and Chipley on straight for Lords Fields, which he skirted then on towards Sturmer Mere when he ran us out of scent and as it was getting dark we gave it up. Time 1 hr 1 min. 'A Good days Sport' Rode Reindeer.

1896–7 season   *Master:* MR W. H. PEMBERTON-BARNES
From Mr Thomas Purkis's diary

Oct. 22.   Met The Thurlow at Pampisford Hall. Found in the cover against the Brewery, ran with a good scent through the Hall grounds by Pampisford Station right handed up to Hildersham Wood by Catley when he tried the drain but too much water for him so he went on by Hadstock Wood to Nunn Wood, pointing for Great Hales when they ran into him a field from Nunn Wood. Time 50 minutes from find, 45 minutes in the open, a good run. Rode Reindeer.

Nov. 23.   Met The Thurlow at Thurlow Common, drew Lophams and Carlton blank, found a good fox at Hart Wood, ran very fast up to Northwood then through Cadges and Over Wood across the Horseheath Road on by Prenns Farm and to Liddigates when we had a check close to Bumpstead. Got on him again and raced across to Bendysh then through Little Bendysh when the hounds could only show a faint line in the direction of Tyrall Springs, but as it was getting late we gave up. Time 1 hour to first check, 30 minutes from then to Bendysh. This was a great run but lacked only blood to make it A.1. Rode Mercia.

From Mr Reginald Hicks's diary

Dec. 10th.   [A meet at Stradishall Park]. Found in Denston Park and had a sharp spin of about 10 minutes to ground in Appleacre Wood. Chipley Wood and one or two more blank. Found in Cavendish Easty and had a ripping run to Reed Grove. 5 mile point through Stansfield, North Wood etc. Very good day.

Jan. 24th.   Met The Thurlow at Hawkeden Green, bolted a brace of foxes from Garrett drain, ran one across Boxted then along the bottom to Stanstead Big Wood then a lot of covers to

Shimpling and lost him close to Alpheton Wood. A nice hunting run, time 1 hr 30 mins. Found 2nd fox at King's Wood, ran across to Long Wood then back thro' Kings along the bottom by Hermitage Farm nearly to Cavendish village, then he bore up hill for a time but finally crossed the river close to Glemsford Station with hounds hunting up to him the pace improved and we drove him along and ran into him at Foxsmith. Time 1 hr 15 mins. A rare good days sport. Rode Reindeer.

1897–8 season *Master:* MR W. H. PEMBERTON-BARNES

Nov. 25. Met The Thurlow at Hinxton Grange, found in Mr. Cooke's plantation, ran with a burning scent down to railway crossing then back and across to plantation against road when he got headed again so the hounds killed him, an old fox. Found 2nd fox at Brabaham Ash Grounds, raced him out the Stapleford end up on Gog Magog, nearly to Shelford when he got headed across the Cambridge road through the plantation nearest Cambridge and then turned right handed again back for Gog Magog and ran from scent to view and killed close to the Roman road. East wind, very cold, Rode Reindeer.

1899–1900 season *Master:* MR W. H. PEMBERTON-BARNES

Nov. 9. Met The Thurlow at West Wickham, found an old fox at Balsham, ran thro' Borley round by King's Hill, across Hildersham big field, round back to Chilfords and killed. Then found at Horseheath Lodge, ran quickly thro' Croats on thro' Northy up to Cardinal's Green on to Limbus then turned right handed through Barsey Groves across to Haverhill Hazel Stubs Farm when he beat us, laid up I think. 3rd fox found at Liddigates which is neutral this season ran with a rare scent across nearly to Helions Bumpstead then left handed towards Steeple Bumpstead, then Sturmers Groves on over the railway round by Mr. Gurteen's house back over the line and killed against Sturmer's Hall. 1st run 35 mins. 2nd run 50 mins. 3rd run 1 hr 15 mins. A rare good day's sport. Rode Reindeer.

1900–1 season *Master:* MR W. H. PEMBERTON-BARNES
From Mr Thomas Purkis's diary

March 1. Met The Thurlow at Bradley Fox. Found a brace of foxes at Hart Wood. Ran with a poorish scent up wind through Lophams across to North Wood then through the Lawn and Over Woods and lost close to Hare Wood. I heard afterwards our fox went on over the Withersfield road towards Horseheath. Time 35 minutes. Then drew Rands and Wratting Park. Found a fox at Weston. Ran out as if for Carlton then turned left-handed round by Willingham Green back through both woods out over the brook across the North Wood quick, through to Littley when we got a holloa up to the Lawns, Over and Hare Wood when he doubled back with hounds close at him through Over Wood on to Cadges then through North Wood across the open to Thurlow Park Groves down to Little Thurlow Hall and killed him in the Garden opposite the Park Gates. Time 1 hr 30 minutes. Rode Reindeer.

1901–2 season   *Master:* CAPTAIN C. BROOK
From Mr Thomas Purkis's diary

Jan. 9.   Met The Thurlow at Withersfield: drew Liddigates and Camps Park and Northy blank. Found a brace at the Croats and ran with a good scent up to Borley where several foxes were on foot and we changed and ran through Balsham across by Wratting Mill, thro' Rands over the road to Leys Wood then thro' the Lawns, leaving Littley just on the left over the hill nearly to Thurlow Mill then along the bottom to Thurlow Park thro' Hart Wood on to Carlton when we no doubt changed again, over the road against Sipsey Bridge through both Widghams on to Ten Wood, the fox went on to Ditton Park, but had to stop hounds as it was getting dark. Very hard day for hounds and horses. Time 3 hours from finding fox at Croats to whipping off. Time from Borley to Hart Wood 1 hour and 30 minutes on one fox. Rode Reindeer.

1902–3 season   *Master:* REVEREND SIR WILLIAM HYDE-PARKER, BT.
From a newspaper account of a meet on 1 December 1902

Fox-hunting on the Suffolk-Cambs Border. Two Packs hunt a fox. On Monday a rather unusual incident occurred in fox-hunting. The Puckeridge Hounds, whilst running a fox from Chesterford Park were joined by the Thurlow Foxhounds also running from Pampisford. The two packs settled down and after half an hour's nice hunt ran their fox into Linton Town. Mr. E. Barclay being the senior Master, handled both packs, whilst Sir W. Hyde-Parker, good sportsman as he is, insisted on taking a back seat. The two packs 'broke up' their fox in the school yard of Linton much to the delight of the rising generation. During a critical part of the run one couple of hounds carried the line of the fox without any hesitation with great speed and dash through several fields full of hares. To these hounds the credit of handling their fox belongs as far as I could see honours were divided between the Puckeridge and Thurlow. We hope the effect of this days sport will induce the Puckeridge to hunt the Walden country on Wednesday as before to avoid clashing and also to give residents a chance to hunt with both packs. As it now stands we feel; How happy would we be with either
Were t'other dear charmer away.

1903–4 season   *Master:* REVEREND SIR WILLIAM HYDE-PARKER, BT
From Mr Thomas Purkis's diary

Jan. 21st.   Met The Thurlow at Bradley Fox. Drew Carlton Wood blank. Found in a field next Hart Wood on Long's land, ran very fast thro' Hart across the Park nearly up to Northwood, then turned right handed by Woodman Spare the Tree up to Hart across the Park to the Walks, where Hounds overran him in the Brook and we lost him. Found 2nd Fox at Gover's Grove ran very fast up wind to Hart when Hounds divided (7½ couple coming away on to the Walks which I followed) the remainder ran at a great pace through Carlton on to Sparrow Grove, Base Field and Marmers then left handed nearly to Brinkley where they lost. A rare good day's sport. Rode Molly.

1905–6 season *Master:* REVEREND SIR WILLIAM HYDE-PARKER, BT
From Mr Thomas Purkis's diary

Feb. 19th. Met The Thurlow at Hawkedon Green. Goddard hunting Hounds. Drew the Bottoms, Horton Grove and Northy blank. Found a fox on a pollard Oak in Meadow between Northy and Easty. Ran with a good scent over the Bottoms up the Hill to Boxted through the Park and over the river against the house cover up the hill on to Stanstead Big Wood on to Kentwell covers where the first real check occurred. Time to here 40 minutes. Then on through the other covers left handed as if for Alpheton then sharp right handed to ground in the big drain in Kentwell Park, time 1 hour. This was a real good run. Came back and drew Easty, Kings, Long Wood and Shadow Bush blank, also Chipley, Appleacre and Hollybud, but a man here told me there was a fox up a tree in Denston Park, so after drawing the Ashdon Plantation we came and I whipped him down. Hounds soon were on his line and hunted towards Boxted Lodge then turned down wind left handed and ran at a great pace through Appleacre and Chipley leaving Long Wood on the right straight through Northy over the Bottoms up the hill to Boxted where we reluctantly had to stop Hounds as it was getting dark. Hounds did not reach Kennels until 8.0 and I did not get home until 9.20. A real good day's sport and hard day for horses. Rode Reindeer.

1906–7 season *Master:* MR RICHARD BOWER
From Mr Reginald Hicks's diary

Nov. 5th. Met The Newmarket and Thurlow at Carlton School. Found at Weston and ran down past Severals, across as if for Brinkley. Lost him owing I fancy to false information. Came back and found again at Weston and killed him as he was headed in all directions. Found again at Hillcroft and ran down past the Severals, across Mr. Foot's Middle bit and then sharp back past Mr. Foot's house and back to Hillcroft where it is possible hounds may have killed him but can't say for certain. Found again in Rands Wood and had a capital gallop going via Mr. Collin's farm and the Lawn Wood across to Littley Wood down into Withersfield Village and across the Haverhill Line down to Withersfield Siding and up to Mr. Gurteens covert where they were shooting and we had to give it up, tho' some people were still holloaing a fox after all the field had gone home. A Capital day's sport. Rode the Mare 1st and Snob 2nd.

1907–8 season *Master:* MR RICHARD BOWER
From *The Field*, an account of a meet on 21 November 1906

Newmarket & Thurlow:
This pack, which is now being managed by Mr. Richard Bower of Stradishall Place, Suffolk, recorded a brilliant gallop in the evening of Nov. 21st. Finding in Cavendish Easty Wood, it was soon evident there was a rare scent for hounds came out of covert right on top of their fox and with a famous cry headed for Northy Wood. A few minutes galloping led to this covert and almost directly forrard away was heard on the other side. Racing through the field found hounds streaming on, pointing for Glemsford; but luckily for some of the stragglers the fox

must have been headed by a labourer for he took a turn to the left, which followers were quick to take advantage of, and bore away for Boxted. Going quickly through these Suffolk coverts the fox led down into the valley below Horsted Mill. Forrard on was still the cry and though there were many signs of bellows to mend the field soon found themselves at Stanstead Big Wood, where they were obliged to stop as it was nearly dark, hounds having travelled about nine miles and made about a seven mile point in fifty five minutes.

From Mr Purkis's diary, an eight-mile point

Feb. 6.   Met The Thurlow at Withersfield. Drew Howe Wood blank. Found a leash at North Wood, ran the selected one very fast across to Hart then out by Bradley Hall on up to Bedfords Grove then left handed over the road to Bradley Park Wood on to Branches when we viewed him and he broke as if for Cowlinge but after going one field headed back through the Park down to the Hulling Road when Hounds got a view and raced him back and killed in the Garden at Thompson's Farm. Then trotted back to Hart and found a travelling fox which went away some few minutes before we got to him as we could make nothing of it. Then drew Cadges blank, found a leash in the Lawn, ran across to Over but he would not leave for some time then ran back through the Lawn across to North out towards Weston but circled back to North where I left them as it was 5.00. Rode Canada.

March 30th.   Met The Thurlow at Worstead Lodge. Drew the Cabbages on Dotterell and found a rare good fox. Got away on his back, ran over the London Road against Havon Dyke, down to within a field of Fulbourne Covers, then circled back over the London Road across to Hicks Gorse then on over Lark Hall Heath up Tilbrooke's Plantation straight away to Underwood Hall into Dullingham Park where he doubled back across by Dullingham Station over the open to the July Course where we were obliged to stop hounds on account of the King's brood mares. Time 2 hours. Hard luck on Master and hounds. Came on to Borough Green Park Wood but did not find. Rode Reindeer.

1908–9 season   *Master:* MR RICHARD BOWER
From a newspaper report

December 3rd: Newmarket and Thurlow Hounds:
In spite of the counter attraction of a meet of the Staghounds at Hargrave there was a good muster at Hawkedon Green on Thursday when Mr. Bower gave his followers one of the best days I have seen with foxhounds for a long time, the evening gallop from Stradishall being of exceptional merit.

Our first fox was found in Northy Wood and that there was a scent was quickly apparent as hounds forced him quickly through Houghton Grove and up the hill to Finstead End. Boxted was evidently his point, but he was unfortunately headed and turned to the right. After running nearly to Glemsford he swung still more to the right and beat hounds in Cavendish Easty after a good run of forty minutes from wood to wood.

Hounds came away from King's Wood on a faint line and going back to Northy found again, but after a ringing hunt of about forty five minutes were run out of scent. Mr. Bower trotted on to Stradishall for an evening fox and at 3.30 23 started on a gallop from Stradishall Plantation, which ended at 4 o'clock in the death the fox at Spring Wood. Getting away on good terms hounds were very close to the fox before he got to New England. Finding little respite here, he broke on the Lidgate side and pointed straight for Ousden, but finding the pace too hot, he turned right handed when opposite Spring Wood where hounds killed him after a really first class gallop of thirty minutes.

Among the few who saw the finish of this smart run were the Master and his Whips, Miss A. Bower, Miss S. Bower, Messrs. R. Hicks, E. Powles, H. W. Claughton, Frink, D. King and about six others. The failing light must be my excuse for not recording their names.

From Mr Thomas Purkis's diary

Jan. 4th.   Met The Thurlow at Thurlow Crown. Drew Trundley first and just as we got to the cover a fox from the adjoining field went into the cover. We got on his line and he took us round the cover with not much scent and out towards Abbacey but could not carry it further than the Thurlow Meadows where he got headed and we lost; Then drew Hart and Lophams blank. Bolted a fox from the Island drain, ran at a great pace up wind through the Grove and Grove's Plantation leaving North Wood, Cadges and the Lawn on our left, through the narrow part of Over Wood down to the Haverhill Road where he no doubt got headed. This was the first check, time here 40 minutes. He now turned back up to Hare Wood through which he went and on by Wickham Church to ground at Streetly Hall Chalk Pit. A very nice hunt of 1 hour and five minutes. Rode Reindeer.

1909–10 season   *Master:* MR RICHARD BOWER
From Mr Thomas Purkis's diary

Dec. 2nd.   Met the Thurlow at Thurlow Crown, found 1st fox in the Old Oak at Little Thurlow Park, ran into the thick Grove then back across the Park to Hart Wood, broke the Carlton end across to Lophams Hall then up nearly to the place where he was found. No doubt went to Carlton Wood but hounds got on the line of no doubt a disturbed fox which they took across to Temple End, when we heard a tired fox was going into the Walks. Hounds hunted by the Hall along to the Earths in the Brook, where they threw up and upon looking in the Ivy Tree the fox jumped down and Hounds ran him straight thro' Hart over the Bradley Brook pointing for Bradley Park then turned right handed, through Bedford's Grove by Wadgell's on towards Thurlow, then left handed up the valley nearly to Abbacey then right handed by Thurlow Vicarage across to Hart where he got to ground. First run 1 hr. second 1 hr 10 minutes. The first 45 minutes without a check. Rode Reindeer.

1910–11 season   *Master:* COLONEL E. DEACON
From Mr Thomas Purkis's diary

Jan. 5.   Met The Thurlow at Little Thurlow Park Gates. Drew Trundley, found at once with rare cry took him round the cover twice then away to Wadgells almost in view, then on towards Stradishall but his heart failed him when he got as far as Bradley Oak as Hounds got a view and raced him back by Wadgells Hall through Wadgells on to Trundley where they killed. Time 25 minutes. Found 2nd fox at Over Wood, ran prettily through Lawn and Littley on over the Withersfield Road up to Abbacey where he beat us. Drew North March and gave up.

Claude rode Digby. I rode Reindeer for the last time as he was taken ill during the night although he fed well when he reached home and died on Saturday morning. Poor old dear, as fine a horse and sensible as any one could wish to ride, no day too long, and there never was a horse fonder of hunting. I think I rode him 18 seasons and only had two falls neither of which were over fences and no fault of his. (A sad blow.)

1911–12 season   *Master:* COLONEL E. DEACON
From Mr Thomas Purkis's diary

Nov. 9. Met The Thurlow at Clare. Found directly in The Osiers; ran at a good pace by Houghton Hall to Cavendish Hall, then bore left handed to within a field of Easty when we had a long check, then left handed by King's Wood down to Maddever's Drain, which was blocked, through North and Stansfield Hall Wood across to Thurston Park, then right handed nearly to Boxted but turned to the left again over the river close to Somerton Hall over the hill nearly to Hartest and killed him in the valley just before reaching Brockley. An old fox and a good hunting run of $1\frac{1}{2}$ hours. 8 miles point. Did not find again, Rode Jane.

Dec. 29th. Met The Thurlow at Clare. Found directly in The Osiers: ran with a good scent up the Hill by Houghton Hall and Cavendish Hall then on by Blacklands across the open towards Stansted, but ran into him just the other side of Glemsford. Time 45 minutes. Then drew Easty, King's and Long Wood blank, then went back to Clare Osiers, found again; ran fast across the meadows towards Poslingford then right handed leaving King's Wood and Easty on the left straight by Glemsford into Boxted Park when he beat us. Time 40 minutes and a five mile point. A real good day. Lovely weather. Rode Jane.

Jan. 25th. Met The Thurlow at Stetchworth; found a brace in the ditch at once. Ran out by the Mansion to Marmers Grove left handed to come at the top of the ditch when hounds came away in view; ran across to Ditton Park round the cover once and broke the Stetchworth side, turning right handed nearly to Lucy Wood, then left handed by Wooditton by Churnlet Green over the Dalham Road and killed in a bullock yard at Ashley. 1 hour 20 minutes. Came back to Little Widghams, found a leash of foxes, ran a great pace through Ten Wood, Ditton Park Wood nearly to Lucy Wood lefthanded by Wooditton to Cheveley Park where he ran us out of scent. 50 minutes. A real good day. Only three of us got away with the last fox. Rode Peter.

March 18. Met The Thurlow at Clare; found at once in The Osiers; ran very fast to Stansfield back by Cavendish Northy to Easty, by King's to Chipley where they got up to him in a hedge and ran very fast back to Stansfield, back to Leywood where they changed and ran very hard leaving Easty on the right to the back of Glemsford and then down to Boxted where they killed him in the woodshed. Hounds were running nearly 3 hours and ran about 30 miles. Rode Peter.

1912–13 season *Master:* MR REGINALD S. HICKS
From newspaper accounts of meets held on 12 and 16 December 1912

On December 12th the Newmarket and Thurlow Foxhounds met at Thurlow Crown. Wadgell's was first tried and a brace of foxes were soon on foot in Trundley. Breaking on the Thurlow side they crossed the river. Hounds stuck to the one that went nearly to Abbacey, but getting headed turned back to Trundley where they lost him. A fresh fox jumped up just outside Trundley and hounds hunted him prettily up to Abbacey and then over the Withersfield road to Norney Plantation; away at the bottom end to the back of Haverhill leaving Wilsey on the left, they sunk the hill and crossed the river at Sturmer to the East Essex country; then over the Colne Valley line, through Sturmer Groves to Bumpstead, where hounds threw up at the brook at the lower end of Moynes Park. The fox was probably drowned in trying to cross the brook which was much swollen as he was seen just in front of hounds after leaving Sturmer Groves. Time 1 hour 30 minutes.

On December 16th hounds met at Hundon Village. After drawing Clare Osiers and King's Wood, Long Wood was tried and a good fox soon broke. Hounds ran nicely across to Northy; leaving Houghton Grove on the left, he ran along the gully to Duck's Hall Plantation, where they got close to him, and ran fast by Glemsford Hill to Boxted, by the Hall, to Bridle Gate Plantation where he was headed. Turning back by the Hall he ran through the Octagon Groves to Thurston Park Wood; from there hounds ran very fast across to and through Houghton Grove and Cavendish Northy; they fairly raced from there to King's Wood, and out on the Clare side; catching a view of him hounds coursed him back to the wood, and after racing him round the cover twice, he again broke away on the Clare side and hounds caught him in Bally Green Farm. Time 2 hours.

1913–14 season *Master:* MAJOR A. C. JAFFE
From a newspaper account (undated)

The Newmarket and Thurlow Foxhounds.

On Monday the Newmarket and Thurlow Foxhounds met at Linton Swan. It was a nice still morning with just a nip of frost in the air. The Master first drew the Rivey, but not finding went on to Borley Wood where a good fox was soon on foot. Breaking at once he crossed the Worsted Road, went through the top end of Balsham Wood and out over the Wickham road, through Bushey Park straight on through West Wratting Park to the Weston covers; hounds pushed him through those, and up the hill to Brinkley Wood and straight through out on the Westley side; leaving Underwood Hall on the right he sunk the valley close to Dullingham Station where he beat us. This was a seven and a half mile point. Time one hour, the first forty minutes without a check. We next went back to Brinkley. Hounds could hardly own to a fox, which was bolted from the Big Wood drain; he seemed perfectly scentless. The Master then decided to try Rands Wood. Finding at once he broke on the Yen Hall side and crossed the road above Wickham village, through Leys Wood. Hounds were hunting with a rare cry and took him through Over Wood and Lawn Wood; leaving Littley on the right, he entered North Wood where he got to ground just in front of hounds after twenty five minutes without a check.

From Mr Thomas Purkis's diary

Feb. 16th. Met The Thurlow at Withersfield. Drew Barsey Groves; a fox stole away from the top Grove while we were trying the Stick Heap in Mastersons Grove, but we got a holloa and hunted up to Liddigates out towards Bumpstead but the fox had got a long start and kept twisiting about. We hunted slowly on to Ballast Wood into Bowes Hall Park, where a hound 'Wildfire' dropped down dead evidently posioned, so we drew the hounds away as soon as possible. We then drew Camps Park blank except Hounds marked a fox in a tree, but we could not get him out and went on to Northy Grove; bolted a fox from the Earth which Hounds settled to at once, running him over the railway as if for Camps Park but running left handed over the road against Grange Farm and soon turned left handed over the railway again when Hounds increased the pace, running up to and through Hare Wood and Over Wood and Lawn Wood by Cadges up to North Wood where he tried the earth, but being blocked ran straight to Weston to ground in the earth; time to this point 45 minutes and hounds had never been touched since leaving Northy Grove and the pace all the way was a cracker. Point five miles. We bolted him and ran across to the top Wood over to Hill Crofts across nearly to Rands then left handed across Wratting Common over the road as if for Leys Wood but his bolt was shot and he turned short to Cadges where they killed this good fox. He was 3 or 4 years old. This was a grand hunt and was quite 12 miles as Hounds ran. Time altogether 1 hr and 10 minutes. Rode May-Be.

1914–15 season *Master:* MAJOR A. C. JAFFE
From Mr Thomas Purkis's diary

March 11th. Met The Thurlow at Bartlow. Drew Mr. Brocklebank's New Farm Plantation, found directly After one turn round the cover he broke the South side with Hounds close at him and ran at a great pace across Nunns Wood through the other Groves to within a field of Grimditch when he turned right handed and headed back to Mitchell's Grove across the open to Linton Mill, there turned to the right and ran straight for Bartlow Pit, but he was headed and went over the railroad into the Small Plantation dead beat, but altho' he was seen just before hounds entered we lost him. I think he swam down the river as hounds could never carry a line out. Then drew Chesterford Common and Hildersham and gave up. A good day's sport as the run was very fast, especially the first 30 mins. Time 1 hr 15 mins. Rode Winifred.

1915–16 season *Master:* MR C. F. RYDER
From Mr Thomas Purkis's diary

Dec. 23. Met The Thurlow at Withersfield Siding. Drew Liddigates blank, found an outlier in Smiths Fruit Plantation, ran over the Bumpstead road straight to Big Bendysh when he got to ground in sight of the pack. Found 2nd fox at Northy Drain, ran at a great pace to Horseheath Lodge parallel to Wean road to the Roman Road up to the Gog when he got headed and turned across Chilfords nearly to Rivey then across Greenditch up to the Keepers House in Borley down to Horseheath Lodge Road and back towards Wood Lane when we lost as there was a storm coming on. I heard afterwards this fox was seen dead beat in Wood Lane. Hard luck on Hounds. Found 3rd fox in Borley after one turn round the cover, broke over the Roman Road and ran at a great pace through Balsham Wood over Pearson's Farm up to within a field of Rands without a check then across the road over Collin's Farm where fresh fox jumped up. Got Hounds back and hunted on to North Wood and gave up. A real good day. Rode Topsy.

Jan. 29th. [Claude Purkis hunting hounds] Met The Thurlow at Bartlow (a nice hunting morning slight drizzle of rain Wind S.E. but mild) Drew Brocklebank's covers blank, found a brace in Mitchell's Groves, ran one across to Shadwell Wood on to Little Hales at a great pace over the Gully up towards Goldstones Farm over the Radwinter Road and pulled him down in the open when going for Langley Wood. 25 minutes of the best! Then came back to Borley, found directly, ran at a great pace up alongside Balsham Wood by Streetly Chalk Pit straight for Hare Wood, ran down the middle drive half way then across to Over through the narrow part over the open until he reached Cadges through which he crossed and pointed as if for Weston; then bore right handed missing North Wood across Weston Wood rough Fields, when I fancy we changed but ran straight on through Gover's Grove on to Lophams under Thurlow grove to the Island when we though he got to ground; bolted him or another, ran through Hart on to Bradley Village across Mr. Long's Ley Meadow up to Bradley Park. Here there was a brace in front of hounds. The body of the pack stuck to a line towards Wadgells at which cover we stopped hounds as the horses had had quite enough and all the field had given up except Mr. D. Webb who joined in when we crossed his Farm. Claude hunted Hounds and killed his first Fox. This was a great day's sport, the run from Borley being the best I have seen for a long while as there was no check from Borley until we reached Thurlow Park. Time to this point 50 minutes, a distance of 7 mile point. Rode Winifred.

1916–17 season   *Master:* MR C. F. RYDER
From Mr Thomas Purkis's diary

Nov. 16. Met The Thurlow at Horseheath Mill; drew Borley first and found directly; ran across Chilfords and Deadman Hill to Dotterell Hall and lost. Found 2nd fox at Borley, ran across Wool Hall, then turned to the left across the Yale and, then turned left handed down the boundary hedge of Chilfords then right handed right across Borocks Farm where we got a view of him across Franklins Farms and Abington Grange over the London Road (where got another view) and old railway when he got headed and turned left handed to the Babraham covers that cross the road; here we got the first check owing to the fox making some funny work owing to his being headed, but the Hounds puzzled the line out and ran through the Babraham covers and along under Gog Magog over the Roman Road nearly to Fulbourne Asylum; then we got another view when he turned sharp to the left back over the Roman Road across the Golf Links through the Plantation on Kents Farm, over the Road and across the fields straight for Cambridge until we got to a field of Cabbage on Towlers Farm when he jumped up in the middle of the Pack, bolted through the hedge and gained a few yards;

but this good fox had shot his bolt as Hounds ran him in view back by Kents Farm and killed him just over the Cambridge main road. This was a great Hunt and a grand performance for the Hounds as it was all light land and lots of hares and although there was a good hunting scent, the high east wind caused the fox to keep dead down wind so they had to really hunt it. A grand old dog fox and I think the same that gave us several good hunts last year. I had his mask set up. A good 10 mile point, time 2 hrs. Rode Topsy.

Jan. 4th. Met The Thurlow at Cavendish; drew the Plantation against Cavendish Hall and the Gully up to Colts Hall blank; found in Easty ran slowly down Truggets Valley and lost, came on to Northy, found and ran up wind very fast to Chipley; he got headed here and turned back over Ships land straight for Long Wood, ran along the valley up to Easty out nearly to Glemsford then right handed over the river between them and Cavendish Station up to Pentlow Tower then bore to the right and ran into him in the open close to Otter Belchamp. This was a great hunt. 1 hr and 15 minutes. 7 mile point, but the fox made a lot of work after crossing the river; there was a strong west wind blowing. Rode Topsy. A very hard day for Hounds and Horses.

March 1st. Met The Thurlow at Three Ashes. Found 1st Fox at the Privet Cover. Ran very fast up wind towards Cowlinge Hall by Branches, leaving it on the right hand straight for Lucy Wood out through Kirtling Towers and killed in the open about a field this side of Cheveley Green Covers. Very fast hunt of 35 minutes; a six mile point. Came back and drew Clickety Appleacres, Fir Plantation, Hundon Thicks, Chipley, Hollybud and Denston Park covers blank; bolted a fox from Bowers Sand Pit Earth, ran up towards Blue Doors but he got headed and turned back towards Stradishall Place through the Sand Pit cover and into Denston Park up to Appleacre where I left them as it was five o'clock. Woodward stopped hounds just short of King's Wood. Rode Winifred.

1917–18 season   *Master:* Mr C. F. Ryder

From a newspaper report of a meet on 14 February 1918

The Newmarket and Thurlow Foxhounds
Meeting at Horseheath Mill on February 14th the Newmarket and Thurlow foxhounds had a real good day's sport. Drawing one or two covers without response, a move was made to Liddigates. Finding at once, hounds went away at the bottom end through Horsham Hall, over the Haverhill Road, as if for Sturmer Groves but bearing to the right, he pointed for Bumpstead Hall, crossed the road to the left of it and entered Ballast Wood, going straight through, he breasted the hill, as if for Spains Wood, but turning left handed entered Bower Wood Plantations, where he was headed, and the first and only check occurred Woodward getting hounds on the line again, he ran back through Ballast Wood, crossed the road and went straight to Hempstead Wood (in the Essex country). The hounds rattled him through this great cover with a beautiful cry and took him away at the bottom end, crossed the brook and ran past Mr. Ketteridge's Farm; leaving Helion Bumpstead Church on the right, he passed Olmstead Green, crossed the Camps Road by Drapers Farm, and again entered Liddigates; running straight through the cover he went by the same line as we started, by Horseham Hall, straight to Steeple Bumpstead (in the East Essex country). Running parallel to the river

135

for some little way, he crossed it opposite Rylands, went up the hill through Rylands Grove to Moyns Park by the Mansion, through the Big Cover when hounds were stopped as it was 5.40 and getting dark and horses were done. Hounds had been running continuously for 2 hours and 50 minutes and really deserved their fox. I afterwards heard that hounds changed foxes in the open against Olmsted Green as a dead beaten fox was seen in the meadow after hounds were gone; but anyhow hounds never checked. It was a great hunt, although circular, the greatest point being about six miles, but as hounds ran about twenty miles and they were running fast all the time.

1918–19 season   *Master:* Mr C. F. Ryder
From newspaper reports of meets on 10 and 13 March 1919

The Newmarket and Thurlow Hounds
The Newmarket and Thurlow Hounds have had an exceptionally good season and sport has been of a very high order since the frost. On Monday last (March 10th) after meeting at Clare, the Osiers were first drawn, but, not finding, a move was made to Long Wood and hounds were soon away on a good fox. Pointing for Stansfield village he turned to the right short of this and went through Cavendish Northey, then to King's Wood, on nearly to Poslingford, turning right handed across to Chipley Wood, through Appleacre, on to Fir Plantation, where, being headed, he turned back, leaving Chipley on the right, through Hollybud, into Denston Park. Getting headed again, he went through Appleacres out at the top end, over the Hundon Road by Mr. Savage's to Three Ashes, were hounds caught him after an hour and fifty five minutes.

On Thursday (March 13th) after meeting at Thurlow, Trundley was first drawn without result, but finding at once in Wadgells, hounds came away at a rare pace, turned to Trundley, out on the Wratting side by the Ganwick, over the Haverhill Road, leaving Barnardiston Church on the right, he entered Glass Wood away at the top end over the Hundon road to Broxted Lodge. Leaving the Privet Cover on his left, he ran the flat to Stradishall Church where the only check occurred. However, Woodward soon had them going again; leaving Stradishall Place on the left he entered Denston Park on by the Mansion. Crossing the road against the church he pointed as if for Wickhambrook, but hounds, getting a view of him, they rolled him over in the meadow against the Plumber's Arms, a six mile point. Fifty five minutes and hounds raced all the way. As they had run right out of the draw and horses had had enough hounds did not draw again.

1919–20 season   *Master:* Lord Wilton
From a newspaper account

Jan. 29th.   The Newmarket & Thurlow Foxhounds
A good sized field met these hounds at Withersfield Siding on Thursday. Northey Grove and Horseheath were first drawn, but were tenantless. However they found a good fox in Borley that was destined to show the best hunt that these hounds have had this season. Breaking at the keeper's house end, he went through Horseheath Lodge up the hill to the gravel pits

and on to Northey Grove. Over the railway line, leaving Camps Park to the right, the fox went through Camps Osiers up the hill through Barsey Groves as if for Liddigates, but turning short of this cover he crossed the railway just above Haverhill, by the rifle range into Northy Wood, through this cover, over the Wratting road, he pointed as if for the Withersfield covers, but turning right handed by the Thurlow road, hounds ran from scent to view and rolled him over just below Abbacey Wood. Time 1 hour and 30 minutes, the first 40 minutes without a check. The distance from Borley to where he turned back near Liddigates was eight miles and from there to where he was killed another four miles, but a very great deal further as hounds ran. It was the same fox the whole way. As hounds had run right out of the day's draw they did not draw again. Going home we heard that a couple of hounds had found and killed another fox in Northy Wood.

From a newspaper report of a meet on 12 February 1920

It was rather a blustery morning when these hounds met at Brinkley, but finding a fox in Weston Top Wood hounds settled down and hunted him at a good pace through the lower cover away at the bottom and to the plantation on the hill. Leaving Carlton Rectory on the left he crossed the road against Lopham's Hall, through Lopham's Wood to Hart Wood. He was headed when pointing for Little Thurlow and turned back to Great Bradley where he ran us out of scent.

Bolting a fox from the long drain at Hart Wood, he went up wind through the Grove, by Temple End to North Wood, through this cover and on to Littley where he turned down wind back through North Wood by Gover's Grove to Hart Wood, out by the kennels, Crossing the river by Little Thurlow Church he breasted the hill to Wadgells, straight through and by Wadgells Hall over the Stradishall Road to ground under a gateway just in front of hounds at Barnardiston Hall. A terrier was procured and he was bolted; hounds caught him in the moat opposite the Hall. Great credit is due both to Woodward and hounds as the plough was dry and quite hard on top in places and scent was consequently very catchy. Hounds must have been hunting their fox for an hour and a half. The longest point made during the hunt was from Littley to when they killed, which was a little over five miles, but a great deal of country was covered during the run.

1920–1 season *Joint Masters:* Mr C. F. Tonge and Colonel J. F. Ryder
From newspaper reports of meets on 27 and 31 January 1921

Successful Runs of Newmarket & Thurlow Hounds:
These hounds had a good day's sport on Thursday week (27th). Finding at Borley, they went away at a great pace by the Keeper's Hut end, over the Cambridge road, leaving Linton to the right, crossing the railway by the windmill as if for Hadstock Wood, but turning left handed through the Bartlow Plantations over the Ashdon road to Home Wood (in the Essex country) through Walton's Park as if for Langley, but being headed Reynard turned sharp back and got to ground just in front of hounds in the gravel pit near Bartlow Station. Time 45 minutes.

Going back to Hare Wood hounds were away at once, through Over Wood and the Lawn, nearly to Northy Wood, but being headed our quarry turned leaving Silver Street to his left and on by Withersfield Siding, where hounds got a view of him and raced him over the railway and killed him in some buildings under Camps Park. Time 35 minutes.

1921–2 season   *Master:* MR C. F. TONGE
From Mr Thomas Purkis's diary

Jan. 30th.   Met The Thurlow at Little Thurlow Cock, drew Hart and Lophams blank. Found at Island Drain, ran at a great pace through Groves and Lophams up wind to North Wood Drain which he tried. Hounds hit a line off just outside Fir Plantation but I think this was a fresh fox for they ran to the Lawn into Over where they got up to their fox and took him round the cover once or twice then out to Hare Wood which he left only just in front of hounds through the Pond Plantation across Horseheath Park Farm over the railway on to Barsey on as if for Liddigates but bore to the right for Camps Park, a Field short of which he turned sharp to the right alongside the Railway to Railway Arch then up the Meadow to Over Wood. Hounds got off the line and we thought he had beat us, but Mr. Lory saw him go into Over after the Hounds had gone through and holloaed us back. Hounds at once got on his line and rattled him round the Lawn and Over for quite 20 minutes before they drove him out of Over and killed in the Valley. This was a fine hunt of 2 hours from the time we left the Island. Miss Rhodes had a nasty fall over timber. Hounds did not draw again. Rode Winifred.

1922–3 season   *Master:* MR C. F. TONGE
From Mr Thomas Purkis's diary

Nov. 23rd.   Met The Thurlow at Branches Park. Found a brace in the Island Cover ran up to the Park where he got headed everywhere and came back to New England where we killed him a nice cub but he never had a chance. Drew the Privett cover next and found a rare big good looking fox, which Hounds simply raced over the road then left handed by Broxted Lodge then parallel with the road and Green Lane to Hundon Hall at times the fox was in view. Hounds went so fast over to the Fir Plantation on to Chipley over Webb's earth then straight to Cavendish Northy through Houghton Grove over the hill, leaving Trucketts on the left along the valley as if for Glemsford up the steep hill by the long meadows on to the Lower Cover at Boxted over the road up the next hill bearing to the left straight to Chadacre when the fox was viewed dead beat and ran through some Gardens and Buildings where I believe he laid up as Hounds could not carry it on and he beat us. Time 1 hr 15 mins. This was an extraordinary fast run and a 9 mile point. I had 20 miles home which I did not reach until 7.15. Rode Topsy.

Dec. 11th.   Met The Thurlow at Wickhambrook Manor. Found a fox in a piece of Roots on Hicks land. Hounds raced him to Wickhambrook Stew and caught him against Slaters Grove. We then drew Denston Park coverts and Hollybud blank. Found a leash in Chipley. Hounds went away towards Stansfield on a fox that was mangy and ran into him opposite Long Wood. There was a holloa back at Chipley and hounds hunted this fox into Denston Park although he had been gone quite 15 minutes, which we did not know until some way in the run, but after leaving Denston Park hounds settled to hunt in earnest and ran over the open to within a field of Reed Groves when he turned left handed and ran by Hargrave then on very nearly to Ickworth Park then turned left handed straight for Ousden but there was a big shoot on there and headed him so he turned across to Dalham but we could not carry it on. After he was headed scent got very bad. This was a fine hunting run of 1 hr 30 minutes with a 7½ mile point and we covered a lot of country. Rode Topsy.

Jan. 1st. Met The Thurlow at Stetchworth White Horse. Found in the first cover above the Park and ran back through all the Paddocks over the road down the Ditch then straight for Cheveley, leaving the Links just on the left but scent was very poor and he beat us against the Park. Came back and drew Ditton Park found at once and ran with a much improved scent very fast across to Ten Wood into Big Widghams then down wind back by the Round House into Ditton Park out to Ditton Plantation, when Hounds got up to him and he broke back towards Ditton Park; but Hounds ran from scent to view and killed him in the Green lane. This was a good hunt of 45 minutes. Then drew Plunder Wood, Widghams and found. Hounds drove him round the cover once when he broke the Boro Green side and ran a circle back to Ten Wood then he ran on to Plunder Wood again and went the exact line as the former back into Widghams and Hounds drove him out the Sparrow Grove end across by Carlton Hall up to Carlton Wood up by Bradley Mill where he laid up somewhere against the Rectory but Hounds could not carry the line further but it was getting dark and we had to say we were beat. This was a great hunt of 1 hr and 20 minutes. Rode Winifred.

Jan. 11th. Met The Thurlow at Pippin Park Lidgate. Drew Howards small cover blank then came on to Lucy Wood and bolted a fox from the earth. Hounds did not settle to him very readily but ran nicely when once outside up the Green Lane towards Kirtling village. The fox got headed on the road and caused a check of several minutes. Eventually they hit it off and ran nicely straight to Branches over the road against the Church and bore to the right as if for Blue Doors, but short of this he turned left handed by Wickhambrook Mill to the Sandpit on into Denston Park through Hollybud on to Chipley by Chipley Abbey; leaving Poslingford Place just on the left he ran by Bally Green on to Houghton Hall along the valley to Cavendish Place, skirting the village through Blacklands then up the hill to Glemsford by the Rectory then bore to the left sunk the valley up the hill by the Glemsford Earths straight to Boxted Hall across the Park and killed him in the Garden. This was a great run of 2 hrs 15 mins. 11½ mile point and ran through 10 Parishes. The same fox all the way, a very small dog fox. We thought it was a vixen when we started. Very hard day. 18 miles home. Rode May Be to Kirtling then Topsy.

Jan. 25th. Met The Thurlow at Hinxton. Drew the covers there blank, also Pampisford, Hildersham Wood, Chesterford Common and Bartlow covers. Came on to Borley, drew the cover blank but bolted a very fine fox from the Braden Earth, ran very fast away through the cover up to the Ring on by the Cellar Plantation down to Little Linton along the river bank to Hildersham Alders then over Cut Throat Lane and by Franklins Farm through Abington Grange Building over the London road up to Signal Hill Plantation. It was 40 minutes to here without a check, but the fox turned back here and caused a check; but we got a holloa back and ran him into Babraham Park where hounds nearly had him but he jumped the wall and ran back towards Abington and Hounds killed him on the old Railway. Time 1 hr 10 minutes. Rode May Be.

Feb. 12th. Met The Thurlow at Withersfield White Horse at 11.30. Drew the Lawn blank; found at Over Wood ran through Cadges to North Wood out as if for Hart but he circled back by Kiddy's Grove into Littley where Hounds re-found him and bustled him out into North out for Lophams when scent greatly improved and they ran very fast by Carlton Wood into Sparrow Grove, then by Boro Green Wood and Rectory into Lady Grove out by Westley and Underwood Hall down to Dullingham Village where Hounds killed a very tired fox in the Brook against the Station Road. This was a good hunting run of 1 hr 45 mins with a 7 mile point. Came back to Hart which was blank. Went on to North Wood and bolted a fox which ran through Littley then circled back through North across Weston Woods Farm on to Rands, where there was a fresh fox that took them on to Weston, but the hunted one came on to Streetly Hall Earths we heard afterwards. This was a very good hard day. Rode Topsy and May Be to the Meet.

1923–4 season   *Master:* MR C. F. TONGE
From Mr Thomas Purkis's diary

Nov. 12th. Met The Thurlow at Shudy Camps Village. Found in a piece of Mustard close to Northy Grove and ran nicely considering it carried on after a sharp frost the previous night along the side of the Railway then bore to the left by Cardinal's Green straight towards the Croats short of which he bore to the right by Town Green at Horseheath, leaving Streetly Hall just on his right straight into Balsham Wood and broke towards Rands, but unfortunately Hounds got off the line for a minute and were holloaed on to a fresh fox which went to Borley and Hounds got off the line but were soon got going again by Will with a fox from Claude's Kale Seed ran through Borley up to Rivey; leaving this just on his left he faced the open across Chilfords and Hildersham, where a fresh fox got up out of some Kale seed, either he or the hunted one came back to Borley but Hounds kept on the one which was in view for a time and ran across Rat Hall on to Dotterel but he got headed in the Dungate Road and turned left handed across Dotterel on to Fulbourne Field ran beside the old Railway over the open to Babraham covers where he beat us. Time from Camp 2 hrs. This was a great hound hunt as they had to hunt every yard except on grass or seeds when they could drive along. He ran through 8 Parishes and covered a great lot of country, the furthest point from Camps to Fulbourne Field was quite 7 miles. We came back to Borley and bolted a fox which the terrier mauled so Hounds took it round the cover about twice and killed. Drew the Croats blank and gave up. Rode Topsy.

Dec. 26th. Boxing Day. Met The Thurlow at Thurlow Crown after a very sharp frost followed by a tremendous lot of snow then rain on Xmas night consequently the covers were soaked and the land in the most rotten dirty state I ever hunted in. Drew Trundley, Wadgells and Hart and the Grove blank; found in Lophams at 11.30. Had to stop the fox going Carlton way as all that side of the Hunt is closed on account of Foot and Mouth Disease. So he broke and ran nicely to North when hounds got off the line, so it is questionable if we changed but Hounds hit a line off almost directly and ran through Cadges on to Leys over the open by Wickham Church on the right straight to Balsham Wood on to Borley breaking against the first Ride down to Horseheath Lodge on towards Croats but he ran us out of scent against

Horseheath Village. This was a very good hunting run of 1 hour and 15 minutes with a 6 mile point but the run was in the shape of a J. Rode Topsy.

1924–5 season *Master:* MR C. F. TONGE
From a newspaper account (undated)

Newmarket & Thurlow. Meeting yesterday at Brinkley Hall by invitation, Mr. King hospitably entertained followers of the Newmarket and Thurlow and had a good fox ready for them in the big wood. Hounds went away at racing pace as if for Carlton Grange. Turning lefthanded by Weston top woods nearly to Carlton Church they continued through Sparrows Grove to Ten Woods and thence through Ditton Park to Basefield and on by Borough Green Park to Little Widghams. Turning right handed again by Sipsey Bridge to Park Wood they worked their fox to ground in the Bottoms at the back of Borough Green. Time exactly 2 hours to this point. The terrier was put in and after some time he bolted the fox. Hounds hunted him nicely through Big Widgams and Plunder Wood and rolled him over in the open at Foxhall Bradley fifteen minutes after he was bolted. It was a great hunt at a good pace and although circular the point from Weston to Ditton Park was six miles and about twenty miles as hounds ran:
([Note by Purkis:] Met The Thurlow at Brinkley Hall the first time since Mr. William King used to welcome them and the first since Mr. D. King has resided there a lapse of 13 years. We had a very good day killing an old dog fox after 2 hours as above described.)

From Mr Thomas Purkis's diary

Dec. 22nd Met The Thurlow at Helions Bumpstead for a day in the Essex country as described in the following cutting:
Newmarket & Thurlow:
Excellent sport fell to the Newmarket and Thurlow field after yesterday's meet at Helion Bumpstead. Finding at once in a little plantation close to the meet, hounds raced away nearly to Camps Village, left handed by the Castle across the road by the Rectory and on into Langley Wood. The fox now bore left handed to the Bourn Plantation and hounds coursed him back to Langley straight through by Camps End and with Greenhouse Farm to the right, away over the brook below Boblows up to Hempstead Wood. The time up to here was sixty minutes. Unfortunately hounds now divided the main body of the pack going away with a fresh fox over the Walden road along the brook to Bulls Bridge and nearly to Bower Hall and then right handed by Horsey Groves, where hounds were beaten forty minutes after leaving Hempstead. Two couple of hounds had meanwhile killed the first fox just outside Hempstead Wood.

From a newspaper account

Jan. 5th: Newmarket and Thurlow Foxhounds
A good day's sport:
One of the brace of foxes found at Hundon was killed at Culverton on Monday (5th) when the

Newmarket and Thurlow kept their appointment at Standsfield Mill. Finding again in Trundley hounds forced a fox away towards Wratting and a very fine hunt ensued.

Crossing the river near Thurlow Hall hounds ran up the hill to Abbacey, over the Withersfield road, and straight along the point-to-point course to North Wood. Not dwelling a moment they were away by Temple End to the Tuft and through Hart Wood. Leaving the Kennels to the left by Little Bradley Hall and Wadgells on the left they crossed the Thurlow road to Ganwick. Going over the Kedington road by the Wash the pack got a view and coursing their fox, killed him by the river Stour after a good hunt of an hour and twenty-five minutes practically without a check. The first hour was very fast over extremely heavy country.

From Mr Thomas Purkis's diary

Feb. 16th. Met The Thurlow at Clare; drew the Osiers blank. Found at Kings Wood ran to Northy then bore left handed leaving Stansfield Church on his left as if for Christlings which he left on his right bearing towards Depden then left handed to Black Groves and then right handed to Wickhambrook Easty short of which a lurcher had coursed him and I should say killed him as Hounds could never make much of it. Time 1 hr 30 minutes 8 mile point. Then drew the Sand Pits and Appleacre and Privet Cover blank and gave up. Rode May Be.

1926–7 season   *Master:* MR C. F. TONGE
From Mr Thomas Purkis's diary

Nov. 22nd. Met The Thurlow at Great Wratting Lion. A nice hunting morning. Drew some roots close by the Black Grove. Found a brace. The selected one ran as if for the Farm then circled round to Wilsey out as if for Trundley but got headed in the road and went through some Mustard when there was a brace in front of hounds, but as they got headed again Hounds got off the line and lost. This was a nice 15 minutes. Trotted round by the road to Wilsey. Found a brace. Hounds came away on the one which bore towards Withersfield leaving the village on his right. He crossed the road against High Noon Farm and went straight to North Wood not dwelling there he ran by Temple End up to Thurlow Park ran along the boundary hedge to the Walks but kept left-handed by the Almhouses through Little Bradley over the Earths there straight up beside the Lane to Norney Moat across to Cowlinge Hall, then left handed for New England but turned into Garrad's Plantation where hounds ran into him. This was a real good hunt of 1¼ hours. Rode May Be.

1927–8 season   *Master:* MR C. F. TONGE
From the *Morning Post*, 2 December 1927

Meet Kedington Dec 1st:
Newmarket & Thurlow. Two excellent hunts resulted from yesterday's Newmarket and Thurlow fixture at Kedington. Finding first in Black Wood hounds crossed the Colne Valley railway into East Essex country and, wheeling right handed at Birdbrook, pointed for Steeple Bumpstead but turned short of Helions Bumpstead and killed their fox by Withersfield Siding

after 60 minutes of the best. A second fox put up in Norney Wood was hunted through Wilsey and in a big circle to ground in view under the Haverhill Great Wratting road. Time 50 minutes.

From Mr E. Cooper-Bland's diary

Thursday Dec. 1st.   Meet Kedington. Found in Blackmere Wood and ran through Wilsey and then nearly into Haverhill the fox came back over the railway line to Woodland Green, he then turned right handed over the main road and railway line betwen Copsehall and Sturmer Hall and then across to Hanut Hall where we killed him in the Long Meadows after 60 minutes a very good hunt indeed. Found again at Norney, ran out towards Great Wratting but turned right handed through Wilsey towards Kedington and eventually ran to ground behind old Mr. Sainsbury's barn after a good hunt of 40 minutes. A very good day, hounds worked very well.

From Mr E. Cooper-Bland's diary

Mon. 30th. January 1928. In the absence of the Master Boore hunted hounds found in Trundley and ran very fast to Avout where we killed him. Another fox jumped up before we had broken the killed fox up and ran very fast across to the gravel pit behind Great Wratting village where we killed him. Found again in some kale and a great hunt ensued. Right through Trundley and Wadgells to Wadgell's Farm where the fox took cover in some bushes, but after being roused he went back to Trundley and then nearly into Great Thurlow along the stream to Little Thurlow and Little Bradley leaving Doley Wood on the right over the road towards East Green then left handed through Great Bradley Hall Grounds then again left handed and eventually we killed our fox in the garden at Little Bradley Hall. A great hunt of 90 minutes. Gave Miss Bedford the mask and Mrs Praed the brush.

Monday 5th March.   Meet Hawkedon Green. The Master (T. Eaton) hunted hounds. Found almost at once in a fallow field near the meet. Ran very fast through the small grove by Stansfield Hall through Northy Wood, leaving Kings Wood on the right and Northy Wood on the left past Robs Farm into Cavendish village. Here the fox was only just in front of hounds who ran him more or less in view back to Robs Farm where they killed him. A Very good hunt. Easty, Kings Wood blank, found a leash in Chipley. Also again in Hundon Thicks and ran through Blackgrove, Appleacres and Denston, killing him near Assington Green, not such a good hunt. A glorious summer's day and grew very dry. Would have bet 100 to 1 against a good scent.

1928–9 season   *Joint Masters:* MR E. COOPER-BLAND and MR T. C. EATON
From a newspaper account of a meet on 26 December 1928

Newmarket & Thurlow Foxhounds. On Boxing Day hounds met at the Rose and Crown, Thurlow, and there was a very large crowd to witness this popular fixture. Hounds moved off with an excellent field in attendance and the first draw – a field of kale belonging to Mr.

Ryder – soon provided a fox which went away into Trundley Wood, where, after hunting around the wood for a short time hounds pushed him away on the Barnardiston side. Pointing for Clare the fox crossed the Great Wratting road at a fast pace over the Haverhill – Bury main road, and leaving Barnardiston on the left passed between Kedington Leys and Taylor's Farm and on to the Kedington–Clare road where hounds checked. The going was heavy and the country stiff and this check was very welcome. Hounds were soon on the line again and pushing on straight ahead crossed the lower Kedington road and made for Lords Wood in the East Essex country. Our fox skirted this covert, and, leaving it on the left bore right-handed in the direction of Stoke. Hounds were now close on their fox, and leaving Crooks Hall on their right, ran well crossing the Kedington–Stoke road at Cains Hill into the cover at Burnthouse Farm, killing their fox in the cover before he was able to reach the Gravel Pits just north of Stoke-by-Clare. A good hunt of one hour ten minutes with a $4\frac{1}{2}$ mile point and once again the hunt is indebted to Mr. Ryder for providing a good fox. Moving on to Kedington a fox was found in some mustard on Mr. F. Sainsbury's farm, close to Black Wood, and, after hunting him round Wilsey and over the Haverhill–Bury road he was given up and hounds went home after a very good day's sport.

From a newspaper report of 28 December 1928

A hunt of one hour 20 minutes without a check, a point of $5\frac{1}{2}$ miles and 13 miles as hounds ran enabled the Newmarket and Thurlow to wind up Christmas Week in fine style, when a large field met hounds by invitation of Colonel the Hon. W. F. North at Kirtling Tower. Snow had fallen in the night, but with a rapid thaw it had nearly all disappeared by the time hounds moved off and scenting conditions were favourable.

From Ditton Park a vixen was viewed away, and hounds hunted slowly into Widghams Wood where they soon got on better terms with another fox. He was away at once into Ten Wood and out again in the direction of Dullingham Ley. Running very fast, hounds reached the road at Dullingham Ley to find that he had been headed, and doubled back towards Stetchworth Ley. On reaching Marmers Wood they bore left handed along the covert into some paddocks at Stetchworth. Running for a bit alongside the Dullingham–Stetchworth road they crossed it before reaching the village.

With a turn to the left hounds raced to Dullingham House, down to the railway, right-handed alongside the line, and across it before reaching the road to the July Course. Missing Hall Farm, hounds ran on still at a good pace over the Dullingham–Swaffham road and through Mr. Taylor's Heath Farm where the fox was only a little way in front. At the back of Hare Park he doubled back left handed across the railway again, through Mr. Oakey's Westley Lodge Farm, and up a belt towards Brinkley, where he was viewed. Turning right handed into Mr. King's Lower Farm, he crossed the Brinkley–Six Mile Bottom road, and circling back, was pulled down in the middle of the road close to Six Mile Bottom Station. He was a fine old dog fox and gave one of the fastest hunts these hounds have had for many years.

From a newspaper account

On February 2nd the Newmarket and Thurlow Hounds had an interesting day's hunting. They met at 'Crockfords' the land farmed by the great Crockford (who actually lived in these offices) and which is now occupied by Major Philip Dawson. After partaking of his hospitality hounds drew his coverts and found in a piece of roots. They ran their fox over the ditch and through the Stetchworth Stud to Lord Ellesmere's racing box, where he was headed back over the ditch to Camois Hall. Here he bore left handed over the Woodditton Hill to Crockford's Farm and ran through the meadows to the railway, which he followed to Newmarket Station, where he crossed the line by the bridge.

The fox went on through Reg Day's paddocks to The Avenue, where he crossed the brook and made for the Sale Paddocks. He could not get over the wall, but went into Sir Murray Scott's gardens. From there hounds drove him in Mr. Reg. Day's exercise ground, where he jumped the wall built by Crockford as his garden boundary. This wall is well over six feet high. The fox then went by the Cemetery and over the gate on to the Heath, where he was killed by hounds in the open. Unfortunately he was worried by a terrier when he got on to the Heath, otherwise he would probably have gone down to the Rowley Mile Stands.

The hunt lasted for over an hour and the fox was well in front from the time he left Stetchworth Park till he reached the Cemetery. Mr. Cooper Bland in conjunction with Mr. Eaton the new Masters, have shown excellent sport throughout the season, although scent has been none too good, a fox being killed nearly every day they have been out.

1929–30 season *Joint Masters:* MR E. COOPER-BLAND and MR T. C. EATON
From a newspaper report of a meet on 14 November 1929

First Rate Sport. Newmarket and Thurlow make a seven mile point: From their fixture at Linton 'Swan' on Thursday the Newmarket and Thurlow had a very good day. Finding in Borley Wood hounds ran by the Rivey to Little Chilford where they turned left-handed and, leaving Linton on the right, ran straight to Horseheath Lodge, but, owing to shooting restrictions, had to be whipped off.

After drawing Wratting Park and Rands Wood blank they found at Weston Wood and ran very fast to Sparrows Grove and on through Little and Great Widghams. Leaving Ten Wood on the left, hounds rattled along up to and through Ditton Park Wood and thence to Upend, crossing the Newmarket road between Kirtling and Saxon Street. After passing Upend, however, the pace was slower and although Hounds hunted on towards Ousden a thick fog descended and they had to be stopped.

This was a fine hunt of an hour and twenty minutes with a seven mile point. Hounds worked splendidly and were unlucky not to kill their fox. Including the hunt staff only eight finished the run.

From a newspaper report of a meet on 21 November 1929

Two Good Runs. Sport with the Newmarket and Thurlow:
Capital sport fell to those out with the Newmarket and Thurlow at Boro' Green on Thursday. Finding at once on Boro' Green Park Wood, hounds went away towards Carlton, and Carlton Wood was held on their left. The fox just touched the corner of Hart Wood before turning left-handed and, crossing the main road, he skirted Little Widghams.

Here the only serious check during the run occurred, but Boore soon hit off the line, and

L

145

hounds fairly raced to Bradley East Green and thence to Cowlinge Village. Swinging left-handed they now made for Branches Park where, owing to shooting restrictions, they had to be stopped. This was a grand hunt of an hour and 30 minutes with a point of five miles, but double that distance as hounds ran.

Later from Lucy Wood the hounds ran at a great pace towards Upend, but, unfortunately their fox turned left-handed and headed for the numerous Studs around Cheveley and again they had to be stooped. This concluded an excellent day's sport from the followers point of view, although a rather disappointing one for both huntsman and hounds.

From a newspaper report of 26 December 1929

Only one Covert touched. Newmarket and Thurlow 7-mile point in 1 hr 10 mins. A large field enjoyed excellent sport with the Newmarket and Thurlow Hounds from their fixture at Thurlow Crown on Boxing Day, Finding at once in Trundley Wood, this very good fox was soon away towards Barnardiston Hall. Leaving this on their right, hounds fairly raced past Blue Doors and High Elms Farms to Branches Park, a distance of four miles. Here the fox was viewed a field in front of hounds, but carrying on through a corner of the park, he crossed the road by Bridgelands Farm and went over the hill towards Lidgate. Holding this village on his right he turned right handed just before reaching Cropley Grove. Here hounds were at fault and although the fox was viewed dead-beat entering the Ousden coverts nothing more could be done and he had to be left.

This was a very good hunt of one hour and ten minutes with a 7-mile point and about eight or nine miles as hounds ran. Branches Park being the only covert touched throughout the run.

From a newspaper report of a meet on 27 January 1930

Newmarket Gallop. Seven miles in 40 minutes without a check and then slows. From their fixture at Hawkedon Green on Monday those hunting with the Newmarket and Thurlow enjoyed excellent sport. After drawing Park, Northy and Easty Woods blank, hounds found a fox in Long Wood and getting away on good terms they ran fast towards Upper Street. Leaving this on the left the fox doubled back through Houghton Grove to Easty Wood.

Without dwelling in this covert hounds raced on towards Glemsford. Holding this village on the right, they crossed Fern Hill and the river Glem and ran on to Stanstead.

Up to this point there had been no sign of a check, seven miles having been covered in 40 minutes. Recovering the line, hounds worked on towards Blooms Hall, but leaving this and Rowhedge Farm on their left, they ran out of scent in the Park behind Kentwell Hall after as capital hunt of 1 hr 20 mins with a point of 6 miles, covering nearly double this distance as hounds ran.

1930–1 season *Joint Masters:* MR E. COOPER-BLAND and MR T. C. EATON
From a newspaper report of a meet on 5 November 1930

Newmarket and Thurlow. Ninety Minutes with 8-mile point over nice line. After a very rough night the weather cleared up for the opening meet of the Newmarket and Thurlow at Thurlow Crown on Monday. An unenterprising cub was killed in a root field in the middle of Thurlow village, but a good fox was soon found on Mr. Goodchild's farm and the large field enjoyed a capital hunt. After running through Abbacey Wood, hounds all but had their fox in a piece of mustard on the point-to-point course, but doubling back through Abbacey Wood he headed straight for Trundley.

Without dwelling in Mr. Ryder's famous stronghold, hounds ran on towards Barnardiston Hall. Leaving this on their right and Blue Doors farm on their left, they crossed the main Haverhill–Bury road and hunted on towards Stradishall Village. Leaving Stradishall Place on his left and Denston Hall on his right, the fox crossed the brook and set his mask for Black Wood, but before he could reach this covert hounds pulled him down just short of Giffords Hall. This was a good hunt of 90 minutes all down-wind, with a point of eight miles over a nice line of country.

From Colonel E. H. Deacon's diary

December 29th: Met Newmarket & Thurlow at The Kennels (1st trailer trip of 19 miles). Nice day scent improving. Found in Hart Wood and hunted him well for some time in cover and killed. Found in North Wood ran fast at times through Groves over Haverhill road, Wratting road, river, through Trundley nearly to Barnardiston, on up to Chipley where fox headed; hunted slowly back to Wadgells. 6½ mile point. Real nice hunt.

1934–5 season *Master:* COLONEL E. H. DEACON
From Colonel E. H. Deacon's diary

Oct. 11th. Met at Stradishall Cross roads. Day fine and warm. Scent serving. A red letter day. Didn't find until Frogs Hall, then ran nicely back to Sandpits on a right handed circle, fox just in front but lost him in roots. Found again Frogs Hall and after running nicely round and nearly getting him went away through Farley Grove as if for Cowlinge but turning right handed he made straight for New England. Checked here but he was holloaed away and then ran beautifully, leaving Frogs Hall on the left on to Blue Doors and Three Ashes then on over Boxted Lodge as if for Barnardiston but right handed at a great pace to Wadgell's pipe. Had him out and eat him. 5½ mile point. 9 as hounds ran.

Dec. 26th. The Newmarket & Thurlow met at Thurlow Crown on Boxing Day. A fox was viewed into Wadgells and going away at once with Wadgell's Farm on the right, hounds ran at a great pace past Cowlinge Hall straight to New England. There they swung left handed over the Lidgate road and reached Branches Park after a fast hunt of 40 minutes. Fresh foxes caused some delay, but going away again hounds ran beautifully round the park to Cowlinge Village and up to New England again. Then they bore left handed and went back to Branches after another fast gallop of 45 minutes. Hounds had run for 2 hours in all, the first and last 40 minutes being really fast.

Feb 21st. Meet Balsham. Showery with high wind. Good scenting. Found at Borley end of Balsham and went straight away to Streetly Hall then right handed over Cambridge road and very fast leaving Croats on the right almost to Northy. Here he turned left and went into the back of Horseheath village and he was almost killed in a chicken run. Ran slowly down to Northy and on through Oven to Croats. G. Long told us he had gone on to Hare Wood and a holloa about Wickham got us up to him and he jumped up just in front of hounds and was chased into Leys and killed. One hour 30 minutes. A good hunt. The record heavy fox and one that is well known at Balsham.

1935–6 season   *Master:* COLONEL E. H. DEACON
From a newspaper report

March 2nd.   Meet Wickhambrook Manor Day fine scent fair. The Newmarket & Thurlow met at Wickhambrook Manor on Monday. A Fox from Denston was hunted slowly to Midlay and was marked to ground. Another from the Sandpits also went to ground, but a third provided a first class hunt. After making for Stradishall cross-roads he doubled back, and going away over the Bury Road hounds settled down to run at a great pace by Denston and Appleacres, hunting on prettily to Hundon Thicks and over Mr. Dennis's land to Chilton Street. Then they bore right-handed to Brickwall Farm where their fox was viewed but escaped after a really good hunt with a four mile point. A slow ringing hunt from Frog's Hall finished the day.

1936–7 season   *Master:* COLONEL E. H. DEACON
From a newspaper account

The 14th January was a hard day on horses and hounds. After meeting at Exhibition Farm, hounds found in Over Wood and hunting slowly down by Hare Wood took the line to the Cambridge road. Here scent improved and running on by the railway they swung left handed and ran on fast by Withersfield siding to Howe Wood and on as if for Norney, but being headed on the Haverhill road the fox turned up the brook, and, scent failing, was hunted slowly through Withersfield Village and on by Lawn Wood to Leys Wood, where scent gave out after a good hunt of an hour. A fox from North Wood next gave us a capital gallop, which also lasted for an hour, but had a more satisfactory finish. Going away slowly at first hounds hunted through the Point-to-Point covert and then settled down to run fast to Abbacey. Scarcely dwelling there they ran on very fast by Thurlow Vicarage to Westend with two foxes in front of them. Here they checked but hitting off the line by Temple End ran fast back to North Wood. Here they changed foxes, but this time the mistake was realised and, being brought back, hounds put up their hunted fox and, racing him round the covert, killed him in the First Plantation. So ended a good day.

Feb. 22nd.   Stansfield Mill. Fine cold day. Good scent. Found in Hawkedon and ran at racing pace to Northy. Twice round and on to Easty, then slowly by Sparrow Wood to Trickett's. 1 hr 10 mins. Found again in a drain and ran beautifully by Stradishall and Clickets to aerodrome and Barnardiston and Glass Woods. Hounds then divided. Half ran on to Brickworth and made a 5 mile point. The others circled to make a 4 mile point, 10 miles. 1 hour.

1937–8 season   *Master:* C O L O N E L E. H. D E A C O N

From a newspaper account of a meet on 30 December 1937

The Newmarket & Thurlow met at Stansfield Mill on Thursday (Dec 30th). A fox from Hawkedon Bottoms got a long start, but hounds hunted well by Thurston Park and Tricketts to Boxted Hall, where scent failed. Finding again in Chipley, they were soon away and pushing their fox through Appleacre settled down to run very fast by Hundon Lodge and the aerodrome to Barnardiston Hall. There they checked but hitting off the line ran on by the Grove to Little Thurlow Church and Thurlow Park. Hounds marked to ground in the Island after a fast hunt of 45 minutes with a 6½ mile point.

From *Horse and Hound*

There was a strong wind on January 13th when hounds met at Balsham. Finding at once in Balsham Wood, they ran very fast up wind to Borley and hunted well through this big wood and out the other side. The wind was too strong to face again, so their fox turned back and a long and interesting hound hunt followed which finally ended at Wratting Park after 1 hr and 50 mins, about fourteen miles having been covered with a four mile point. A good fox from Hillcroft took us at racing pace to Exhibition Farm without a check, but here he turned sharp into Lawn Wood and hunting well hounds pushed him out on the down wind side and killed him in the open at Skippers Hall after a fine hunt of 40 mins.

1938–9 season   *Master:* C O L O N E L E. H. D E A C O N

From a newspaper account of a meet on 15 December 1938

The Newmarket and Thurlow met at Bartlow yesterday and after a disappointing morning hounds found in some mustard below Horseheath Lodge. They ran very fast through Balsham Woods and over the Linton road. Then with Chilford Hall on their left, they continued very fast to the Rivey, having covered this five miles in 20 minutes. Hunting slowly through the covert hounds ran on at a reduced pace to Borley Wood and then by Streetly Hall to Streetly End, where the fox turned sharply back. With Horseheath Lodge on the right hounds crossed the Cambridge road to the Croats and scent eventually failed at Shudy Camps after more than 12 miles of the deepest going had been covered in 90 minutes.

March 17th.   The Newmarket & Thurlow, after meeting in stormy weather at Weston Colville yesterday (Mar 17th), had a disappointing morning, but on finding an outlier on Mr. Read's Farm at Carlton hounds ran well. Putting Carlton Wood on the left he led to Hart Wood, then through the Grove to Lophams and over the Temple End road. Leaving North Wood on the right they crossed the Haverhill road and ran fast over the racecourse with Abbacey on the left. Going on between Norney and Burton's Ley they lost their fox in a snowstorm after a fine hunt of one hour with a five mile point.

From a newspaper account of a meet on 24 March 1939

The Newmarket & Thurlow met yesterday (24th) at Balsham. Finding in Balsham Wood hounds ran fast by West Wickham and Streetly Hall to Croats. They crossed the railway and went on as if for Langleys but, turning back, they ran more slowly up the railway to Cardinal's Green and through the open to Horseheath Lodge. Crossing the Bartlow road they hunted on past Borley to the river and out towards Hildersham, but then turned back through the river and were run out of scent on the Linton road. This was a good hound hunt of two hours ten minutes covering 17 miles of country and including two four mile points.

From a newspaper account

March 28th.   The Newmarket & Thurlow met at Hundon yesterday (28th). After looking for outliers in the morning, hounds found at once in Trundley and, running the length of the wood made a ring by Wratting to Thurlow Hall, where they crossed the river. Then they ran on well by the Vicarage to North Wood and after some delay went away again. Hunting slowly by Littley and Exhibition Farm they ran through Lawn and Over Woods to Hare Wood where they marked their fox to ground after a good hound hunt of 70 minutes with a point of more than five miles.

1953–4 season   *Master:* Mr Harvey Leader
From Mr J. D. Webb's diary

March 7th.   Stansfield. Warm sunny morning after overnight white frost. Heavy rain Sunday night. Best scenting day of the season. Stansfield Bottom not holding went on to Gravel pits from whence a fox had been viewed away out of a ditch just before we arrived. Taking hounds down and over the road end, casting over the meadows hounds picked up the line of a fox which turned back over the road towards the Gravel pits. Hounds had just started to settle down and hunt nicely when our fox was headed by cars on the road side by the Gravel pits. Whilst casting to pick up the line information was received regarding a fox at Farley Green but owing to delay in confirmation it was given up. Going back to the pits a fox got away from the drain on our approach. It went away towards Denston, and hounds were soon over the road and settling down to hunt well across the ploughs. It was soon apparent that there was a scent and turning right handed short of Denston village hounds were soon over the road and hunting in the meadows towards Denston Park and to keep up with them it was necessary to sit down and ride straight. Taking a line straight up the hill into the Park ileaving the Hall on the left hounds raced on through the Copse, through the plantation on to Goymers Farm (Being no time to open gates we had all the thrill of riding the one Day Event Course with hounds in front.) Hounds were still racing across the plough and leaving Goymers on the right raced on into Appleacre without having had the slightest check (Only L. Woolard and myself on Hamlight[?]were with hounds at this point) swinging right handed over the drain our fox broke as if for Appleacre but wire netting turned him back into the road and, doubling back through the wood, he broke covert at the point he entered where he was viewed by late arrivals. When turning about with every move still relentlessly hunted on and passing through the copse by Goymers Farm coursed him down the hedgerow towards Denston Park, bowling him over just before entering the plantation on the edge of the Park.

All hounds on (except Dainty which got hung up in Appleacre). A hunt of 35 minutes at racing pace throughout without ever a check.

A red letter day. L. Woolard, Charlie and self all took it as it came. W & C jumped gate out of Park and fence into the Plantation. Hounds, Horses and Riders all dead beat. Being warm and thirsty adjourned to the Hall where everyone refreshed themselves at the Masters. Hounds at the water trough. Going back to Goymers a fox bolted out of the bale straw stack, took us back practically the same line as our first fox had gone and just as hounds had again settled down to hunt quite as well and fast as the previous hunt our fox got to ground in an Elm tree in the Park by our one day event starting post and had to be left. Black Grove and Coping blank so Home. A great day.

1954-5 season *Master:* MR HARVEY LEADER
From Mr J. D. Webb's diary

Nov. 15th.   Kirtling Green. White frost. A fox in a field between the cross roads and Long Meadow was found at once and ran to Mr. Howards Alder Bottom, where he got to ground. Leaving it to Mr. Fenwick and his terriers, drew the rest of Upend Coverts blank. As Mr. Fenwick was still a long way off his fox went on to Mr. Cooper Bland's Plantation where a leash of foxes were viewed: going away on a fox towards Kirtling Towers (1.0 clock) ran the side of the road into Lucy, and skirting the wood broke as if for the School, headed on the road ran the side of the road through a field of beet, crossing the road into Meadow by Parsonage Farm, turning right handed to Kirtling Green crossed the road and on to Horse Pasture Farm where it was headed back, but circling round it made its point by crossing short of Longacre Green up to Bradley Park Wood. Plenty of grief over ditch, wire & fences by Cowans lane, but after making good round Bradley Park hounds hunted on down towards Great Bradley to the meadows by the river here the line was foiled by cattle, but a timely holloa put us on the alert and soon after the fox was viewed returning to Bradley Park from the Waterfield Barn direction. Up to then scent had been very catchy on the plough but the air was keener and hounds raced on up to Bradley Park, but turning short left handed crossed Water Lane into Plunder Wood and hunting with a great cry through Widghams to Sparrows Grove took the line out to the drain below where they marked to ground after a great hunt of 2 hrs 40 mins. Later Fenwick reported after a four hour dig getting to his terrier which had hold of the fox which it had killed.

Dec. 30th.   Cheveley Old Hall. Pony Club. Very pleasant day, slightly hazy. A fox viewed from Dainsley's took a line over the road to L. Ditton on to Saxon St., turning right handed up to Brickyard through as if for Ditton Park, headed on road swung right handed up Esc Stud Paddock, but away through Lt. Ditton left handed at Ditton Church leaving Camon's Hall on right with Pickmores wood by which time they had raced clean away from the field. Thinking hounds had carried straight on the field after being held up by locked gates, got round and could hear nothing of hounds. They had however swung right handed down the ditch; racing on and then swinging right handed by Court Barns were last seen going toward Cheveley. At some point they either ran their fox to ground or killed; eventually they were found returning from the original draw. Going on to Ditton Park a fox was twice headed on the road trying for Brickyard and took a deal of putting up. Thanks to a view hounds were soon on the fox and backing towards Charcoal Wood, swinging right handed through the paddocks across the road to Houghton Green right handed by Parsonage Farm through Brickworks on to Old Park House where, headed making a circle back to Brickyards, it took the lane back to Lucy. Here other foxes were on foot but hunting with great cry round and out hounds nearly had him in Toll Yard Plantation, but breaking back to Lucy went round again breaking at the Bottom. Hounds courses him up to Old Park House across the big plough Field at Bottom of Plantation. Here hounds were at fault, everyone's horse dead beat; while casting round information came that it had been viewed crossing the road to Densley but although hunted down to the Stetchworth–Cheveley road had to give up as horses all dead beat. A great day's hunting. Very unlucky not to have caught one.

1955–6 season *Master:* MR HARVEY LEADER
From Mr J. D. Webb's diary

Dec. 11th. Stansfield. Drawing Hawkedon Bottom one of four foxes was soon on foot and hounds hunting towards Gallowgate Farm pushed the fox out right up the hill over the lane through Thurston End Court over the road down to Bottoms behind Houghton Grove, left handed through rough meadows leaving Houghton Grove on the right along the Cavendish side of Northy, left handed at the top as if up the Lane then right handed down to deep ditch; here hounds had difficulty in owning the line but seemed to try for Kings Wood. Pushing on this Wood hounds spoke once of twice in here and seemed to take a line out towards Shadowbush but could not own the line. (Hounds may have been at fault and our fox made for Southy.) Holding hounds into Shadowbush one hound spoke to a line in here, eventually marking to ground in the drain. From this a fox was evicted (but don't think it was our hunted one), breaking through Shadowbush Farm ran on as if for Chipley but crossing the road and leaving Chipley on the right ran side of grass then turned left handed along the track into kale by Chipley Abbey farm straight through along by Culverton Farm along ridge to old Gravel Pit left handed to Windden Dairy Farm behind Poslingford. Here hounds were at fault, but going on they ran as if for Clare Osiers but swinging left crossed over road by Wentford Farm up over hill down to Bottoms; here our fox was viewed standing still broadside on listening (See Lionel Edwards Book on the Fox); turning left handed, hunted it down back to Poslingford over the stream and through the dairy farm, right handed along the meadows parallel to the road where hounds appeared to have either marked to ground or caught their fox in a ditch (Charlie getting off his horse), but our fox evaded hounds again by running the ditch bottom and was viewed out of the ditch behind hounds; however they were soon after him and hunting him again almost in view the whole time marked him to ground in the old earth by Chilton Hall. Taking hounds away commenced digging for it but as usual (Too Many Cooks) the fox bolted out of another hole along the ditch and catching Charlie on his feet without and hounds anticipating the kill escaped back to meadows and was lost. (The fox deserved his brush and we deserved to lose it) I think hounds if left alone with Charlie would have had it at the earth as some hounds were almost out of sight. Did not draw again. great hunt.

Mon. Jan. 30. Kirtling Green. Pleasant day after heavy rain Sunday. Drew along Meadows to Upend Bottoms found Hicks Plantation. Good dog fox going away right as if for Lidgate, swinging right handed after two fields crossing Lidgate–Cowlinge road short of Lidgate Belt and going straight on crossed the Lidgate–Wickhambrook road just right of Lidgate Village, going on at great pace as if for Spring Wood but turning left handed short of the wood. Charlie held hounds over the road into some fields of kale ($\frac{1}{2}$ hour without check), viewed and headed by some hedgers as he was heading for Easty Wood and turning left handed circled round and was again viewed over the road back into Lidgate direction. Holding hounds right handed round back of farm at Court. Hounds picked up a line and raced on back to Lidgate Hall. Here our fox ran through Boyces, pigs running out in meadows and what with delay due to wire, gardens, etc lost our fox. Going on to Upend road hounds drew the plantations right of the road and putting up a vixen hunted it down to Old chalk pit where they were at fault and could not pick up the line. A fox was later viewed into Upend coming from this direction, but although these coverts & later Lucy were drawn did not find again. First hunt $1\frac{1}{2}$ hours first $\frac{1}{2}$ hour very fast without check. Charlie's horse dead beat and my chestnut the same. I think the best scenting day of the season.

Thurs. Feb. 9th.   Horseheath. Bitterly cold. Croats blank. Northy appeared to be blank but the drain held and terriers soon bolted our pilot who was soon away towards Shardelows, keeping left of the railway. Hounds were at fault at Cardinals Farm by the railway cutting, but quickly putting them right Charlie had them over the road and swinging right took the line over the railway cutting parallel with the road for a field and then swinging left took the line down to the plantation at the side of the railway embankment. Here a train ran right through the pack without damage and our fox twice tried to cross the main road but was headed back by traffic, but hounds sticking to their fox took the line back over the railway and along the bank. Here I think our fox again tried to cross the line but although Charlie cast hounds all round he could not touch the line. (I surmise that our fox did cross the line but under the culvert under the road.) Leaving this, Gage Wood proved blank though a lot of riot with hares. Going on to Lawn and Over whilst galloping forward left handed a fox was headed back and was again viewed by Charlie. Some hounds took a line up to the top but Charlie not hearing wasted a lot of time before being fetched up to the top. Here he was informed that there appeared to be a line out to Cadges but whilst trying down to Cadges a fox was viewed going away from Lawn towards Ley. Taking hounds quickly forward they soon picked up the line and hunted nicely to Ley; quickened in Ley where they were soon out and racing away towards West Wickham Old Rectory, hunting nicely along the wire of Neals poultry meadow they came through a small hole over the road and as if for Rands. Here our fox, taking a line out on stubble scent, was never so good again, but pressing on to Rands ran into riot, but casting on beyond took the line out as if for Wratting Park then right handed along ditch and again left along ditch to Wratting Park. Here turned right short of Park ran up to pond by Wratting Common road and ran out of scent. Unfortunately Charlie did not try left at the road. Later information that a fox, very tired, was seen on the road by men coming out of Cherry Tree and was in fact so beat that one man was able to catch hold of it but was bitten and let go. As the pace and time was not sufficient to tire a fox between Lawn and Rands it seems that we put up in Lawn our original fox from Northy so again very unlucky not to catch it. Did not draw again.

1956–7 season   *Masters:* A COMMITTEE, UNDER THE CHAIRMANSHIP OF MR J. D. WEBB
From Mr J. D. Webb's diary

March 7th. Weston Green. Drawing Weston Woods first Dick Taylor going ahead through the wood saw a fox sitting listening in a ride. Quickly getting hounds on to it after once round the top were soon away across the road to Hillcroft and running straight through swinging left handed, crossing the Weston to Wratting road by Muir Farm then right handed across Wratting Common Road with the Park on the right as if for Rands Wood but . . . on passing Yen Hall on the right pointing as if for Benly Farm but being headed in the road, turning left short of D. Taylors Barn and pointing as if for Wickham Church but again right handed crossing the road above Bottle Hall on to my Chalk Pits when hounds dwelt; but one hound took a line up towards Hudson and holding hounds on put up the fox in Hudson Bank where they nearly had it but for the old wire fence and breaking back by my Pits hounds coursed it up 14 acres by Parsons to Balsham Wood where they hunted it round and were at fault at the top end. Holding them all round the wood again, touched the line on my boundary hedge and running on put it up in the ditch by Browns little field below Balsham where hounds soon had him out and killed him. 1 hr 20 mins. Very good hunt fast. Going on to Fairheads kale . . . and Hare Wood did not find until Lawn where hounds put up a fox, hunting it up top side of Over, out as if for Cadges but turning left ran up side of road to Hangars by Wratting Wickham cross roads; swinging right crossed runways, being headed left towards Woodman Spare the Tree but being right ran on through Govers Grove with Lophams wood on the right as if for Lophams Hall where hounds ran out of scent and gave up as all horses had had enough. A very good day.

1966–7 season   *Joint Masters:* MR AND MRS E. H. VESTEY

January 26th. Cowlinge. Found in 4 Acre but could not do much with it owing to foot followers and bad information. Drew Branches Park blank and found in Bradley Park Wood. Had a wonderful hunt of two hours to Branches Park, Hobbles Green, Norley Moat, Little Bradley and on to East Green. Finished at 5 o'clock. Tony Champion on the Master's horse for the last hour as his was cooked. Weather bright and warm.

February 5th. The Kennels. Found in the boundary hedge below Deersleys. Ran to Hobbles Green, through Norley Moat and down to the Little Thurlow road. Back to Deersleys where we lost. Found in Lophams and ran through Hart Wood to the Island. On through the Walks, past Mill Cottage and over the rides to Church Farm and up into Trundley. Straight through Trundley to Great Wratting left handed to the Ganwick and then right handed towards Barnardiston. Checked after crossing the Bury St. Edmunds road and then the fox jumped up and ran down to Hilly Grove to ground. One hour from Lophams with a 4½ mile point and between six and seven miles as hounds ran. Weather warm and fine.

February 2nd. Withersfield. Found in a scrubby place by the Melbourne Bridge. After a bad start, through some people holloaing in quite the wrong direction just because they heard hounds speaking, hunted up towards Northey Wood right handed into the middle of the building works in the new housing estate in Haverhill to everyone's astonishment. On to Wilsey, left handed between Cocked Hat Wood and Northey and lost by Abbacey. Found again in Lower Wood and went to ground in the pipe in Over Wood. Bolted him and after running him the length of Over and all round Lawn Wood again went away very fast to the Roman Road on to Park Farmyard through Hare Wood, Ley Wood, Cadges and North Wood, skirted the Spinney at High Noon and lost a field short of Littley Wood. Hounds going like smoke. Tony Champion took the Master's horse after Hare Wood as his was finished. Weather mild, slightly cloudy, light S.W. wind.

1967-8 season   *Joint Masters:* MR AND MRS E. H. VESTEY

December 30th.   Waltons. Hunted on foot because of thick snow. Found in Home Wood and ran through Olmsells, down to the Bartlow Belts, where he went to ground in an old barn under some hay bales. Killed him and bolted a vixen with which they could do little. Drew Woolpack blank, and then marked at the pipe in Langley Wood. Bolted him quickly and went away towards Sandons, left handed to Great Bendysh, on to Little Bendysh and to ground by Plumtree Grove after ninety minutes with only Mr. Phil Brown and me there. Very stiff after running so many miles.

February 17th.   Great Bradley Hall. Found in Bradley Park Wood and ran through Base's Wood towards Branches Park. Headed on the road swung back right handed and then headed on the Bradley road, went into the pipe under the concrete road at East Green. Bolted from there he ran into College Grove and doubled back into a ditch and killed him.
Found again in Bloomfield Wood and after a slow start all round Branches Park ran through Cowlinge and Catley to the II Acre. Checked inside and took some time to get him away, when we ran back through Cowlinge and Branches out towards Kirtling, right handed through Vicarage Farm on to the Lidgate–Upend road. Checked in the brook and then slowly took the line back across the road between Pippin Park and Lidgate Belt and finally lost. An hour the first hunt, one hour and three quarters the second. Only a $2\frac{1}{2}$ mile point but 9 miles as Hounds ran. Weather, faint sun at times, mainly cloudy with not much wind, rather cold.

1968–9 season   *Joint Masters:* MR AND MRS E. H. VESTEY

January 13th.   The Temple, Great Wilbraham. Drew the Temple coverts blank, and then found a good fox in Colonel Francis's covert in Wilbraham Fen. Ran through Fulbourne Fen and left handed to the road just short of Great Wilbraham, picking up a fresh fox en route. Sticking to our original line, ran back through Little Wilbraham, right handed over the road and lost just short of the A II on Allington Hill. Meantime some hounds had killed another fox on their own in Wilbraham Fen. Found again in Bottisham and had another little hunt, but scent had gone and could not do much with him. Hounds hunted well all day on a patchy scent. The first hunt a good six miles with a $3\frac{1}{2}$ mile point. The first time Hounds had been in Bottisham since the Great War.

155

1969–70 season   *Joint Masters:* MR AND MRS E. H. VESTEY

March 25th.   Brent Pelham Hall by invitation. The Newmarket & Thurlow's last day. Drew a couple of coverts blank and then found in Oxbury. Went away nicely over the River Stort by Roast Green to Wood Hall. Got in a muddle with deer and lost eight couple of hounds. The rest picked up the line again and hunted nicely by Chardwell and Clodmore Hill where we checked. Ran on into Rockall's to ground the far end. Hacked back and found again by Brent Pelham. Hunted round these coverts and then went away from Oxbury finishing on a poor line going into Roughway Wood, after ninety minutes with some very tired horses. A high note on which to finish with hounds hunting well throughout.

The Puckeridge Hunt Diaries

1838-9 season *Master:* MR NICHOLAS PARRY
from *Bell's Life*, 16 December 1838 An account of the famous Sandy
Warren run, 1 December 1838

THE PUCKERIDGE HOUNDS

We are happy to be able this week to supply our omission of the week previous and to present our readers with an authentic account of the extraordinary run these hounds had on Saturday the 1st inst. The glory of Hertfordshire (as we some weeks ago ventured to prognosticate it would be) is restored under the able management of Mr. Parry, seconded by the talent and energy of Simpson one of the most promising young huntsmen that ever entered the field. The sport of the season has been brilliant, but Saturday was a day the like of which few look upon twice in their lives even though they live to the age of the veteran John Chapman, who, though upwards of seventy, was one of the few in at the death. The meet on Saturday was Sandon, when after drawing several coverts blank, a leash of foxes were found at Broadfield; the hounds settled well to one of them and hunted him very steadily to Sandon Fryers and on to Wallington Springs; here they divided for a short time, but the greater part of the pack stuck to the hunted fox, got away close to him, and went across the open to Bygrave at a racing pace, the fox being in view nearly all the way; luckily for the nags, they checked for an instant here and off again at much the same pace through Mr. Hill's plantations at Newnham, where there was another slight check to Hinxworth, Edworth and over the Millow Bottoms; the country throughout all this line was dreadfully heavy, and it was curious to watch the caution of the leaders, for although the hounds were a field or more ahead, no one dared to make play; each one looked at his neighbour as much as to say, we can't stand this long; and many were the ironical cautions not to ride over the hounds. From Millow the line was taken by Dunton Fen, leaving Biggleswade and Stratton Park (The Cambridgeshire kennel) to the left, to Sutton through Sutton Park, where the pace considerably abated from the sheer inability of hounds and horses to go faster, leaving Potton to the right and on towards Everton. The fox here changed his point and, turning to the left, tried to reach Sandy Warren on the Hssels; in this he failed and was killed a short distance from the Warren. The line taken is estimated at from 23 to 24 miles and the distance from point to point cannot be less than 16 to 17 miles; the time was two hours and five minutes and out of a very fine field not more than twenty saw the finish. It is useless to mention names on an occasion like the present, as frequently some are up who have not borne the heat and burden of the day, but we must say that Mr. Parry went a right good one and saw as much of the run as anyone, if not more.

157

Simpson stuck to his hounds well and killed his fox mounted on his third nag (a mare lent him by Mr. Rayment). In returning home horses were to be seen in all directions and very many were left in the neighbourhood. We have since heard of the death of three, one of which we regret to say was Simpson's.

1847–8 season *Joint Masters:* MR NICHOLAS PARRY AND MR WILLIAM WIGRAM

Extract from *Bell's Life,* 5 December 1847

The Puckeridge Hounds:
Mr. Editor I am a reader of your paper and find that authenticated accounts of good runs are acceptable. Yesterday the Puckeridge Hounds met at Stanstead, Essex; after drawing several coverts blank, they found a fox in a turnip field adjoining Northy Wood, behind Rickling Green. They went away through Broom Wood, over the London road and through Quendon Wood, crossed the railway and through the Jock, through the further part of Widdington High Wood, under Park Springs and away over fine country to the Chickney Brook, which he crossed then nearly up to Horham Hall which he left to the left, and over the Thaxted River to Little Easton, leaving Lord Maynard's Park on the right; here the fox was viewed, being ten minutes before, on to within one field of Big Wood (Bigods) and away to Stebbing, where he ran the line of the meadows and crossed the brook. Here he was viewed again and was twenty minutes before the hounds; they then hunted on to Saling Long Green: the fox then bore to the left and was lost between Fox's Wood and Luberhedges, a distance of not less then 14 or 15 miles from point to point! The ground gone over must have been nearly 20 miles, and this fine run lasted nearly two hours! I beg to remain your obedient servant. An Old Sportsman. Saffron Waldon: Dec. 2. 1847.

1850–1 season *Master:* MR NICHOLAS PARRY

Extract from *Bell's Life,* 16 February 1851

The Puckeridge Hounds
Mr. Editor . . . The meet Hazel End; found a brace of foxes in Birchanger Wood; the hounds divided; part went with Simpson (the huntsman) and the whips and ran their fox to ground in Stanstead Park. The other part of the hounds settled on the fox, who broke covert and went in the direction for Lord Maynard's park; he, however, crossed the road on to Takeley Forest, ran direct to the farther end, and broke for Hatfield Heath, at a tremendous pace; he crossed the road, and set his head for Row Wood, but being hard pressed he bore to the right to Down Hall, the seat of – Selwin, Esq., crossed the pastures by Matching Church, & from thence he went straight across country to Potter Street, near Harlow-bush Common; at this point some sheep crossed the line, and caused a check of a few minutes. The Master of the hounds (Mr. Parry) with great judgement made his cast beyond Mark Hall Wood, where he hit off the scent again, but by some accident the fox was headed in Mr. Arkwright's Park; he then ran in the direction for Down Hall again, but did not quite reach that point; he turned to the right across a fine country, and ran into Man Wood in the parish of White Roothing, where there was a fresh fox, but the hounds sticking to the old scent, compelled him to break covert again in the direction of Matching Green, where he was pulled down in first-rate style, about

a mile and a half from Man Wood. So fine a run has not been witnessed for many long years; the superior horsemanship of Mr. Parry and the judgement displayed by him in hunting the hounds (having no assistance from his own men) was beyond all praise. Yours etc. An Eye Witness.

1879–80 season *Master:* MR ROBERT GOSLING

February 23. Manuden. Found at Sion Osier Bed; away nearly to Stansted, round Coppice, through Taylor's Wood Street Coppice on to Monk Wood, pointed for L. Hallingbury Hall, Hatfield Heath on the right to Lancaster Springs, nearly to Man Wood, then to Down Hall; away again to Man Wood, back to Down Hall & after a lot of work killed him. From find to finish 3 hrs 20 minutes.

1880–1 season *Master:* MR ROBERT GOSLING
From *The Field*

December 8th. Wednesday the 8th saw these hounds at Langley Green and an extraordinary good run ending with blood was the result. Found at Roughway. The fox never hung a moment, went through Clavering Park and Earl's Wood like lightning, from which our Master viewed him away, leaving Barkway just on his right, set his head as if for Capons, which he went within a field of, then, bearing to the right, left Reed Wood to the right and went straight to Hawkins (the same covert where we found such a good fox on Saturday) Through it like a shot without hanging a moment, and the same through Sandon Park Wood on to Sandon Roe Wood, where he got headed by some ploughmen, so turned to the right, but made his point a little deeper. Hounds took him into the covert, where, owing to our fox lying down, and the covert being very thick, they were at fault for a short time. They soon got him on his legs again, rattled him round the covert from which he broke, and hounds pulled him down in the open one field off; time up to our fox entering Sandon Roe Wood, one hour and thirty minutes going the whole time. Very few saw this really fine run, the pace being so fast there is no catching these hounds if once left behind, when with a good scent they really drive, as only well made and well-bred hounds can do – the great difference between a first and a second-rate pack. The distance from point to point in the ordnance survey map is nearly nine miles and the way they ran thirteen miles.

1902–3 season MR EDWARD E. BARCLAY
From Mr Thomas Purkis's diary

Dec. 24th. Met The Puckeridge at Clavering Hill Green; drew for an outlier first then the Arkesden covers blank found at Quendon ran very fast up wind across the open by Berden to the Beeches on to Furneux Pelham time 35 mins to here then he turned downwind to Scales Park when I think we changed foxes, however hounds hunted very prettily on through Clavering Park on to Roughway across to the Lower End of Langley High Wood through Pond Street Wood up the hill to Elmdon village then as it was getting dark I gave up as they were holding the hounds towards Quendon to see if they could hit the line off. A very fine day's sport, only lacked blood, which was hard lines as they doubtless changed at Scales. Rode Reindeer.

Feb. 4th. Met The Puckeridge at Debden Cross; drew Rowney, Cessny, Peverells, Sykello Springs, Little and Great Hales all blank; found in Grove close to Pounce Wood, ran across to Pounce Wood when he got to ground in a drain close to Walden Road, poked him out then ran on with a good scent across to Great Hales, then over the Railway across to Grimmage over the Little Walden Road nearly to Chesterford Park then turned right handed up to Mitchell's Grove on to Sheddle Wood when he got to ground close to the Railway and had to leave him. Time 1 hr. Rode Reindeer.

1904–5 season   *Master:* MR EDWARD E. BARCLAY
From Mr Thomas Purkis's diary

Jan. 4th. Met The Puckeridge at Debden Cross; found a good fox at Rowney, ran with a very catchy scent by Wimbish Green and Radwinter Rectory across by Tickle Springs when we had a long check but got a holloa and ran thro' the top end of Big Bendysh across to Helion's Bumpstead village then left handed to ground in Ketteridge's Drain. Time 1 hr. 30 mins. Rode Reindeer.

Feb. 7th. Met The Puckeridge at Elsenham, a wet morning and a good scent. Found a fox at East End Wood, ran to Chickney and lost. Found 2nd fox at Funnell Wood, ran nearly to Bassingbourne and lost. Found third fox at Mr. Maitland's covers at Stanstead, chopped one but could not make anything of the 2nd; found 5th fox at Absey ran with a much improved scent to ground against Oakley Hall Farm; found 6th fox at Widdington High wood, ran very fast to Debden Hall across the Park to Rowney where we lost him dead beat. Rode Reindeer.

1906–7 season   *Master:* MR EDWARD E. BARCLAY
From Mr Thomas Purkis's diary

Dec. 19th. Met The Puckeridge at Debden Cross; draw Rowney first, found a good fox which broke at once towards Thaxted but could not hunt him further than the Thaxted and Walden Road. Came back to Rowney and found again ran with a rare cry round the cover for 30 minutes and killed then drew Widdington High and Jock Wood blank when we came home. Rode Reindeer.

Feb. 11th. Met the Puckeridge at S. Walden; did not start until 12.0 as the frost was still very bad under hedges; found at Pounce Hall, ran with a poor scent thro the Hales on to within a field of Bendysh then came and drew all the covers up to Emannuel Wood blank, found there and ran fast (as it began to freeze again) across through Gremmage to Nursen Wood back to Chesterford Common on to Hildersham Wood where they stopped hounds as it was 5.15. A very good 40 minutes. Rode Reindeer.

1923–4 season *Joint Masters:* MR EDWARD E. BARCLAY AND
MAJOR M. E. BARCLAY FOR A COMMITTEE

From Major M. E. Barclay's diary

January, Wednesday the 16th. Found the lady pack at Patmore Heath with a large field out. Patmore Hall Wood was blank, but a leash of foxes got off a stubble field at the Battles end of the wood and the selected one ran a loop round by Hixham Hall and back into the wood. Trying to break at the Bogs End he was headed short-back by motor-cars and this lost some valuable time, but hounds ran him well back through the wood, across into the Gravel Pit Plantation and away at the top right hand corner. Crossing the Pelham–Albury Road to the right of the hamlet, the fox sank the valley, and going over the river Ash, ran the whole length of Oaken Spring. Coming away at he top, he left Hole Farm buildings just on the right and passing through the long spring, crossed the Cockhampstead Farm and ran down nearly to the back of Braughing; but swinging left-handed he went over the Braughing Little Hadham road and hounds checked for the first time just outside Gatesbury Covert after a fast forty-five minutes from the time of finding. The fox had turned sharp left-handed and some little time was spent before the line was recovered. Hounds then ran through Sacombe Wood and over the valley up into Upp Hill Warren where the fox had waited. They hunted him all round the Warren, across the road into New Wood, round this, back into the Warren and away again at the bottom corner pointing for Standon. Running on well, they crossed the Standon–Hadham road leaving Standon just on the right and down to the railway, alongside of which the fox went, being then in view of all the field, and only about 300 yards in front of hounds. Crossing the railway by the lane leading over the river to Lordship the fox followed the river bank and then crossed the river, about half way between the Lordship and Latchford Ford, and went on up into Plashes Wood. Hunting him well round the Standon quarter unluckily there were two lines, but the main body of the pack drove a fox without checking back through Plashes and Hanging Wood and Blackie Mead, away over the road at the bottom and straight on for Youngsbury, leaving the long strips of covert away on the right. On forcing their fox well into a little spinney just outside Youngsbury Buildings, however, they failed to recover the line, after an excellent gallop of an hour and fifty five minutes, making a seven and a half mile point. It was a long trot back to draw Ringsbury and Burrell Woods blank but hounds found again at once in Upwick Wood and went away at the bottom pointing for Patmore. At the end of the first field the fox was badly headed and the line was not recovered and with Shaw Wood and Lye Wood proving blank they went home.

1925–6 season *Joint Masters:* MR EDWARD E. BARCLAY AND
MAJOR M. E. BARCLAY, FOR A COMMITTEE

From Major M. E. Barclay's diary

Jan. 2nd. [At Walkern Hall]
On January 2nd Miss Cotton-Browne dispensed generous hospitality to a large field and a good day's sport ensued. Her St. John's Wood at once produced several foxes, the selected one going away through Lord's Wood across Walkern Park Farm and through Woodcrofts. Then, sinking the valley and crossing the Bourne, the lady pack (holding Bugby's Farm on the left and Libury Hall on the right) running well, crossed the Munden road for Levens Green,

hounds checking on the road by Brockolds Farm. It was a fast forty minutes up to here. Hitting off the line, hounds hunted over the Levens Green–Old Hall Green road, through Beggar, and leaving Righgrounds on the right and Riggery Farm to the left, pointed for Standon Green End. But bearing short right-handed by Potters Green, they left Rowney Prior on the left to be run out of scent near Surtees Gorse after a good hunt of seventy-five minutes, making a four and a half mile point. On the way back to draw Moor Hall, a travelling fox was holloaed by Great Munden Church hounds running him hard, with Bugby's Farm on the left and Stag Hall on the right, over the Rush Green–Haultwick road. Leaving Woodcrofts on the left they went on through Thrift, holding Wood End on the right and through a corner of Lords Wood. Then with a right handed turn the pack left Pigs Foot on the right, crossing Moor Green and the old Roman road with Drinkwater Spring on the left, and going on over Cottered Warren Farm. Leaving Tannis Court on the right and Buttermilk Hall on the left, hounds still ran hard across Aspenden Park, with the hall on the right, as if for Buntingford, but turning sharp left-handed by Aspenden Thicket, the hunt crossed the Buntingford–Cottered Wood, going on with Thricking Hall on the left by Balderose and through a corner of Broadfield Wood, to be stopped entering Friars Wood with all the hunt horses beat, having missed the second horses. Only ten of the original large field got through this very good hunt, hounds running hard most of the time of ninety minutes, with a six mile point and quite fourteen miles as hounds ran, the country riding awfully deep.

February 3rd. [At Chrishall Grange Wood]. On Wednesday the bitch pack brought off a great hunt in a thick fog. The fox would not leave the wood for a considerable time and scent was bad. At last, breaking at the top corner, he ran through Ickleton Grange farmstead, over the Elmdon–Chrishall Grange road and pointed for Chrishall village, but swinging left-handed passed through Park Wood, going away at the church corner. Hounds were now running well. Chiswick Hall was held on the left, and again swinging left-handed, leaving Pond Street Wood just on the left, the fox went nearly up to the Langley–Duddenhoe End road. Then with a sharp right-handed turn back he passed through a corner of Langley High Wood, running the rides all the way, to come out to the Langley road at the top corner. Crossing this hounds went on with the Cosh on the left, then crossing the old blind lane leading to Bird Green about half way along, the fox ran through Scotts Wood. Breaking with Thurrocks Farm on the right, hounds crossed the road between the two Clavering Mills, sinking the valley and crossing the Brent–Pelham–Clavering lower road and brook at Deers Green. The hunt now went on over the upper-Clavering road with Starlings Green just on the right, for Berden Priory, but holding this on the right, crossed the Berden–Manuden road near the chalk pit. Then, leaving Little London just on the left, hounds had to be stopped in this fine hunt, with the fox viewed only three minutes in front of them, when pointing for Battles Wood, as they had now entered the prohibited foot and mouth area. It was a fine piece of hound work, and for their first half-hour they had to pick the line out but after Park Wood, when the pack worked up to their fox, they kept running at a nice hunting pace. The time was one hour and fifty five minutes, measuring a nine mile point and many more as hounds ran, for the fox twisted about a good deal. During the whole of this long run not a single strand of wire was encountered and the line was over a good piece of enclosed country, but it rode terribly heavy. The fog was so thick that till just before the end of the hunt it was difficult to see fifty yards.

1927–8 season *Joint Masters:* MR EDWARD E. BARCLAY AND
MAJOR M. E. BARCLAY FOR A COMMITTEE

From *Horse and Hound,* an account of a meet on 12 March 1928

On March 12th the dog pack met at Audley End Station. Cornwallis Hill and the Ring were blank, but on going on to the rough thorny fields near Green Wood hounds soon found a fox. They went through Green, Lee and Free Woods, and, after a turn round the latter, went away down the strip, swinging right-handed, with Lofts Hall on the left, into Park Wood. Pushing their fox through this large covert, they came away with Chrishall Church on the left and went to Barnes Wood. Running along the outside, hounds went away through Needles, Chishill Great Wood, James's, Widney and Pond Bottom, and then away, with Abbot's Bury and Smith's End on the right. They crossed the London–Cambridge road, with Newsells on the left, went through Long Pen and, bearing away right-handed over the Barley–Royston road, with Burloes on the left, went on to Noon's Folly, Crossing the main road again, leaving the 'Coach and Horses' on their left, the pack hunted on to Dacre's Gorse, where they were beaten. This was a fine hunt of two and a half hours, making an eight mile point. There was a useful scent on the heavy land, but when hounds got on to the open dry land they had to hunt.

1930–1 season *Joint Masters:* MR EDWARD E. BARCLAY AND
MAJOR M. E. BARCLAY FOR A COMMITTEE

From Major M. E. Barclay's diary

Friday January 16th. P.H. (doghounds) at Hadham Park Gates. Drew Blood-hounds blank. Found in Hoggets & came away with Wickham Hall on the left, also Bailey Hills, & on by Farnham Church, across Hassobury Park, by the Old Kennels & on to Battle Wd & lost after a nice hunt of 45 minutes. Found in Patmore Hall Wds & went away through the Gravel Pit Plantation, crossed the Albury–Furneux Pelham road by High Farm as if for Albury Park but turned sharp left up the valley through Ninna Wd & Upwick Wd, where several foxes were on foot & hounds divided. Got them together & hunted across to Shaw Wd & marked to ground there. Killed him. Found again in Patmore Hall Wd & for 30 mins the fox refused to leave & I think we were on a vixen, but at last he went away by Hixham Hall, crossed the Furneux Pelham–Manuden Mill road & on to Berden Park. Here the fox ran a long way down the cart road, where we had before come along to draw Patmore Hall Wd form Battles Way. Overcame this difficulty, ran on over the Park & crossed the Berden–Stocking Pelham road by the Council Cottages. Here Douglas made a very good hit, where the fox had gone down the Parsonage Farm lane. Ran on for a bit & got a good holloa near Curls Manor; then turned right-handed & crossed the Clavering–Manuden road & the Allotments, with Clavering just on the left, crossed the valley & ran up the old green lane. Here the fox ran the ditches, either one side or the other of the lane, hounds hunting it beautifully; left Moat Farm on the left & hunted up to our fox in a small pond close to the farm buildings opposite the Old Rectory at Rickling Church End & killed him there. Wilfred had him first. A great hunt of 1 hr & 40 mins altogether. 1 hr 10 mins from leaving Patmore Hall Wd & a 4¾ mile point. I *was* proud of my hounds. I think it was about the greatest triumph they & I have ever had. They hunted magnificently. We had many difficulties to overcome. Rode 'Jackal' through this hunt.

1931–2 season *Joint Masters:* MR EDWARD E. BARCLAY AND
MAJOR M. E. BARCLAY FOR A COMMITTEE
From Major M. E. Barclay's diary

Saturday January 23rd. P.H.(Bitches) at Brent Pelham. The Annual Hunt Meeting – which was much more largely attended than usual as a special whip had been sent round, since, owing to the financial crisis, our subscriptions have dropped (also several good subscribers have either left the country or died). They asked us to go on, but we shall probably only be able to do 3 days a week & shall not keep a 2nd Whip. A satisfactory meeting. Drew Chamberlains blank. Hunted a stale line away fron Meesden Hall Wood to Oxbury & lost. Several foxes in Beeches Wd. Hunted one away by Old End & Parish Acre to Meesden Hall Wd. Away over the road to Chamberlains & away at the top & up our boundary fence & then left handed over the Anstey road & on by Gipsy Lane, over the Buntingford road, through Three Acre Wd & Arney Spring into Hormead Park. Out to the Thrift & back to the Park & then away through Arney Spring; left Three Acre Wd & Borley Green just on the left almost to the Vicarage, but turned left by Bury Farm, left Cole Green on the right, crossing the Anstey road across New Closes; left Ladylike Spring on the right, through Five Acre Wd as if for Sacles, but luckily John Sworder happened to be on the road & turned our fox left-handed; left Hale Farm on the right & on over the road & Anstey Castle Mound & into Northey. Straight through this & away with Bandons Pit on the left, crossed the Cave Gate–Anstey road & on over the Cambridge road, with Biggin Farm on the left, crossed the Buckland–Barkway road to Rookey. Did not enter this, but turned left handed through Bush Spring to Reed village, skirted round this left handed, left the Church just on the right & Reed Hall on the left & then swung left-handed to Reed Wd. Only went through a corner of this & away over the main road, through Braunish, crossed the Therfield–Buckland road, through Hawkins & into Philpotts. Away from here to Kelshall village, through some cottage gardens & on to Therfield village. Hunted up to our fox in some gardens near the Church, but he got away and left the village where he had entered it, near the Rectory, & then turned left-handed over the Therfield–Reed End road, with Hay Farm on the left & then turned left again; left Park Farm on the left & hounds ran hard over the open as if for Royston, but our fox was beat & hounds ran from scent to view & killed him in the open near Mile End Bottom, a field away from the Old North Road on the west side, opposite to Seven rides. A glorious finish to a really *Great* hunt. Time 2 hrs & 30 mins and an 8 miles point & 23 miles as hounds ran. Scent seemed to get better and better as hounds ran on. Hounds did magnificiently, as also did Bob. From Hormead Park it was fast practically all the time, a real good holding scent. The best hunt for a long time for pace, distance covered, point and the right finish.

1933–4 season *Joint Masters:* MR EDWARD E. BARCLAY AND
MAJOR M. E. BARCLAY FOR A COMMITTEE
From Major M. E. Barclay's diary

Saturday January 13th. P.H. (Bitches) at Barkway Mill. Drew Rookey & other coverts & Reed Wd blank. Found in Capons & went away towards Cave Gate straight into a flock of ewes & no more good was done. Found an outlier near Dell Field. Spring, Cornerbury, but could only hunt him across a few fields & lost. Alswick Hall Wd blank. Chopped a fox in Camps Wd. Found an outlier near by & ran fast through Room Wd & Hay Lodge Covert & away left handed to Dassels, where the fox was headed & ran back by Stonebury & through Dog Kennel Spring (2 foxes in front of us now) through Camps Wd & marked to ground on the bank beyond. Meanwhile our original fox had gone on & Willie Sale gave us a very good holloa, & hounds ran on with him through Alswick Hall Wd, crossed the Buntingford–Hare St. road left Beauchamps Farm on the right, crossed the Wyddial–Cave Gate road, through Forty Acres, over Biggin Moor, crossed the Buckland–Barkway road to Bush Spring, where our fox was headed & turned towards Reed Wd; was headed again & ran nearly to the Buckland–Barkway road & turned left again, completing a circle, back to Bush Spring. There was a longish check here, but Bob made a very good cast round Rookey & hit him off near the Chalk Pit. Crossed the Joint, through Coopers Green, left Newsell's Barns on the right, crossed the Royston–Barkway road & hounds ran from scent to view and killed their fox in the open on Whitely Hill, after a great hunt of 1 hr 30 mins & an 8 mile point. Bob and his hounds put up a great performance as scent, though useful, was not first-rate. Very few people left at the end. Many went home at the check by Bush Spring.

Saturday January 20th. P.H. (bitches) at Monteagle, Sandon, Found a brace in Roe Wd & after several turns in covert went away with one over the lane to Park Wd & on over Gannock Bourne to the Thorns by Rain Hill; then turned left-handed back over the Sandon–Slip End road to Roe Wd. Away again through Park Wd & over Gannock Bourne through the Thorns & over the Therfield–Slip End road by Coombe Farm, left the Thrift Farm on the left, into Church Hill, Royston Heath, & lost him after a good hunt of 1 hr 35 mins. Found in Tichneys & away to Friars, where some time was spent in hunting various foxes. At last got a fox away & through Broadfield Wd & ran fast, going away by the old chalk pit & across Potato Lane; crossed the Cottered–Cumberlow Green road at Lodge Hill, left Cottered & Hare Street on the left, crossed the Cottered–Cromer road with Cromer Mill on the right, through Church Field Common up to Ardeley Village, where the fox was headed & turned right-handed through Markhams & on nearly to Walkern Rectory but bore right-handed crossing the Walkern–Cromer road, through Howells Wood & on by Dane End into Box Wd. Hounds ran well all round this covert & away through the small springs as if for Stevenage, but swung round right-handed through Well Wd, left Botany Bay on the left as if for Howells again, but the fox ran into a line of beaters & turned back towards Broxbury. Here the fox got out of a hedge & hounds getting a view, coursed him down & killed him in the open, in the middle of a field, by the Broxbury–Walkern lane, just in fron of a line of guns – they took it very well! This was another great hunt of 1 hr 55 mins. Bob and his hounds put up yet another fine performance. A 6 mile point.

1936–7 season *Joint Masters:* MR EWARD E. BARCLAY AND MAJOR M. E. BARCLAY FOR A COMMITTEE
From Major M. E. Barclay's diary

Monday March 1st. P.H. (Doghounds, 18 couple) at Berden. A sharpish white frost & a slight fall of snow. There was an inch or so of snow on Saturday night. Looked for outliers on Highlands & Clavering Hill Farms without success. Came back to our coverts; drew Little Flexlands blank, but found a real old customer in Beaches Wd. Went away by Shonks Moat & over the Clavering road & across Arsley, left Dews Green & Berden Priory just on the right, left Parsonage Farm on the left nearly to Clavering Hall, but turned right-handed, crossed the Clavering–Manuden road with Berden Lodge (late Highlands) on the right, through the kale on Highlands Farm through the Fir Covert above Potash, onto a big plough a field away from Northey Gorse. This had been a very fast 20 mins to here. Scent seemed to deteriorate all of a sudden & hounds could only hunt on, with Calendars just on the left, over the brook & the fox did a lot of twisting and turning between the brook & the Manuden–Clavering road, before he at last crossed the latter, then pointed for Maggots End, but turned right for Battles Wd. Ned (Ned Paxton, then 2nd whipper-in) got a good view of our fox away by Blakins Lane & then left-handed, leaving Brickhouse End on the right & Pump Spring on the right, crossed the Manuden–East End road & on, with Up End on the left, nearly to Farnham Green. He made a very sharp turn left-handed away from the Green. I was holding hounds on for Home Wd, when I got a holloa opposite Thrift Farm & hounds hunted up to their fox in a clump of bushes on the edge of Farnham Green. They got a view of him crossing the road & they ran on well, with Thrift Farm on the left & Farnham Hall on the right; over Thrimley Lane & right-handed leaving Thrimley Barn on the left up to Upwick; left Newman's house just on the left, crossed the road & ran in between Upwick Hall & Upwick House, through the Fir Trees and right-handed into Upwick Wd. Ned viewed our fox away & hounds hunted on, with Inset Spring on the right, through Shaw Wd & on by Up End & Lye Wd, recrossed the East End–Manuden road, left Pump Spring on the left & Ned viewed our fox back into Battles Wd. Away at the bottom & over the Manuden–Clavering road, crossed the brook with Calendars on the left & over the Rickling–Manuden Lane, through Wakelands & Bury Springs, left Oughty on the left & into Hargraves Park. Hunted round the Shrubberies for some time, but he beat us in the end – there are so many back gardens etc. Very bad luck as hounds richly deserved him. This was a really great hunt of 3 hrs 20 mins, the first 20 mins very fast. It measures a 5½ mile point from Beaches Wd. to Hargraves Park, a 4½ mile point from near Clavering Hall to Upwick Fir Trees & a 4 mile point across from Hargraves Park to Upwick Wd. Hounds were magnificent. They hunted perfectly wonderfully . . . We were all on at the end of the hunt, which was very satisfactory. This is the best hunt of the season so far & for several seasons . . . As hounds ran it was quite 25 miles.

1937–8 season *Joint Masters:* Mr Edward E. Barclay and Major M. E. Barclay for a committee

From Major M. E. Barclay's diary

Monday February 21st: P.H.(doghounds, 15 couple) at Clanver End. It looked like a good hunting day & was. We found a fox in the Rough Field below Green Wd & hounds ran hard as if for Lea Wd., but swung right-handed through Green Wd & away over the lane as if for Cornwallis Hill; but soon turned left over the Littlebury Green–Littlebury road & threw up all of a sudden near How Hall & we could make no more of it. I afterwards heard that there was a drain there. No doubt he got in. Time 10 mins. Drew Howe Wd & Strethall Wd blank. Found a brace or a leash in Free Wd & after a turn in covert hounds raced away to & through Lea Wd & Bitchets Spring & marked to ground in the deep ditch between there & Ann's Wd. Time 15 mins: killed him. Drew Rockells & the Woodhall, Arkesden coverts blank. Hounds hit off a line out of Morley Wd & ran hard by the Cosh Farm & over Lawkins Lane & the Langley–Duddenhoe End road & into Langley High Wd just above the middle ride & they fairly flew down through the wood (I have never seen hounds get through it so quick) & away straight through Pond Street; left Duddenhoe End School on the right & over the Duddenhoe End–Elmdon road above the chalk pit, through Dowes Grove & into Rockells; a loop here & away as if for Hobbs Eyrie, but bore right-handed, with Newland End on the right, nearly to Arkesden. It had been a brilliant, racing 30 mins to here. Our fox had put in a good deal of work here, but hounds worked it out beautifully, crossed the Arkesden–Duddenhoe End road & on by Chardwell Farm into Stocking Grove at Wood Hall (the Long Spring). Hunted slowly through this & away right-handed almost down to the brook, as if for Scotts Wd., but could not get on. But just when it looked as if we were done, there was a holloa back towards Sticklers Green. Hit off the line of our fox near there & ran on well again, leaving Clavering Place Farm on the left, up to the Valance. Here the fox had put in some more work, but hounds again unravelled it & ran on well, crossing the road, with Clavering Mills on the left as if for the Lower Road to Clavering but short of it bore right-handed, with Deers Green on the left; crossed the brook, left Ford End just on the right & ran on into Beaches Wd., entering it at the Oxbury End. Ran straight up it, 3 couple got onto a fresh fox, but luckily the main body stuck to their hunted one. They came away right-handed with the Fir Trees just on the right, & on up to the Hall Wd. Hounds checked at the gate into the Sanctuary & there was a holloa at the bottom of the young wood. As I was taking hounds to this they hit off another fox & raced away over to Westley, leaving Black Hall on the left, through Meesden Hall Wd; left Meesden Hall on the left & luckily checked on some sheep stain between the Church & Meesden Bury. I got them here & took them back to Hall Wd. Hit off our now very tired fox where he had been seen to go back into the covert & hunted slowly through it & on to the pond in Nicholas. As I was going up to the gate into the stables, I viewed our fox going away towards the dog kennels. Put hounds onto him in the shrubberies by the Raquet Court, but he climbed the wall into the back stable yard! Hounds raced him down Cut-throat Lane, crossed the road with Down Hall on the right, through Laundry Gorse & over the Furneux Pelham road & into the Bourne. Frank Edward Debenham viewed him come out & go back there with one hound close to him; then Ned viewed him with his back to a tree & Barrister baying him! He holloaed the other hounds on & they killed him. A grand finish to a truly great hunt. It is, I think, almost the best hunt I have ever had with my doghounds. It was a great performance on their part. Time 2 hrs 25 minutes & a 5½ mile point. Twice we were very nearly done – once at Wood Hall & again at Hall Wd when hounds changed, but luck was with us. Hounds in tremendous form, making the most beautiful swinging galloping casts led by Turpin. He is a brilliant foxhound. There is really nothing to choose between most of them… Rode Pilot & Reuben. I rode the latter all through this hunt & he went brilliantly. Only two people finished the hunt besides Ned & myself & they were Norman Pryor & Frank Edward Debenham. A great scenting day. This hunt was all over some of our best & most sporting country.

1938–9 season *Joint Masters:* MR EDWARD E. BARCLAY AND
MAJOR M. E. BARCLAY FOR A COMMITTEE
From Major M. E. Barclay's diary

Saturday April 1st. P.H. (doghounds, 18½ couple) at Anstey at 12.0. A mild warm but cloudy day & wind S.E. Drew Northey blank. Found in the East Wd quarter of Scales Park & ran well on a good scent in here for some time & then away over the Woodman Inn lane, crossed the Nuthampstead–Langley Lawn Lane, running hard through Oaks Bushes & Doctors Grove, leaving the Lake covert on the left. The fox was headed on the Little Chishill–Langley road & turned back into Clavering Park. Hunted slowly through this covert & away through Lady Grove & by Up End to the Rough by the Fir Covert. Hounds got a view of their fox here & ran him onto the Fir Covert & killed him. A good hunt of 55 mins. While breaking up the fox, Ben brought news of a fox being viewed away from Whitehill, crossing the Meesden–Anstey road. Hit him off where he crossed the road & hunted him back over the road & into Scales, but he had got too much lead & was lost in the wood. Found in some cut wood in the middle of Scales & ran hard in a ring here, round by Jacks Grove & the Rough Field, back over the main road & away through Up End Thorns, hounds running very hard, through the Fir Trees; crossed the Langley–Meesden road & the Brook & pointed for Bocking, but turned right-handed over the Meesden–Clavering road, with Further Ford End on the left, recrossed the brook with the White Bridge on the right & raced on with Meesden Hall on the right, through Meesden Hall Wd & over the Brent–Pelham–Meesden road & through Chamberlains & away over Bucmust. This was the only time I touched hounds throughout this hunt. Ran hard on over the Brent-Pelham–Anstey road & pointed for Brick House, but our fox was turned by a man. Hounds turned beautifully with their fox, right-handed by Puttocks End, recrossing the Brent-Pelham–Anstey road, left Coltsfoot Farm just on the left & Five Acre Wd on the right & bore left handed leaving Hale Farm & Anstey Rectory on the right & on to the Castle Mound at Anstey Hall. Got up on our now beaten fox here & after chasing him round Anstey Hall garden hounds killed their fox in the open in a meadow. This was a brilliant gallop of 57 minutes from finding in Scales & 40 minutes from leaving Scales. The best finish to a season I ever remember. It is the last proper day's hunting . . . Hounds were in grand form, everyone doing his bit, practically nothing to choose between any of them. Rode Reuben all day as I missed my second horse . . .

1939–40 season *Joint Masters:* MR EDWARD E. BARCLAY AND
MAJOR M. E. BARCLAY FOR A COMMITEE

Nov. 4th.   Found in Capons and Hounds ran very hard by Anstey and Meesden to Bocking and thence to Brent Pelham where they were stopped. A very good hunt of 1 hr ten minutes and a 5 mile point.

December 6th.   Found in Broom Wood and ran by Manuden to Upwick Wood and lost. A very good hunt of 1 hr 25 minutes and a 5 mile point.

December 12th. Found in Hassobury Home Wood and after running a ring out by Manuden Village and back ran by Patmore Hall Wood and Uwpick Wood through the Upp Hall coverts and on to Rectory Springs and lost. A very good hunt of 2 hours and 30 minutes and a 6 mile point.

1940–1 season *Masters:* MR EDWARD E. BARCLAY AND MAJOR M. E. BARCLAY FOR A COMMITTEE

February 12th.   Ben Wilkinson ill and Mr. Charlie Barclay hunting hounds: Found in Beaches Gorse and ran by Chamberlains, just touched a corner of Scales Wood and killed in the open at Shaftenhoe End. A first rate hunt of 1 hour and 25 minutes and a 5 mile point.

1943–4 season *Masters:* MR EDWARD E. BARCLAY AND MAJOR M. E. BARCLAY FOR A COMMITTEE

October 9th.   Found in Upwick Wood and ran by Albury Park nearly to Patricks Wood, thence by Stocking Pelham and Berden Park up to the Hassobury Park fence and hounds were finally stopped at Farnham Green. A first rate hunt of 1 hour 50 mins and a 4½ mile point.

October 30th.   Found in Rogers Wood and hounds ran very hard indeed by Hormead Park to Capons where they got among fresh foxes and had to be stopped. A very good 47 mins and a 5 mile point.

Dec. 4th.   Found in Hazel End and hounds fairly raced for 35 mins and finally marked to ground below Upwick. Time 35 mins.

Dec. 18th.   Found in Broom Wood and had a good hunt by Quendon Springs and Newport Osiers and lost near Clavering. Time 1 hr 15 mins and a 4 mile point.

1944–5 season *Masters:* MR EDWARD E. BARCLAY AND MAJOR M. E. BARCLAY FOR A COMMITTEE

Nov. 11th.   Found in Beaches Wood and ran by the Hall Wood, Laundry Gorse, Patricks Wood, Hormead Park, Corinna Plantation, Patient End, Albury Park to Patmore Hall Wood, where hounds lost. Time 1 hr 35 mins and a 4 mile point.

February 20th.   Found in Patmore Hall Wood and hounds raced through Shaw Wood, skirted Bloodhounds, left the Hadham Park Coverts on the right and marked to ground by the Bishops Stortford–Much Hadham Road. This was a brilliant hunt of 20 minutes in which time hounds covered 4 miles.

1945–6 season *Masters:* MR EDWARD E. BARCLAY AND MAJOR M. E. BARCLAY FOR A COMMITTEE

Nov. 3rd. (The Opening Meet).   A brilliant 35 minutes without a check from Meesden Hall Wood and killed in Great Hormead Village.

Dec. 29th. Found in Great Wood, Moor Hall and ran by Aspenden, Tannis Crt, St. John's Wood and hounds were stopped at Bennington Park. A first rate hunt of 1 hr and 55 mins and a 4½ mile point.

February 2nd. A first rate hunt of 2 hrs 10 mins from Hazel End Wood to Bloodhounds and on by Farnham, Bentfield Bury, Potash Farm, Battles and the fox was lost near Patmore Hall Wood. The point was 4½ miles.

February 12th. A fox found in Broom Wood provided a very good hunt via Battles, Potash Farm, nearly to Quendon Hall and he beat hounds at Coneyacre. Time 1½ hours and a 4 mile point.

1947–8 season   *Masters:* MR EDWARD E. BARCLAY,
MAJOR M. E. BARCLAY AND CAPTAIN CHARLES BARCLAY
FOR A COMMITTEE

Nov. 29th. A very good hunt of 1 hour and 58 minutes from Rogers Wood via Patricks Wood to Laundry Gorse. Slow up to this point and then hounds ran well by Beaches Wood as far out as East End, Furneux Pelham, then back by Stocking Pelham to Whitebarnes and thence to Laundry Gorse and killed.

Dec. 9th. An exceptioanlly good hunt from Newport Osiers via Arkesden and Oxbury Wood to Beaches Wood and killed. Time 1 hour and 10 minutes and a 5 mile point.

1948–9 season   *Masters:* MAJOR M. E. BARCLAY AND
CAPTAIN CHARLES BARCLAY FOR A COMMITTEE

December 24th. Found in Patmore Hall Wood and ran through Upwick Wood and on by Albury End through the Warren, Upp Hallon by Standon Lodge and lost west of the Railway near Arches Hall. A very good hunt of 1 hr and 17 minutes and a 5 mile point.

January 5th. A very good hunt with a fox found in Bloodhounds which was eventually killed in the open near High Wych. Time 1 hour 55 minutes and a 5½ mile point.

Jan. 15th. Hounds found at once in Clothall Great Wood and were running continuously for 4 hours and 45 minutes. At one time the hunt reached Weston and finally hounds were run out of scent near Reed Mill, 2 miles short of Royston. The furthest points were 7½ miles apart.

Feb. 12th. With the pack numbering only 6 couple a very good hunt took place with a fox found in Sun Wood, Little Hadham which was killed near Furneux Pelham. Time 1 hour and 10 minutes and a 4½ mile point.

1949–50 season *Masters:* MAJOR M. E. BARCLAY AND CAPTAIN CHARLES BARCLAY FOR A COMMITTEE

Jan. 14th. Found in Coldash and ran via Clothall Great Wood nearly to Bygrave. Then swung back righthanded via the Wallington Wireless Station to Clothall Great Wood. Away at once to Friars and lost near Roe Green Sandon. Time 2 hrs and 10 mins and a 4 mile point. The next fox was found in Park Wood, Sandon and after a good 40 mins was killed close to Capons making a 3½ mile point.

March 1st. A fox found in Bloodhounds provided a really good hunt of 1 hr and 25 mins, going through Bailey Hills across Hassobury Park and on by Bentfield Bower and Oughty to Broom Wood, where hounds changed foxes. This was a point of 5 miles.

1950–1 season *Masters:* MAJOR M. E. BARCLAY AND CAPTAIN CHARLES BARCLAY FOR A COMMITTEE

January 3rd. In the snow from Clavering Park a fast 35 minutes via Langley Upper Green and Morley Wood to ground short of Clanver End. A 4 mile point.

March 10th. A very good scenting day. A fox from Albury Park provided a fast circular hunt of 25 minutes before being lost. The next fox from Upwick Wood was raced for the first 20 minutes to near Battles Wood and hunted more slowly to the Clavering–Manuden road and lost. A five mile point and 45 minutes altogether. A fox was killed in Patmore Hall Wood and another provided a good hunt of 1 hour and 40 minutes in a ring and was lost.

March 14th. A fox from Battles Wood provided a fast 22 minutes to ground by Pinchpools Farm. The next fox, an outlier near Manuden, gave a very good hunt to Oxbury Wood, Brent Pelham and was killed. Time 50 minutes and a 4 mile point.

1951–2 season *Masters:* MAJOR M. E. BARCLAY AND CAPTAIN CHARLES BARCLAY FOR A COMMITTEE

November 7th. From Battles Wood via Berdon Park and East End by the Albury Hall coverts. Time 40 minutes and a 3½ mile point.

Dec. 22nd. Found in Earls Wood and ran through Clavering Park and away without touching a covert and over the open country nearly to Anthony Hill and back by Heydon Village, the Needles, Little Chishill Great Wood and into Clavering Park where hounds divided. A very good hunt of 2 hours and 10 minutes and a 4½ mile point.

March 1st. Found in Park Wood, Sandon, and hunted on a poor scent through Reed Wood and Rookey and away over the open country via Coopers Green to Burloes and killed in the open. A very good persevering hunt of 2 hours and 50 minutes and a 5 mile point.

1952–3 season *Masters:* MAJOR M. E. BARCLAY AND
CAPTAIN CHARLES BARCLAY FOR A COMMITTEE

November 5th.   From Hazel Wood End via Bloodhounds and Stocking Wood and killed at Kate's Green. A very good 35 minutes and a 4 mile point.

February 23rd.   From Quendon Wood via Quendon Springs, Newport Osiers, Clanver End and marked to ground in Rockalls. A very good hunt of 1 hour and 50 minutes and a 6 mile point.

1953–4 season *Masters:* MAJOR M. E. BARCLAY AND
CAPTAIN CHARLES BARCLAY FOR A COMMITTEE

November 23rd.   Littlebury Green. Found the first fox in Green Wood and after a very good 45 minutes killed in the open at Howe Wood. Got on to another fox from Howe Wood and hounds hunted very well for an hour and 10 minutes and killed in the open.

January 11th.   Barkway. Found in Cannon's Bushes and ran to Needles, thence via Roughway to Langley High Wood. Back through Roughway and hounds ran hard to Scales Park. Away at once by Whitehill. Smaley Wood and Meesden Hall Wood to Oxbury and killed. A very good hunt of 2 hours and a 4 mile point.

March 17th.   Elsenham. Found in Ailsa Wood and hunted through Oughty, Broom Wood, Catherine Grove, over the Rickling Church End–Rickling Green road on to the hill above Wicken then right handed through Quendon Springs to Coneyacre and killed. A very good hunt of 1 hour 50 minutes and a 4½ mile point.

1954–5 season *Masters:* MAJOR M. E. BARCLAY AND
CAPTAIN CHARLES BARCLAY FOR A COMMITTEE

November 17th.   High Wych. Found in Perryfield Spring and hunted by Thorley Wood to Maddams. Back through Thorley Wood to Great Plantings and on by Cradle End to Bloodhounds and on to Hoggetts and killed near Wickham Hall. Time 2 hours and 37 minutes. A 4 mile point.

December 6th.   Rickling Green. Found in Broom Wood and ran for the rest of the day. Forty minutes of it was very fast. Time 5 hours and 25 mins. Hounds were finally stopped back in Broom Wood having changed foxes. A great day's hunting.

December 27th.   Washall Green. Found in Beeches Wood and had a good show hunt in that district and killed. Time 2 hours. Found in Meesden Hall Wood and ran by Starlings Green to Stocking Pelham Hall Wood. Got close to our fox and ran straight through Beeches Wood and on by Meesden Bury through Clavering Park and stopped hounds short of Little Chishill Great Wood. Time 1 hour and 45 minutes and a 5 mile point.

January 10th.   Chrishall Grange Wood. Found in Strethall Wood and hunted slowly into Free

Wood. Ran hard from here as if for Chrishall Grange and then swung left through Park Wood, and Langley High Wood to Roughway and back to Langley High Wood and stopped. A very good hunt of 1 hour and 30 minutes and a 4 mile point.

January 24th. Elsenham. Found in the Lake Covert and had a very good hunt of 2 hours and 5 minutes and a 5 mile point, losing the fox near Woodhams Farm Debden.

1955–6 season *Masters:* MAJOR M. E. BARCLAY AND CAPTAIN CHARLES BARCLAY FOR A COMMITTEE

November 20th. Anstey. Found in Oxbury and ran through Beaches Wood to Col. Le Hardy's house at Furneux Pelham, then swung back left through Beaches Wood to Scales Park and marked to ground. A very good hunt of 1 hour and 45 minutes and a 4 mile point.

January 30th. Toggs, Clothall. Found in Clothall Little Wood and a good hunt ensued via the Old Roman Road, Luffenhall, Cromer Mill, St. John's Wood, Lords Wood and Walkern Park to ground in Shouts. Time 1 hour and 40 minutes and a 5½ mile point.

March 3rd. Sandon. Found in Roe Wood and had a good 40 minutes and lost in Clothall Great Wood. Found in Philpotts and hounds ran hard through Hawkins and West Wood to Burrell. Away left handed straight through Capons through Bushey Ley to Northey. A very good hunt of 1 hour and 20 minutes and a 5 mile point.

March 7th. Hazel End. Found in the Ash Planting and hounds ran very hard indeed across Hassobury Park, Huds Hill, Hoggets, left Stortford Park on the left to Warren Farm on to the road. This had been a 5 mile point in 30 minutes. Hunted on by Tye Green and Perry Green, left Hadham Towers on the right into Marshland Wood and Eastwick Wood. Away through Battle Wood nearly to Home Wood, Gilston and back to Eastwick Wood where there were two lines and we had changed foxes so hounds were stopped. This was a wonderful hunt of 2 hours and 30 minutes and an 8½ mile point.

1956–7 season *Masters:* MAJOR M. E. BARCLAY AND CAPTAIN CHARLES BARCLAY FOR A COMMITTEE

December 12th. Widdington. Found an outlier near Littley and had a very good hunt to the Hunt Covert in the Essex country. Time 2 hours and 45 minutes. A 4½ mile point.

December 16th. Therfield. Had a good 50 minutes to start with from Hawkins to the Church Mill covert, Royston Heath and to ground. Found in Roughfield by Broadfield and hunted the fox through Balderoe's to Throcking Hall. After a check hounds raced away up a strong wind by Arney Wood and Youngloves to Clothall Great Wood and hounds were stopped at dusk. A very good 50 minutes and a 4½ mile point.

February 6th. Bedlars Green. Found in Beggar's Hall Coppice, scent good and hounds ran hard all round the Forest to Elgins Coppice and then away off the Forest; left Canfield Hart on the left, ran between Cannon's and Taverners Green to Broomshawbury, a very fast 40 minutes to here. Then hunted on, left by Thorpe Roothing on the left nearly to Langley's Farm. Then left and hounds were stopped at Lords Wood. A first class hunt of 1 hour and 30 minutes and a 6½ mile point. Later had a very fast hunt on and off the Forest and the Park and hounds were stopped at Ladywells.

1957–8 season *Masters:* MAJOR M. E. BARCLAY AND CAPTAIN CHARLES BARCLAY FOR A COMMITTEE

November 6th. Manuden Mill. Found in Battle's Wood, over the Clavering–Manuden Road' by Pinchpools and Wakelands into Broom Wood. Away by Bunny Wood and on by Bollington Hall and Oughty over the Main Road by Orford House to Ugley Osiers. A very good hunt of 1 hour and 40 minutes and a 4 mile point.

December 26th. Washall Green. Found in Meesden Hall Wood and went away through Chamberlains; left Hall Wood on the left, through Beaches Wood to the Clavering Road. Then turned back left handed to Ford End and Deers Farm over the two Langley–Clavering roads, over Thurrock Farm; left Scotts Wood on the left, left Wood Hall, Arkesden well on the right and on by Chardwell Farm, over Clodmore Hill and hounds were stopped out of Rockells. A first rate hunt of an hour and over a 4 mile point.

January 18th. Brent Pelham. Found in Oxbury and hunted into Beaches Wood, the fox had left before we got to Oxbury. Got up to our fox and came away through Oxbury, through Meesden Hall Gardens and on through Dimsdale Gorse and Lady Grove and on through the Ash Pightle, Oaks Bushes and The Lake Covert on through James's and lost by Mincing Bury. A very good hunt of an hour and a 5 mile point.

March 26th. Bedlar's Green. After hunting on the Forest for 2 hours hounds hunted slowly on to Wall Wood where they got close to a fox and ran well through Monk Wood and away by the Ryes and hunted on by Lea Hall; left Hatfield Broad Oak on the left and on by Crabs Green; left Woolard's Ash on the left and Broomshawbury on the right and on by Wilson's Springs to Poplars where we gave up. A very good hunt of 1 hour and 20 minutes and a 4 mile point.

1958–9 season *Masters:* MAJOR M. E. BARCLAY AND CAPTAIN CHARLES BARCLAY FOR A COMMITTEE

January 24th. Brent Pelham. Found a good fox in Chamberlains and hunted him via The Hall Wood; left the Kennels on the left, left Patrick's Wood on the left, through The Thrift and Turks on through Roger's Wood and Ferricks. Away by Braughing Friars and marked to ground in The Warren Upp Hall. A very good hunt of 1 hour and 30 minutes and a 6 mile point. Found in Meesden Hall Wood and went away by Meesden Church and on by Further Ford End left Clavering Rectory on the left also Clavering hall and on by Berden Priory nearly to Beaches Manor. There hounds checked for the first time after running very hard for 45 minutes. Then hunted on leaving Beaches Wood on the left and swung right-handed to Stocking Pelham Hall Wood to ground there, but Hounds came away on a fresh fox through Beaches Wood and were stopped in the moonlight at Little Flexlands. The whole time of this first-rate hunt was 1 hour and 30 minutes. It was freezing.

March 11th. At Cumberlow Green. Found in Clothall Great Wood and went away through Coles Wood; left Wallington on the left, over Roe Green, through Roe Wood and Philpots nearly to Therfield, but turned back right handed through Hawkins and lost near West Wood. A good hunt of 1 hour and 15 minutes and a 5 mile point. Found again in Clothall Great Wood and had good 40 minutes. Away to Coles Wood and thence through Bury and Spital Woods and lost in The Happy Valley near Bush Wood.

March 18th. Aspenden. Found in Capons and hunted slowly through Burrell Wood and Hawkins to Philpots. Got close to our fox here and hounds ran hard through Tichney, Friars and Bachelors across Julians Park through Shaw Green Springs nearly to Wallington, but turned right handed to Roe Green where hounds were stopped. A very good hunt of 1 hour and 20 minutes, the last 40 minutes hounds ran hard. A 5 mile point.

1959–60 season *Masters:* MAJOR M. E. BARCLAY AND CAPTAIN CHARLES BARCLAY FOR A COMMITTEE

November 11th. Manuden Mill In the afternoon found in Hassobury Home Wood, went away by Saven End and on by Farnham Green, Lye Wood, Bray's Spring and killed in the open by Stocking Pelham Hall Wood. A very good hunt of 1 hour and 30 minutes and a 4 mile point.

January 30th. Therfield. An outlier was found by Gannock Bourne and hounds ran hard for 30 minutes and killed their fox at Fire Houses Farm. Found in Burrell Wood and went away by Green End, through Tichneys to Roe Wood. Away by Lodge Farm, crossed the road, left Wallinghams on the left, also Quicks Wood, and marked to ground in The Happy Valley. A first rate hunt of 1 hour and 25 minutes and a 6 mile point.

March 5th. Sandon. Found in Roe Wood and went away over Roe Green and ran well by Redhill through Coles Wood and into Clothall Great Wood and thence through Spital Wood and marked to ground just beyond. A good hunt of 50 minutes. Found in Friars and hounds ran hard leaving Tichneys on the right, through Roe Wood and on by Lodge Hill to Slip End where they killed their fox. A very good 35 minutes and a 5 mile pt.

March 16th. Elder Street. Found in Rowney and went away by Cabbage Wood left Yardley Hall on the right to West Wood and thence to Great Sampford. Up the brook to Clay Wood and thence over the Radwinter–Great Sampford Road as if for Bendysh, but swung back and marked to ground in a sand pit near Great Sampford. A very good hunt of 1 hour and 25 minutes and a 5½ mile point.

1960–1 season *Masters:* MAJOR M. E. BARCLAY AND CAPTAIN CHARLES BARCLAY FOR A COMMITTEE

December 19th. Westmill. Found in Turks and went away by Dassells, crossed the Cambridge

Road and the Old North Road through Cobs Park and lost by Cherry Green. A good hunt of an hour and a 4 mile point.

1961–2 season *Masters:* MAJOR M. E. BARCLAY AND CAPTAIN CHARLES BARCLAY FOR A COMMITTEE

January 24th.   At Little Chishill. Found in Canons Bushes and had a good woodland hunt in a ring by Roughway and Langley High Wood and killed by Langley Hall Spring. Next found in Walk Wood and ran to Oaks Bushes and thence ran via Shaftenhoe End Bourne; left Barley on the left, crossed the Cambridge Road and on by Noons Folly to the Royston–Newmarket road opposite Gopher Hill where hounds were stopped at dusk. A 5 mile point and a first rate 45 minutes.

March 4th.   Washall Green. In the afternoon found in Oxbury and ran hard through Beaches Wood, Hall Wood Chamberlains, left Meesden on the right and into Scales Park and round it to the Dump a good 35 minutes to here. Then hunted on through Doctors Grove and Little Chishill Great Wood and finally gave up at Shaftenhoe Bourne. A very good hunt of 1 hour and 40 minutes and a 4½ mile point.

1962–3 season *Masters:* MAJOR M. E. BARCLAY AND CAPTAIN CHARLES BARCLAY FOR A COMMITTEE

March 23rd.   At Little Chishill. A good hunt from Pond Bottom with an outlier, hounds being stopped at Capons after a good hunt of 1 hour and 15 minutes and a 5 mile point.

March 27th.   At Green Man. Thorley Houses. A good slow hunt from Maddams of 1½ hours and a 6 mile point to ground short of the Furneux Pelham–Manuden road.

1963–4 season *Masters:* CAPTAIN AND MRS CHARLES BARCLAY

January 25th.   Brent Pelham. Found in Chamberlains Wood and hounds ran well by Oxbury, Beaches Wood via Battles to ground short of the Clavering–Manuden road. A good hunt of 1¼ hours and a 4½ mile point. Found again in Laundry Gorse and hounds were stopped out of Scales Park after another good hunt of 90 minutes.

March 30th.   Rickling Green. After finding a fox in Broom Wood and killing him in the middle of the A11, hounds found in Wakelands and had a brilliant 45 minutes and were stopped short of Bishops Stortford town. A four mile point.

1964–5 season *Masters:* CAPTAIN AND MRS CHARLES BARCLAY

November 28th.   Little Chishill. Found a big old dog fox and ran him very fast to Langley High Wood and killed him in the open near Duddenhoe Grange. Found in Roughway and ran well for an hour to ground at Coltsfoot Farm, Anstey. Finally found in Needles and had a very good hunt with a 5 mile point by Rockells and gave up short of the railway at Cornwallis Hill.

December 12th. Westmill. Found in Col. McMullen's rushes by the railway. The fox soon went to ground but being bolted hounds ran very hard to Hare Street and then more slowly to ground at Lincoln Hill. A good hunt of 1 hour and a 4 mile pt. Found again in Hormead Park and hounds ran nicely to lose in pouring rain in Earls Wood; another 4 mile pt.

1965–6 season   *Masters:* CAPTAIN AND MRS CHARLES BARCLAY

December 4th. Washall Green: Hounds found in Oxbury and divided, one lot being stopped at Thurrocks and the others ran to Meesden Hall Wood where both packs were reunited and hunted a fox by Puttocks End to the Great Hormead–Brent Pelham road where the fox turned shortly back to Cole Green and Chamberlains and was killed at Whitebridge. Finding next in Beaches Wood hounds ran by Oxbury to Meesden Hall Wood where they were at fault on foiled ground and on being held quickly on to Whitehill they ran well across the aerodrome to Crossley's where they were stopped owing to shooting, after a good hunt of 1 hour and 20 minutes and a 4½ mile point.

January 26th. Brent Pelham. After finding 3½ brace in Chamberlains Wood, hounds hunted one via Beaches Wood and killed at Patricks Wood. With an outlier found near Stocking Pelham Wood hounds ran to Violets Lane and then back by Stocking Pelham Wood and Beaches Wood through Oxbury, Scott's and Morley Wood and hounds were stopped out of Langley High Wood after 1 hour and 25 minutes and a five mile point.

1966–7 season   *Masters:* CAPTAIN AND MRS CHARLES BARCLAY

December 17th. Curles Manor. Hounds found immediately in Mr. Talke's rough orchards at Starlings Green and had a very good hunt of one hour and thirty minutes and a six and a half mile point via Morley Wood, Rockells and Clanver End and hounds were stopped from the main railway line at Cornwallis Hill. Later, hounds found near Clodmore Hill and ran very fast nearly to Langley High Wood by Scotts Wood and Woodhall to ground in the Castle Mound at Clavering; a very good hunt of 55 minutes.

January 21st. Thorley Church. After a busy day's hunting from Madam's and the Plantins area hounds found late in Bloodhounds and ran slowly to Lye Wood, from this point hounds absolutely flew via Patmore Hall Wood, Oakum Spring and hounds were stopped in the moonlight from Hormead Park. A brilliant hunt of 1¼ hours and a five mile point.

February 18th. Layston Church. After killing an outlier following a circular hunt of 30 minutes hounds found a brace in Northey Wood and ran the vixen to ground at Lincoln Hill. Hounds were taken back on to the dog fox and had a really great hunt with the pace increasing the further hounds ran through Scales Park, Whitehill, nearly to Chamberlains and on via Puttock's End to Bradbury Farm. Racing on from here nearly to Layston Church they swung right handed by Widiall to Capons and from here they raced on over enormous ploughed fields by Buckland to be stopped out of Reed Wood as no horse could go any further. The fox had been viewed by car followers only just in front of hounds. A truly great hunt of 1 hour twenty minutes and a five mile point nearly all at racing pace.

1967–8 season *Masters:* CAPTAIN AND MRS CHARLES BARCLAY

February 9th.   Starlings Green. Hounds found at Woodhall, Arkesden and had a really good hunt of 2½ hours and a 4½ mile point covering a great deal of country. They ran hard back to Beaches Wood and after a ring round by Meesden Hall Wood and Oxbury marked to ground at Chamberlains. The fox bolted and hounds ran very hard by Langley Lower Green to Scales Park. Hounds hunted beautifully round this and forced the fox away back to Chamberlains where he was killed.

March 20th.   Elder Street. A fox was found at Rowney Wood and hunted on a very bad scent as far as Clay Wood. Near here the fox took refuge up an ash tree. On being disloged he ran on towards Hempstead and was eventually marked to ground near Great Sampford after a good hunt of 1½ hours and a 5 mile point.

1968–9 season *Masters:* CAPTAIN AND MRS CHARLES BARCLAY

October 23rd.   Widdington. An exceptional scenting morning. Hounds found in Littley and after two turns round the coverts were away through Debden Park, The Howe and Peverills Wood to ground on the edge of Saffron Walden. The fox was bolted and hounds raced their fox back to Peverills Wood where he was accounted for on the edge of Debden aerodrome. A wonderful hunt of one hour and thirty minutes and a five mile point. Hounds were never cast once and ran with a really grand cry.

December 26th.   Washall Green. After finding in Beaches hounds hunted very well through Oxbury to Woodhall Arkesden and on by Wicken Bonhunt and Rickling Church and to ground at Clavering Hall. A good hunt of one hour fifty minutes and a six mile point.

The Puckeridge and Thurlow Hunt Diaries

1970–1 season   *Masters:* CAPTAIN AND MRS CHARLES BARCLAY AND
MR AND MRS E. H. VESTEY

February 6th.   [Hunts Park] Found quickly in the young trees on Jarvis Hill. Ran fast towards Pelican Farm, swung right towards Northey and then left handed through Burton's Ley. Ran almost to the Bury road but turned left again through Great Wratting to the Wash. Turned left for Trundley but he was headed back into the cottage gardens where they caught him. About 3½ miles flat out.

Found quickly in Trundley, ran down to the Gravel Pit, turned up the river over the Hall meadows and back into Trundley. Away again down through the Hall garden over the river and the Wratting road, up the brook and righthanded through the Vicarage belt, Wastelands, past Temple End into Lophams. Without a pause ran straight through to Carlton Wood and on to Sipsey Bridge, where they checked for the first time on the road. Soon had the line again and ran through Sparrows Grove, drove on right through the thick young trees in Widghams, through Ten Wood and into Ditton Park Wood where we stopped as it was full of pigeon shooters. Just over eleven miles as hounds ran and very fast.

Hacked back, changed horses and found immediately in Trundley. Raced away to the Ganwick, House Farm, past Barnardiston Hall, turned short of Harlica Farm back to Sowley Green, Weathercock and back into Trundley with Hounds just behind to ground in a pipe and killed him. 4½ miles. A little drizzle early, clearing later. Mild and cloudy.

Feb. 15.   Clavering Mills. Hounds found at Woodhall Arkesden and killed at Stickling Green. Getting on to another fox at once, hounds had an historic hunt of one hour forty five minutes and an 8½ mile point via Scotts Wood, Cosh Lane and Langley Upper Green to Meesden Hall Wood. They hunted on without changing through Oxbury, Beaches Wood and Merlin Plantation, then on by Patient End, Oakum Spring to ground in the sand earths at the Brickfields, Little Hadham.

1971–2 season   *Masters:* CAPTAIN AND MRS CHARLES BARCLAY AND
MR AND MRS E. H. VESTEY

27th December. (Boxing Day.)   Two packs were out. Ned Paxton had a busy day from the Rose & Crown, Great Thurlow, while Capt. Barclay had an excellent day from Washall Green. The first fox gave an excellent hunt from Beaches Wood with a 4 mile point to Woodhall

Arkesden. Getting up with their fox hounds ran hard back and killed at Starlings Green. Finding again at Laundry Gorse hounds ran very hard for 25 minutes and killed in the open.

15th January. Brent Pelham Hall. Ted Barclay hunted hounds for the first time; a great hunt of 1 hr 45 mins and a 7 mile point from Beaches Wood via Chamberlains, Needles and Great Chishill to ground at Heydon Valley.

26th February. Cave Gate. Hounds found a brace behind Silkmead Poultry Farm; they ran one to ground at Hare Street and took the other over the main A.10, marking a fox to ground at Broadfields, making a 6 mile point; some hounds ran on to Clothall Great Wood an 8 mile point, where a very tired fox was seen with hounds close at him, but it is not known whether he was killed. Hounds found again in Scales Park and killed one fox after 25 mins woodland hunting and ran another to Clavering where hounds were stopped after a great day's fox-hunting.

1972–3 season *Masters:* CAPTAIN AND MRS CHARLES BARCLAY AND MR AND MRS E. H. VESTEY

December 28th. at Hundon. A great day's sport. Hounds found in Mr Mizon's kale and had a great hunt of 1 hour 50 mins, and 5 mile point by Range Hills and Black Grove, finally killing in the brook by the Denston – Wickhambrook Road. Another good hunt took place from Mr Brook's rough hedges on to Stradishall Aerodrome.

January 6th. at Bedlars Green. After a good start on the Forest where one fox was killed and two run to ground, hounds found in Ladywells and ran at a terrific pace through the Forest via Webbs Earths nearly to Row Wood, but twisted back to the Chelmsford main road, and skirted Hatfield Heath Village; our fox tried to make his way back to Monk Wood but he was beat and was killed in Mr Albert Harris's garden after a brilliant 55 mins.

March 14th. at Elsenham. Hounds got on to a travelling fox near Holden Wood and ran to Horham Hall and thence, via Tilty Hill Farm to Dutton Hill where hounds marked a fox to ground. Hounds hit off the line in the rough by the river and ran over the Thaxted–Dunmow roads to Hunts Covert where the fox was given up as we were well into the Essex country and a lot of spring farming work was in hand.

1973–4 season *Joint Masters:* CAPTAIN CHARLES BARCLAY AND MR AND MRS E. H. VESTEY

December 29. Cave Gate. Hounds found a leash in the fences between Anstey Hall and Anstey Bury. The first fox took us straight to Scales Park where hounds were stopped because of shooting. They were taken back on to another fox who had a very long start. They hunted slowly by Brick House over the main road by Hare Street. A very long cast forward enabled them to come up with their fox at Pinners. Hounds ran at a very great pace by Barkway and Rookey to Reed Wood. Here large herds of deer foiled the scent, but hounds were able to hunt slowly and were stopped coming away from Capons to the A.10. with all the Hunt staff horses exhausted and only one grandmother in attendance.

February 13. Sandon. While hounds were drawing Roe Wood, a fox was on the move at Wheat Hill. Unfortunately he got a long start and the hounds could only hunt slowly in the direction of Gannockbourne and Philpotts. Hounds got up with him here and another fox and hunted both away, killing the hunted fox on the Sandon–Kelshall road. They ran the other one hard through Roe Wood and on by Julians to Friars. After running hard in covert, hounds came away, close to a fox, to Broadfields and away to Lodge Hill. Our fox was headed on the Cottered Cumberlow Green road and hounds raced back by Youngloves and Munchies and were stopped, as all horses were exhausted, at Coles Wood. A fine hunt for $2\frac{1}{4}$ hours.

February 25. Weston Colville. After a hunt form West Wratting Home Wood, a fox was bolted from a straw stack by Smoothies and absolutely raced as hard as hounds could go through Littleys, Lawn and Over Wood, just touched Hare Wood, crossing the main A.604 by the Montford Arms. Hounds raced on without a check, to Shudy Camps, where a very tired fox just beat them into a drain beside the road. After hounds had left, he was seen to come out and curl up in straw stack in Mr Kiddy's farmyard. I hour 10 mins at fastest possible speed.

1974–5 season *Masters:* CAPTAIN CHARLES BARCLAY AND MR AND MRS E. H. VESTEY

Dec. 28th. Layston Church. Finding an outlier by the Roman Catholic cemetery, hounds hunted prettily to Anstey Bury, through Five Acre Wood into Scales Park. On hounds being held round on the down wind side, they came away close to a fox and ran by Meesden Church nearly to Oxbury, but turning left handed over the brook by Thurrocks and Cosh Lane they were stopped in Langley High Wood after a good hunt of 3 hours and a 7 mile point.

Jan. 1st. Walkern Hall. A fox slipped away behind the hounds from St. John's Wood and hounds ran well by Farm Wood and Witnesses to ground at Shouts. Later hounds found in the rough behind Moor Green and had a wonderful hunt over some wild country in a series of big circles before being stopped in the dark at Buttermilk Hall.

Feb. 12th. Aspenden Church. After a lengthy draw, hounds found in Friars Wood and ran very hard by Batchelors and Julians Park to Roe Wood. Through this, and the fox circles out to Gannock Farm and back by the village. Coming away again over the Gannock bourne, hounds ran on almost to the Royston border road, but the fox was headed by traffic and turned back. Hounds rolled him over in the open on Mr Howe's farm after a first rate hunt of 1 hour and 5 minutes and a 5 mile point. This fox was one of the biggest ever killed by the Present Master.

Feb. 17th. Boxbury. Walkern. Hounds found in the High Grove and a nice but slow hunt was enjoyed to ground at Clobbles. Finding again in Lords Wood, hounds came away on the brush of their fox to Benington and thence via Benington Park, Walkern Park, Moor Green, Wakeley and Graves Wood. Hounds were eventually found by Mrs Streeter, Mr Allen, the Master and Ned Paxton, having killed their fox at Westmill Bourne. Hounds hunted the entire course of this entirely unaided and were only seen by one person. A great hunt of 1 hour 20 minutes and a 6 mile point.

1975–6 season *Joint Masters:* CAPTAIN CHARLES BARCLAY AND MR AND MRS E. H. VESTEY

November 29th: 1975: Puckeridge & Thurlow
The fog was thick when Hounds met at Washall Green on November 29th. With a large field Captain Barclay decided to hunt even so; a risk which led to a memorable hunt. After drawing some artichokes by Furneux Pelham and Rogers Wood, Hounds picked up the stale line of a fox above Bozens Green and rather hesitantly headed for Hormead Park. Mrs. Vestey and her two elder sons, hotfoot from Eton on St. Andrew's Day, then loomed out of the clearing fog with news of a fox on the move that they had met a few minutes earlier while trying to find Hounds. That lucky encounter was really the start of the day. Captain Barclay lifted Hounds and they were soon away very fast to Patrick's Wood, where deer caused a slight diversion. Hounds retrieved the line and ran on past Brent Pelham, almost to the Kennels, and swung lefthanded through the Dairy to Cole Green. A short check, before Mrs Streeter spotted the fox going away to Meesden Hall, where he bemused some pigs, but without delay they took the line out to Further Ford End. Here Virgin, a pure English Hound, put them right, across the Stort, and they then ran past Ruttels to Clavering Place, through Wood Hall, Severals, Wicken Osiers and Whiteditch Farm, to Wendens Ambo. Left handed just short of the village, they hunted nicely back towards Arkesden, where Mr. Ted Harvey viewed the fox not far ahead. By this time Ron Quarmby was hunting Hounds as Captain Barclay had been badly baulked by wire by Clavering Place. A long check by Severals, complicated by a stag, and then some shooters put us right when they spotted our fox, who had lain down, pick himself up out of the middle of a stubble field. Captain Barclay's horse had blown up; Ron Quarmby was retrieving the young Hounds who had gone staghunting, so Mr. Vestey hunted them from then on. Retracing his steps, the fox ran through Wood Hall, past Clavering Place, Valence, Roast Green, Further Ford End, to Meesden Hall Wood, where he did a circuit and then decided to take refuge under a pile of logs in Mrs Tyler's garden where he had to be left. Hounds first picked up the line at 12.30. They put him to ground in the dusk at 4.15. An eight mile point. Nineteen miles at least as they ran, with only two grass fields from start to finish, and on neither of these could Hounds really hunt. Starting with a field of ninety, seven saw the end; Mr. and Mrs. Vestey and their sons Timothy and James, Mr. Pat Lloyd, Captain Barclay's daughter, Diana Pyper, and Mr. Christopher Sporborg, the field master. A marvellous plough country hunt, with several of the progeny of the Duke of Beaufort's Beadle '66 prominent throughout.

RULES OF THE THURLOW HUNT CLUB.

At a meeting held at the Crown Inn, Great Thurlow, on Friday, the 16th day of April, 1858; and a meeting held at the Rutland Arms, Newmarket, on Tuesday, the 31st day of May, 1859, the following resolutions were agreed to:–

1st. – That the Club called the Thurlow Hunt Club be revived and re-established.

2nd. – That the object of the club shall be the preservation of foxes in the district known as the 'Thurlow Country' which extends on the Suffolk side as far as Dalham, Denham Thicks, Barrow Wood, Easty Wood, Denston Groves and Cavendish Covers; and on the Essex and Cambridgeshire sides as far as the Suffolk Hounds Hunt.

3rd. – That the Club consist of President, Vice-president, Treasurer and Secretary, Committee of Management, and general subscribers.

4th. – That Mr. Edward Frost be President; Mr. John Webb, Vice-President; and Mr. Grimwood Cooke, Treasurer and Secretary.

5th. – That the following Gentlemen, having consented to attend to the preservation of Foxes in the covers attached to their respective names, form a Committee of management. viz:

J. R. BROMLEY, Easty wood and Bansfield Hall wood.
THOMAS WEBB, Hildersham Abington, Babraham, Linton woods
JOHN WEBB, Mr. Ratson's Covers, Borley wood.
R. SIMOND, Balsham wood
JNO. FOSPIN, Still, Yennan, Over, Lays, Cadges and Haugh woods.
JNO. SIGGS, Rands and Weston covers
HENRY KING, Wilbraham and Fulbourne covers
R. W. KING, Brinkley, Widgeons, Boro' green wood
THOMAS NASH, Carlton wood
T. NICE, Bradley Park and Lamprells Groves

F. KING, Lucy woods and Branches Park
JNO. OSLAR, Ditton Park woods and Stetchworth Covers
L. SNAZELL, Duke Stand's Covers and Chevely Green
THOS. GARDNER, Moots, Chippenham and Kentford covers
JAMES KING, Dalham
GEO. DOSITO, Lidgate and Onsden Covers
FREDERICK HALLS, Denham and Barrow covers
GEO. SPARROW, Denston covers, Chipley, Applesere &c
GEO. PALMER, A.B.C. wood, Trundly and Wadgells
W. TRAYLER, Hart, Temple, Lophams, Thurlow Groves

6th. – That subscriptions be received from Gentlemen residing in the Thurlow Country, and others disposed to contribute; (no one subscription to exceed the sum of £5) and such subscriptions to form a fund for carrying out the objects of the club.

7th. – That Cubs shall be purchased, and turned down at such parts of the Thurlow Country and in such covers as the Committee may determine.

8th. – That one sovereign shall be given to any keeper, woodman, or servant, who shall take care of and rear any of the purchased Cubs.

9th. – That the sum of £2 shall be given to any keeper, or woodman, in whose woods or covers a litter of foxes shall be bred and reared.

10th. – That a donation of a sovereign shall be given to every keeper or woodman, in whose woods or covers there shall be 'a find' and more than one 'find' on the same day shall not entitle the same keeper or woodman to more than one donation.

11th. – That an annual general meeting shall be held at the Crown Inn, Great Thurlow, or such place as the committee may at any time determine, on the Friday in the week between the first and second Newmarket Spring meetings, of which due notice shall be given by advertisement in the Bury and Cambridge papers, and on which day the accounts shall be audited, and other general business of the club transacted.

12th. – That at such annual meeting the conduct of any keeper or woodman, who may not have had during the preceding year any claim for a 'find' may be considered, and the meeting shall have full power, if the members present think proper, to award any compensation to such keeper or woodman, for care or trouble they may have had in the preservation of Foxes.

12th. – That if any complaint of the loss of fowls &c, by any person not being a member of the club, be laid before such meeting, such complaint be considered by the members present, who shall have the power, if they think proper, to award compensation out of the funds of the club.

LIST OF SUBSCRIBERS

Mr. Batson	Mr. Eagle	Mr. J. Goodchild	Mr. Mitchell Junr.	Mr. W. H. Sams	Mr. M. Townie
,, W. Barrow	,, Flatman	,, J. Hammond	,, T. Nash	,, J. Siggs	,, G. Traylen
,, Bromley	,, Francis	,, Haylock	,, F. Nice	,, J. Simmonds	,, Turpin
,, T. Chalk	,, C. Francis	,, Hicks	,, T. Nice	,, R. Simmonds	Capt. Tyson
,, S. Clayden	,, Freeman	,, F. King	,, J. Oslar	,, M. Slater, Junr.	Mr. H. Webb
,, W. Collin	,, E. Frost	,, H. King	,, Partridge	,, G. Smith	,, J. Webb
,, G. Cooke	,, H. Frost	,, R. King	,, H. Pearl	,, J. Smith	,, T. Webb
,, W. Danby	,, T. Frost	,, J. King	,, W. Purkis	,, L. Snazell	,, W. Webb
Capt. Dench	,, W. Frost	,, W. King	,, Rodgers	,, G. Sparrow	,, A. Witt
Mr. G. Dobito	,, S. Gardner	,, H. Long	,, Robinson	,, W. Staples	,, B. Witt
,, Du Chesne	,, T. Gardner	,, R. Maulkin			

BIGMORE, PRINTER, HAVERHILL

List of Masters

Masters of the Newmarket and Thurlow Hunt

1605–1625: James VI & I
1625–1649: Charles I.
  Hunting virtually stopped during Commonwealth until Restoration
1660–1685: James, Duke of York
1685–1689: James II
1690–1757: Charles, 2nd Duke of Grafton
1757–1770: Augustus Henry Fitzroy, 3rd
  Duke of Grafton
1770–1800: Mr Thomas Panton
1800–1804: Colonel John Cook
1804–1822: Reverend Dacre
1822–1823: Mr George Osbaldeston
1827–1845: Mr George Mure
1845–1864: Mr John Josselyn
1864–1867: Mr John Ord
1867–1871: Mr John Josselyn
1871–1875: Mr Edward Greene, M.P., and
  Mr Walter Greene
1875–1880: Mr John Josselyn
1880–1883: Sir E. Walter Greene
1883–1884: Mr Jesse Coope
1884–1890: Mr James Gardner
1890–1892: Captain J. Gordon Miller
1892–1894: Mr Edward Molyneux
1894–1895: Mr George Bowen
1895–1896: Mr Edward Molyneux
1896–1901: Mr W. H. Pemberton-Barnes
1901–1902: Captain C. Brook

1902–1906: Reverend Sir William Hyde-
  Parker, BART
11906–1910: Mr Richard Bower
1910–1912: Colonel E. Deacon
1912–1913: Mr Reginald S. Hicks
1913–1915: Major A. C. Jaffe
1915–1919: Mr C. F. Ryder
1919–1920: Lord Wilton
1920–1921: Mr C. F. Tonge and Colonel
  J. F. Ryder
1921–1928: Mr C. F. Tonge
1928–1931: Mr E. Cooper-Bland and Mr
  T. C. Eaton
1931–1934: Mr E. Cooper-Bland and
  Mr A. M. Praed
1934–1942: Colonel E. H. Deacon
1942–1946: A Committee. Chairman Mr.
  H. C. Leader
1946–1947: Brigadier M. W. Selby Lowndes
1947–1948: A Committee. Chairman Mr
  F. B. Taylor
1948–1956: Mr. Harvey Leader
1956–1957: A Committee. Chairman Mr
  J. D. Webb
1957–1958: A Committee. Joint Masters
  Mr J. D. Webb and Colonel D. R. B. Kaye,
  D.S.O.
1958–1959: Colonel D. R. B. Kaye, D.S.O.
1959–1962: Mr Neil Parker

1962–1964: Mrs R. H. D. Riggall
1964–1965: Mrs R. H. D. Riggall and Mrs
E. H. Vestey

1965–1966: Mrs E. H. Vestey
1966–1970: Mr and Mrs E. H. Vestey

Masters of The Puckeridge Hunt

1727–1756: Mr Felix Calvert
1756–1770: Mr John Calvert, the Elder, Mr
Thomas Panton and Mr William
Plumer, M.P.
1770–1780: Mr John Calvert, the Elder and
Mr William Plumer, M.P.
1780–1783: Mr John Calvert the Elder
1783–1785: Mr John Calvert the Elder and
Mr John Calvert the Younger
1785–1799: Mr John Calvert the Younger
1799–1826: Mr Sampson Hanbury, Mr John
Calvert the Younger and Mr Nicholson
Calvert
1826–1832: Mr Sampson Hanbury
1832–1835: Lord Petre
1835–1838: Mr John Dalyell
1838–1842: Mr Nicholas Parry and Mr
William Wigram and Mr John Archer
Houblon
1842–1854: Mr Nicholas Parry and Mr
William Wigram

1854–1875: Mr Nicholas Parry
1875–1885: Mr Robert Gosling
1885–1894: Two Packs hunting the country
1885–1894: Mr Frederick C. Swindell
hunting The Puckeridge
1885–1890: Mr Gosling's, hunted by Mr
Robert Gosling
1890–1894: The Herts and Essex: Hunted by
a Committee with Mr R. Gosling
1894–1896: The Hon. J. L. Bathurst
1896–1910: Mr Edward E. Barclay
1910–1922: Mr Edward E. Barclay and Major
M. E. Barclay
1922–1947: Mr Edward E. Barclay and Major
M. E. Barclay for a Committee
1947–1948: Mr Edward E. Barclay and Major
M. E. Barclay and Captain Charles
Barclay for a Committee
1948–1963: Major M. E. Barclay and Captain
Charles Barclay for a Committee
1963–1970: Captain and Mrs Charles Barclay

Masters of The Puckeridge and Thurlow Hunt

1970–1973: Captain and Mrs Charles
Barclay and Mr and Mrs E. H. Vestey

1973–1975: Captain Charles Barclay and Mr
and Mrs E. H. Vestey

Bibliography

ACTON, C. R., *The Modern Foxhound*, London, 1935
   The Foxhound of the Future, London, 1953
AFFALO, F. G. (Ed.) *The Sports of the World*, London, 1905
ALKEN, Henry, *The National Sports of Great Britain*, London, 1825
APPERLEY C. J. (Nimrod) *Hunting Tours*, London, 1835
   The Horse and the Hound, London, 1842
Badmington Library: *Hunting*, London, 1885
Baily's Hunting Directory.
BEACH THOMAS, Sir William, *Hunting England*, London 1936
BECKFORD, Peter, *Thoughts on Hunting*, Salisbury, 1781
BERRY, Michael F., *Foxhunting from The Times*, London, 1933
   More Foxhunting from The Times, London, 1937
   A History of the Puckeridge Hunt, Country Life, London, 1950
BOVILL, E. W., *The England of Nimrod & Surtees*, Oxford, 1959
   English Country Life, 1780–1830, Oxford, 1962
BRANDER, Michael, *The Hunting Instinct*, Edinburgh, 1964
   Hunting & Shooting, London, 1971
   The Georgian Gentleman, London, 1973
   The Victorian Gentleman, London, 1975
   The Country Divine, London, 1976
British Hunts and Huntsmen, Ed. *Sporting Life*, (4 vols), London, 1909
BROMLEY DAVENPORT, W., *Sport*, London, 1868
BROOKSBY (Capt. E. Pennel-Elmhirst), *The Hunting Countries of England*, (2 vols) London, 1883
BURROWS, George T., *Gentleman Charles: A History of Foxhunting*, London, 1951
CARLISLE, R. H., *Fox-hunting Past and Present*, London, 1908
CHALMERS, Patrick, *The History of Hunting*, London, 1936
COATES, A. W. (Ed.), *British Hunting: a complete History*, London, 1910
COCKAINE, Sir Thomas, *A Short Treatise on Hunting*, 1591
COOK, Colonel John, *Observations on Foxhunting*, London, 1826
COOPER–BLAND E., *Diaries* 1928–32
DEACON, Col. E. H., *Diaries*, 1928–39
DELME RADCLIFFE, F. P., *The Noble Science*, London, 1839

DIXON, H. H. (The Druid), *The Post and the Paddock*, London, 1857
  Silk and Scarlet, London, 1859
DIXON, William Scarth, *Hunting in the Olden Days*, London, 1912
  Foxhunting in the Twentieth Century, London, 1925
GREAVES, Ralph, *Short Histories*, inc. Newmarket & Thurlow and Puckeridge
HICKS, Reginald S., *Diaries*, 1890–1913
LONGRIGG, Roger, *The History of Foxhunting*, London, 1975
Lonsdale Library, *Fox Hunting*, London, 1930
  The History of Hunting, 1936
McNEILL C. F. P., *The Unwritten Laws of Foxhunting*, London, 1910
OSBALDESTON, George, *Autobiography*, Ed. E. D. Cuming, London, 1936
PURKIS, Thomas, *Diaries*, 1880–1932
THORNMANBY, J. Wilmitt Dixon, *Kings of the Hunting Field*, London, 1899
THORNTON, Col. Thomas, *A Sporting Tour*, London, 1804
  A Sporting Tour through Various Parts of France, London, 1806
WEBB, J. D., *Diaries and Notes*, 1930–1957

Index

Compiled by Patricia Utechin

Adams, Charles, 51, 53
Allen, Robert, 65–6
Anderson, H. A., 87
Andrews, Thomas, 10, 21,
   30, 104
'Ansty', 6, 25
Apperley, Charles J., 35
Archdale, R., 79
Archer, F., 61
Archer, Fred, 94
Ashton, M., 119
Austin, Stanley, 107

Bailey, James, 80, 85
Barclay, Charles G. E., xii,
   104, 113, 115–16, 118–19
Barclay, Mrs. Charles G. E.,
   116, 118–19
Barclay, Edward E., 50, 69–70,
   76, 84–8, 99–100, 102,
   113–14, 116
Barclay, Maurice E., 86–8,
   99–104, 108, 113, 115–16
Barwick, George, 25–6, 32–5
Bathurst, Earl, 69
Bathurst, Hon. L. J., 68–9
Beaufort, Duke of, 56
Beckford, Peter, xiv–xv, 42
Beddington, Sir Edward,
   115–16

Bell's Life, 14, 38, 48–9
Berry, Michael, xii–xiii
Binney, Mr, 64
Blackwell, George, 94
Blair, T. Hunter, 111
Blank, Terence, 118
Boore, Jack, 95–6
Bowen, George, 63, 85
Bower, Richard, 77–8
Braybrook, Lord, 21
Briggs, Sir Charles, 93, 95,
   97, 99, 107–8
British Field Sports Society,
   90, 106
British Hunts and Huntsmen, 62
Brook, Charles, 74–6
Brown, Ted, 104
Browne, Edward, 60
Broxbourne, 13, 22
Budd, James, 69
Bull, Dick, 104
Bull, Fred, 79
Bury St Edmunds, 11, 21,
   32, 46, 60

Calvert, Felix, 5
Calvert, Felix (of Albury
   Hall,) 5–6, 13
Calvert, Felix (of Furneux
   Pelham), 5, 67

Calvert, John, (the Elder),
   11, 13–14
Calvert, John (the Younger),
   14–16, 24–5
Calvert, Nicolson, 16, 24
Canning (huntsman), 25
Cannon, Walter, 82
Cantile, James, 87
Capel, William, 18–19
Chafy, William W., 37, 48,
   52–3
Champion, A., 111
Chapman, John, 38–9
Church, Will, 25
Cockaine, Sir Thomas,
   xiii–iv, 1, 3
Cockayne, James, 69, 84–6
Collins (landowner), 80–1
Collins, Bob, 94
Conyers, H. J., 32
Cook, John, 6, 19–25, 28–30,
   39, 43
Coope, Jesse, 60
Cooper-Bland, E., xii, 95–7
Cooper-Bland, Mrs. E., 99,
   107, 109
Coote, T., 109
Cotton, John, 14
Cotton-Browne, Miss G.,
   86–7

Cotton-Browne, George, 87
Cowell, Bob, 108
Crane, Will, 14
Croft, Page, 88
Custerson, Bob, 99

Dalyell, John, xi, 35–7, 50
Davers, Sir Charles, 11, 22
Davers, The Rev., 22, 28,
  30, 75
Deacon, Edmund, 78–81, 97
Deacon, E. H., xii, 97–8
Deacon, Mrs. E. H., xii,
  97–9
Deakin, J., 110
Debeham, Frank, 100–1
de Rothschild, Leopold, 82
Dinnicombe, John, 51
Dixon, William, 57
Duschene, Jack, 75

Earl, Walter, 94
Eaton, T. C., 95–6
Edwards, Lionel, 102
Ellenborough, Lord, 18
Ellis, Dick, 64
Elwes, Sir Gervase, 10
Elwes, Sir Harvey, 10
Elwes, John, 10
Enever, Tom, 58
Engaine, Thomas, xiii
Essex, Earl of, 18

Field, Charlie, 108–10
Field, The, 51–3
Fielden (landowner), 85
Firr, Abraham, 50
Firr, Tom, 50
Fordham, Barbara, 101
Fordham, Joan, 101
Forest Laws, xiii, 3, 57
Forsyth, Alexander, 18
Foster, George, 79–80
Fox, Charles James, 44
Foxhound Kennel Studbook, xiv,
  56, 72

Gardiner, Bob, 86, 88, 100–2,
  104, 110
Gardner, James, 60–2, 65
Gibbs, J., 96
Goodchild, Colonel, 63, 80
Gordon-Miller, J., xi, 62
Gosling, Robert, 65–9, 87
Gosling, Robert Cunliffe, 87
Gosling, W. S., 102, 115
Grafton, Dukes of, 8–9, 11,
  24, 30, 47
Grant, Sir Francis, 39, 52
Greene, Edward, 46
Greene, Harry, 79
Greene, Sir Walter, 46–7,
  58–60
Guiness, Linette, 101
Guiness, Mrs, 101
Gurney, Dick, 33

Hanbury, Sampson, 6, 16,
  24–6, 32–4, 50
Hargreaves, D., 110
Haverhill, xvi, 105, 111–12
Hedges, Alfred, 52–4, 65
Hibbs, Sam, 30, 32, 44–6
Hickly, Jane, 101
Hicks, Reginald S., 63–5,
  73–82
History of the Puckeridge Hunt,
  xii
Holmes (huntsman), 25
Horse and Hound, 85
Hort (huntsman), 34
Houblin, Jacob, 14
Houblon, John A., 37
Howe, Countess, 71
Hubbard, Tom, 14–15, 25
Hunting in Herts & Beds, 54
Hunts:
  Avon Vale, 78, 111
  Bedale, 34
  Belvoir, 66, 95
  Berkeley, 93
  Bicester, 37
  Blankney, 97

Bramham Moor, 50
Burton, 50
Cambridgeshire, 37, 54,
  59, 65, 73, 82
Cambridgeshire Harriers,
  79
Cattistock, 75
Colonel Croft's Stag-
  hounds, 88
Craven, 97
Devon and Somerset
  Staghounds, 82
Duke of Cumberland's
  Staghounds, 25
East Essex, 23, 32, 59–60,
  73, 78, 82
Eggesford, 69
Enfield Chace Staghounds,
  88
Essex, 19, 32, 50, 52, 59, 65,
  73, 80, 82, 85, 94
Essex Union, 30, 34–5, 109
Eton Beagles, 73
Exmoor, 68
Fitzwilliam, 73
Forfarshire, 35
Grafton, 50
Hambledon, 19
Hampshire, 119
Hatfield, 13, 25
Hempstead Invincibles, 10,
  21, 24, 30, 104
Hertfordshire, 6, 13, 15,
  25, 34, 50, 66, 110
Herts and Essex, 68–9
Holderness, 37
Newmarket, 5, 8
Newmarket Drag, 65, 82
Newmarket and Thurlow,
  xi–xiv, xvi, 6, 9–14,
  18–19, 21–4, 28, 30–2, 46,
  56, 58–65, 73–9, 82–5, 91–2,
  94–100, 102, 107–12, 117–18
North Warwickshire, 85
Old Berkeley, 18
Old Berkshire, 68

Portman, 93
Puckeridge, xi, xii–xiv, xvi, 5–6, 10–14, 16, 18, 21–2, 24–6, 32, 34–40, 47–54, 56, 59, 63, 68–70, 73, 76, 82, 84–8, 91, 93, 95, 99–104, 108, 110, 112–19
Puckeridge and Thurlow, xii, 112, 117–20
Pytchley, 31
Quorn, 23–4, 30, 50
Radnor and West Hereford, 119
Royal Buckhounds, 25
Rufford, 65
South Pembrokeshire, 110
Suffolk, 8–9, 24, 28, 30, 32, 44–7, 58–60, 65, 73, 112
Surrey Union, 37
Talents, 11, 30
Thurlow Farmers, 60
Tickham, 110
Trinity Foot Beagles, 73, 75, 79, 116
York and Ainstey, 37
Hyde-Parker, Sir William, 75–8, 81

Jackson, W., 102
Jaffe, A. C., 82
James I and VI, King, xi, 1, 120
Jarvis, Basil, 94
Jarvis, Will, 32
Jones, Herbert, 82
Jones, William, 13, 22
Josselyn, John, 32, 44–7, 58–60, 110
Judd, J. P., 66

Kaye, D. R. B., xii, 110–11, 117
Kentucky, 111.
King (huntsman), 13–15
King, Robert W., 59, 63, 74, 82–3, 93

Kirkby, Tom, 101, 110

Leader, Colledge, 94
Leader, Harvey, 94, 99, 107–10
Leader, J. W., 67
Leader, Thomas, 82
League Against Cruel Sports, 106
Leech, John, 50–1
Linton, xi, 59–60, 73, 76, 85
Lucas, W., 54

Macadam, John L., 12, 27
Mann, T. J., 74
Manuden, 65, 67–8, 101
Marriage, Miss, 101
Master of Game, xiii
Masters of Foxhounds Association, 42, 56, 68, 72, 84
Millbank, Mark, 34
Milne, Jack, 75, 80
Molyneux, E., 62–3
Monk, John, 25–6
Morris, Richard, 37
Munnings, Sir Alfred, 107
Mure, George, xi, 24, 28, 30–2, 82

Newman, Charles, 23–4, 30
Newman, G. C., 110, 116
Newman, Sam, 96
Newmarket, xvi, 1–2, 9, 11–12, 19, 27, 30–1, 45, 62–3, 94–6, 98, 111, 120
New Sporting Magazine, The, xv, 6, 23–5, 32, 35, 39
'Nimrod', see Apperley, Charles J.

Observations on Foxhunting, 6, 19–20, 22, 29, 43
Orbell, Joseph, 51–2, 87
Ord, John, 46
Orford, Third Earl of, 9

Osbaldeston, George, 23–4, 28, 30–1, 45, 58, 60

Panton, Thomas, 11–14, 19, 21
Parker, J. P. N., 110–11
Parry, Nicholas, 32, 34, 36–40, 47–54, 65, 67, 69, 87
Parry, Segar, 37
Patten Saunders, W. H., 67–8
Paxton, Ned, 110, 113, 118–19
Pearce (second whip), 77
Pemberton, Leigh, 116
Pemberton-Barnes, W. H., 63–4, 73–5
Pemberton-Barnes, Mrs. W. H., 63–4
Petre, Lord, 34–7, 50
Pigg, Russell, 102
Plumer, William, 13–14
Poole, C. S., 94
Praed, A. M., 96–7
Pryor, Norman, 101
Pryor, Peter, 101
Pudney, T., 109
Puller, Arthur G., 54
Purkis, Anthony, 73
Purkis, Claude, 73, 83
Purkis, Thomas, xi, 59–66, 69–70, 73–4, 77, 79–86, 92–5
Purvis, C., 109

Quarmby, R., 119

Radcliffe, Delme, 34, 58
Raper, E., 96
Riggall, Mrs R. H. D., 111
Rivière, H. G., 88
Rose, Will, 30, 32
Routledge, M. G., 117
R.S.P.C.A., 106
Royston, 5, 38, 48, 51
Rutland, Duke of, 60
Ryder, C. F., 75, 80, 83–4, 92–3, 95, 97–8, 107, 109, 111

Ryder, J. F., 84, 92
Ryder, Stephen, 111–12, 117

Saffron Walden, xvi, 21, 68
Sale, Mollie, 101
Sale, Willie, 101
Salisbury, Lady, 13, 25
Samways, George, 97–9
Sefton, Lord, 15
Selby-Lowndes, M. W., 108
Sharp, George, 25
Short, Ted, 85–6
Short Treatise on Hunting, A, xiv
Simpson, Richard, 37–9, 47–53
Six Mile Bottom, 2, 12, 61
Skinner, John, 35–6
Smith, Sydney, 101
Smyth, George, 86–7
Smyth, Hugh, 87
Sporborg, H. N., xii, 116–17
Stacey, Frank, 100–1
Stevenage, xvi, 5, 51, 105, 112
Stobbert, Sam, 77

Stubbing, Thomas, 87
Stubbings, N., 119
Surtees, R. S., 24, 62
Swindell, F. C., 67–9, 84
Sworder, John W., 53, 88

Talbot hounds, 1, 4
Taylor, Edward, 50
Taylor, F. B., 99, 107–8
Telford, T., 27
Thornton, Thomas, 26
Thoughts on Hunting, xv
Thurlow, 12, 22, 31, 45, 47, 59, 62, 64, 83, 93, 118
Thurlow Farmers' Purse, 46–7, 111
Thurlow Hunt Club, 30, 45–6, 58, 82, 95, 111, 120
Thwaites, Hannah, 101
Tonge, Charles F., 84, 92–3, 95–6, 111
Tonge, M., 94
Tonge, Miss, 96
Tongue, Cornelius, 56
Turner, Harry, 97
Turney, Miss, 101

Vestey, Edmund H., xii, 111–12, 118–20
Vestey, Mrs Edmund H., xii, 110–11, 118
Vestey, R. A., 109–10

Walker, A., 111
Walls, J., 21
Ware, 5, 12, 68, 87
Way, R. E., xii, 96
Webb, Henry L., 82, 95–6
Webb, Jack D., xii, 95, 108, 110–11, 118
Webb, Jonas, 82, 95
Wells, William, 66
Wigram, William, 37
Wilkinson, Ben, 102–4, 113
Williams, Albert, xii, 83, 97, 109, 120
Willis, George, 10, 21
Wilton, Lord, 84
Woodward, Frank, 83
Woodward, Joe, 83
Woodward, Will, 82–4, 92–3, 95–6
Wright, F., 96